Books are to be returned on or before
the last date below.

Ou

LIBREX-

Out of the Shadows

Managing self-employed, agency and outsourced workers

Patricia Leighton, Michel Syrett,
Robert Hecker and Peter Holland

AMSTERDAM • BOSTON • HEIDELBERG • LONDON • NEW YORK • OXFORD
PARIS • SAN DIEGO • SAN FRANCISCO • SINGAPORE • SYDNEY • TOKYO
Butterworth-Heinemann is an imprint of Elsevier

Butterworth-Heinemann is an imprint of Elsevier
Linacre House, Jordan Hill, Oxford OX2 8DP, UK
30 Corporate Drive, Suite 400, Burlington, MA 01803, USA

First edition 2007

British Library Cataloguing in Publication Data
A catalogue record for this book is available from the British Library

Library of Congress Cataloguing in Publication Data
A catalogue record for this book is available from the Library of Congress

ISBN-13: 978-0-7506-6524-7
ISBN-10: 0-7506-6524-6

For information on all Butterworth-Heinemann publications
visit our web site at http://books.elsevier.com

Typeset by Charon Tec Ltd (A Macmillan Company), Chennai, India
www.charontec.com

Printed and bound in Great Britain
07 08 09 10 11   10 9 8 7 6 5 4 3 2 1

Working together to grow
libraries in developing countries

www.elsevier.com | www.bookaid.org | www.sabre.org

ELSEVIER   **BOOK AID** International   **Sabre Foundation**

Contents

1

Introducing the topic

Prescient tales

In 1999, British Telecom outsourced the delivery of a number of key HR services to a leading international consultancy, Accenture. Like many outsourced agreements, a significant number of the workers recruited by Accenture to undertake the work were former BT employees. They enjoyed good existing relationships with the line managers inside BT who were the internal 'clients' for the services encompassed by the contract, and they understood the context which determined the levels of service against which the contract was determined.

Within three years of the agreement, the arrangement started to degrade. Many former BT staff, unhappy with the terms of employment they were being offered, left Accenture, and the consultants who replaced them were unfamiliar with BT's internal HR needs. Gaps started to appear in the quality of the service. The group's HR department lacked the IT infrastructure and focused attention to spot these early enough to make an effective intervention.

By 2003, the situation had deteriorated to the point where renewal of the contract between BT and Accenture was seriously under question. Equally worrying, the negotiations were conducted in the public eye and were subject to 'real time' coverage by UK professional journals such as *Personnel Today* and *People Management*. It took a 'back to basics' review of operational procedures to convince BT to renew the arrangement.

In an interview with one of the contributors to this book (Syrett, 2004), Jenny Arwas, Director of BT Group Operations, admitted:

When we made the decision to move service delivery out of BT's direct hands, we initially disassociated ourselves from that part of the operation. We outsourced our expertise and know-how and entrusted a core feature of our reputation to a third party. The potential for overlap and double handling went undetected and unchecked in those early days, until we sat down with the supplier and established realistic goals as well as clear lines of responsibility and accountability.

British Airways' group HR practitioners would empathize closely with this statement. In 1997, British Airways (BA) outsourced its in-flight catering provision to a US-owned company called Gate Gourmet. This company employed several hundred staff, largely living near Heathrow Airport. The workforce was drawn from various ethnic groups, especially Asian.

As in the British Telecom/Accenture contract, many were former BA employees. Gate Gourmet recognized trades unions, in particular the Transport and General Workers Union (TGWU). The contract was a long one and, importantly, BA sourced all its in-flight meals from Gate Gourmet. The contract was due to be renegotiated during the spring of 2005. Profit margins were always low, and by 2005 Gate Gourmet's Heathrow operations were running at a significant loss. Its parent company, Texas Pacific, remained highly profitable.

In an effort to deal with the losses, Gate Gourmet proposed changes to working practices and the increased use of agency temporary workers. In June 2005, the TGWU and other unions agreed a restructuring deal. This was rejected by members. The workers affected took unofficial strike action – that is, they did not follow the required legal procedures prior to taking strike action. The TGWU provided advice and support.

Those who went on strike were sacked by Gate Gourmet, as the company was entitled to do under UK law. Baggage handlers and other staff employed directly by BA then went on a 'sympathy' strike, leading to the cancellation of large numbers of BA flights, while those flights that went ahead were often delayed and did not have meals for passengers. There was widespread publicity regarding the situation at Heathrow Airport. The disruption continued for several weeks. In the immediate aftermath, investigative journalists apparently discovered unhealthy and unsafe working conditions at the Gate Gourmet factory premises. There had anyway been major complaints by BA in 2004 about poor hygiene and safety standards.

The case achieved international publicity. The industrial dispute lasted for months, and the damage to BA's business and business reputation is incalculable. The lesson BA learned was summarized effectively by Rory Murphy, a Director of Morgan Chambers, who, when commenting on the dispute in *Personnel Today* (23 August 2005) said:

BA's case highlights the need for early HR input. When you have no control over how a business is run or its people management strategy – when it views its workforce differently from how you view yours – disaster is inevitable.

It is a sad but inevitable characteristic of time-pressed, resource-hungry managers that they rarely find the mental space to anticipate issues that will dominate their work in the future, until those issues are sufficiently immediate to smack them in the face.

HR practitioners are no exception to the rule. In 2001 and 2004 respectively, the people policies of two of the UK's flagship companies, British Telecom and British Airways, received unexpected and extremely unpleasant 'smacks' that did very public damage to their reputation and cost them millions in lost revenues. Both were the direct result of the wave of outsourcing and increased use of agency temps that has characterized business operations in the past decade. Both were caused by a failure, by no means confined to BA and BT, to anticipate the people-management implications.

It is thought that part of the unexpected nature of the problem lies in the fact that the temps, the workers of an outsourcing company (and, one might add, the thousands of consultants and freelance staff typically employed in most employing organizations) are not seen as part of an organization's people management. We undertook many case studies for this book, and two quotations from respondents stand out:

You ask how many temps and consultants are working here today. I haven't got a clue.

They [the non-employees] do not count in this organization. This is because they are not counted.

What this book aims to do

This book is about a rarely discussed topic: the management of people who are not typically seen as a central concern of HRM – the 'non-employees'. Like the Accenture staff who delivered key HR services on behalf of British Telecom, or the Gate Gourmet workers who provided an integral component of BA's customer service, their role is vital in sustaining the organization's performance, reputation and 'brand'. They often constitute up to 50 per cent of a workforce, yet they are not typically considered to be the direct remit of that organization's people management. They work 'for' the organization, yet are not 'of' it.

Freelancers, associates, consultants, contractors, agents, sole traders and other self-employed workers all fall into this category. Even more numerous and problematic in terms of their impact on conventional HR policy are people who perform key functions on behalf of the organization but who are employed by someone else. They may be agency temps or interim workers, work for an outsourcing company or, perhaps, be employed in a shared business service.

This process whereby staff are supplied to an organization by a third party is often referred to as 'intermediation'. Some of those supplied in this way work outside the country that houses the organization that uses their skills, and are part of the phenomenon referred to as 'off-shoring'.

Non-employees may be employed a long way away; on the other hand, they may work alongside the client organization's own employees. They may work for the company for a few days or for many years. The freelancer or consultant may also be working concurrently for other organizations in the same area of work. An agency 'temp' may have previously worked for a rival or, perhaps, be looking for a permanent job at the organization.

Most of these non-employees will likely be using the equipment and facilities at the organization. They may also be representing the organization to clients, customers and, for example, patients, and perhaps be the first 'port of call' for those clients, customers and others.

Where non-employees are employed by an outsourcing company to provide, say, catering for the organization, there are in effect at least two employers operating on the same premises. In countries where outsourcing is highly developed there may be tens of employers on the premises, performing specialist functions ranging from IT, reception and occupational health through to building maintenance, hygiene services, cleaning and security services.

The subject of this book is therefore both complex and important. It presents particular challenges to HRM, but also many opportunities, especially in terms of the function's strategic dimensions.

It is also recognized that there are other groups of non-employees which are beyond the scope of this book. They also raise important, though conceptually different, issues for employers. Included here are volunteers, domestic and family workers, and those on work experience.

However, many of the points made in this book can have relevance for at least some of these groups.

What this book aims to achieve

The book's main aims are as follows:

- To raise awareness of the extent of the contribution made by non-employees to employing organizations.
- To identify the distinctive needs and expectations non-employees have of employing organizations.
- To highlight the need to redress the absence, or low-key role, of HR in the management of non-employees, particularly in ensuring that people issues are dealt with in the supply of non-employees by third parties.
- To highlight good practice in how non-employees are selected, inducted and trained for their roles, and how existing management systems are adapted to accommodate their needs.
- To set the use of non-employees into their appropriate regulatory framework.
- To examine the broader issue of how the greater use of non-employees can be reconciled with the need to ensure the quality of product and service provided by the employing organization as a whole, particularly in the context of the professional and regulatory standards applying to the work activity. This might include standards for food production, transport, health, child and elder care. Quality issues increasingly cover ethical standards and business reputation.
- To explore the nature and workings of the employment relationship between the non-employee and the employing organization, particularly in the context of existing assumptions about the 'psychological contract' governing all employment relationships.

Where non-employees are employed alongside the organization's standard employees, experience tells us there is a vast range of managerial and legal issues that need to be addressed.

Research shows that in many (typically large) organizations there are not only frequent problems with communication and coordination systems, but also the managers, including HR managers, simply do not know how many contracts for services exist and how many people are involved.

Pressures on 'headcounts' have similarly led many line managers to resort to using agency staff rather than employing staff directly. Senior managers are often unaware of the extent of this practice and the numbers of 'temps' working for them. Sometimes the pressure to outsource or otherwise employ non-employees is motivated by a wish to avoid labour costs, especially the costs of the employment protection rights available to employees in most legal jurisdictions.

There is a perception by some that employment legislation is simply a 'burden on business' and inhibits flexibility, innovation and productivity. The evidence on this is far from clear. However, many see attractions in using non-employees for skill needs, as lower legal responsibilities can reduce non-wage labour costs. This, it is argued, can have major 'bottom line' benefits. However, where decisions such as this are taken without thinking through the full implications of using non-employees, the consequences – as illustrated by some of the case-examples in this book – can be disastrous. Unfortunately, it is not just a matter of 'out of sight and out of mind'.

By contrast, research and analysis also shows that there are many and increasing examples of good practice – practice that has evolved from careful assessment of skill needs and evaluation of the most effective ways they can be delivered. These analyses often lead to a conclusion that employing specialist freelancers or outsourcing companies to perform (in particular) non-core tasks can make real sense. It can also enable an organization that employs a carefully selected and prepared intermediator to focus on what the organization does best – be this manufacturing, health care, education or, perhaps, operating an airline or ferry service.

One of our case studies illustrates well these attitudinal changes.

In mid-2004, a former jam factory in Hobart, Tasmania was transformed into a fifty-bed hotel. It is called the Henry Jones Art Hotel, and displays art by Tasmania's best and emerging artists. It has won many prestigious awards, including being in Condé Nast's *Hot list of the Top 60 best Hotels in the World* in 2005. The hotel industry is traditionally known as a user of contingent or peripheral labour. However, Richard Crawford, one of the hotel's owners, explained his change of philosophy regarding employment. He says:

> I think of my staff as customers. We employ genuine tourism leaders. We do have a few part-time staff, but the core are tertiary trained

and interested in a career in tourism. We wanted to avoid this transient nature of people coming for a holiday job and then leaving us. We had to think hard about what staff wanted and respond. We need to treat them as core, regardless of their type of employment relationship, and it's paying off.

Such organizations also recognize that when skills are employed on a non-standard basis in this way there are repercussions in terms of the need to adapt management systems, especially HR management systems. The decision to maximize skills delivery through optimizing the services of employment agencies, freelancers or outsourcing companies also opens up the possibility of HR professionals playing a key role in this central business strategy. The 'people' issues are vital to the process, and many organizations have adopted partnership management models with the outsourcing organizations and agencies so that the latter's staff are appropriately integrated into the 'host' organization and work within a coherent management framework. These practices will be explored and analysed here.

However, as will be seen from our case studies and other evidence, HR's role in the management of non-employees is often limited or seen as unconstructive. It is clear that even where non-employees provide a significant proportion of the skills needs of an organization, the HRM department's role may be marginal or marginalized. It seems that more typically the key 'players' in the management of non-employees are other professionals, such as in purchasing/procurement, or perhaps line managers play the dominant role.

It is also necessary to take a wider view, and this book addresses such matters as how to ensure the quality of product and service provided by the employing organization as a whole. This is especially important where there are professional and regulatory standards applying to the work activity. This might include standards for food production, transport, health, child and elder care. Quality issues increasingly cover ethical standards and business reputation.

There is also the vital issue of training and development. How will this be provided in a work situation where more are self-employed or work on an intermittent basis for an agency, or where outsourcing companies move from contract to contract, facing the constant risk of contracts being summarily terminated when things to wrong? How can training be planned and funded? Who should or could be paying for it?

This book examines the development and implications of using 'non-employees', and follows through the key management decisions and tasks that underpin it. It uses a wide variety of examples and case studies, taken from several countries. The major focus will be on the UK, other EU states and Australia. The specially developed case studies from multinational companies are a particular feature. The book aims to abstract good practice from the case studies and provide advice, especially regarding the key decisions organizations make about their skills needs.

How is this book different?

First, the focus of most writing on HRM is on the internal management of people and on harnessing their skills for the efficiency of the organization. Literature emphasizes recruitment and retention issues, career management, performance management and, most importantly, the increasing need for flexibility and competitiveness. Here, some of the issues are different or have different emphases.

There has been a growing emphasis on organizational flexibility for over two decades and in most developed economies. As described in more detail on page 14, the so-called 'Atkinson model' of functional and numerical flexibility (Atkinson, 1984a) has been built on by many writers so as to include such matters as financial, geographical and organizational flexibility (Sparrow and Marchington, 1998). In this respect, the challenge to become more flexible and responsive is recognized as significant, perhaps compounded by the need to resolve the 'conflict between the need to operate in today's hyper-competitive environment and the current reliance on bureaucratic forms of organization' (Sparrow and Cooper, 2003).

However, this book argues that recent trends are not just towards more flexibility and different work patterns; they also challenge very basic assumptions of why and how people work. If, say, core tasks are performed by non-employees and an increasing number of employees display a strong sense of mobility and entrepreneurism, we may be moving to an 'inside out' model of employment (Holland and Hecker, 2003). There is evidence from Australia and elsewhere that so-called 'gold-collar' workers, who are apparently standard employees but who exhibit many of the characteristics of the self-employed, are an increasing feature of employing organizations. Their motivation and expectations are critical. This book, therefore, does not rely on statistics and macro-aspects of flexibility and change at work, but explores individuals at the workplace.

Second, the book reflects the challenges of globalization and competition, the need for organizational flexibility, and the need to maximize skills. However, its focus is on the 'external' human resource management function in relation to flexibility provided by non-employees – a distinctive form of HRM. It also explores decision-making – for example, deciding whether or not to outsource, or how best to select an agency. However, as well as considering business factors, this is done in a context of placing considerable emphasis on the aspirations and expectations of the individuals who actually work as non-employees, agency temps, etc., for the organization.

Research on such people often challenges assumptions and preconceptions. They are generally clear about their employment aspirations and expectations and how they want to be managed (Drucker and Stanworth, 2005). These people are certainly not just 'failed' employees or 'failed' permanent workers. Research is increasingly indicating that younger and typically highly skilled people are rejecting standard employment and standard management frameworks in favour of more varied, often more entrepreneurial, work patterns, and are consciously selling their skills (Lammiman and Syrett, 2004). Such workers will often have a cool-headed and strategic approach to their own career, and want to take more ownership of it.

Third, the book emphasizes the role of national and international regulation of work and the workplace. This is a topic often neglected in HR publications. Indeed, many writers on HRM explore management practices as though employers are able to take any decisions in a legal 'vacuum'. This is patently not the case. The debate about the impact of regulatory frameworks and the extent to which they inhibit or facilitate innovation and competitiveness has been both intense and long-running. Many cite the USA as an example of a deregulated labour market, and argue that that fact has been a prime cause of its economic success. However, Sweden has a highly regulated labour market and can also claim fame for the success of its economy (OECD, 2003). The jury is still probably out on the precise impact of regulation. No-one should deny, however, that its role is critical, and affects every day decision-making.

By way of example, it can be noted that many employers that have moved to using intermediaries, outsourcing, off-shoring, etc., have openly stated that they were strongly influenced by employment regulation. Sometimes they sought skills in particular places or in particular ways because of perceived weaker regulatory frameworks. Legislation may provide highly developed employment rights and protection for pay, but only for employees; thus non-employees who have lesser or few protections can be seen as attractive to employ. By moving to outsourcing or using an agency, many legal obligations can, many think, be avoided entirely. As will be seen later, this is rarely the reality, but the 'lure' of using non-employees remains intense.

However, sometimes, as in the case of the EU, there are regulations that establish minimum standards across many countries. Some of those provisions also have impact beyond the boundaries of the EU. However, it is important to recognize the role that regulation plays, even where there is little or no regulation from legislation. This is regulation through a contract. The key obligations and protections are obtained from contracts that are defined and applied according to their precise wording. These contracts are especially important where traditional industrial/employment relations structures are missing, declining, poorly developed or highly contentious; thus the contracts need to carefully planned for and devised. Chapters 6 and 7 consider these important legal issues.

Fourth, the book explores the nature and workings of the employment relationship between the non-employee and the employing organization, which are often highly complex. This is especially the case where employment agencies are used. Unsurprisingly, the role of the psychological contract will also be carefully reviewed. It is generally taken for granted that it is the standard employment contract that is susceptible to such analysis. This stresses the aspirations and expectations to the parties, in a context of an assumed interdependent relationship with a joint endeavour. The psychological contract, it is argued, can express more subtle issues than a legal one, and can respond more easily to changing policies and priorities.

Such assumptions, however, cannot be made where the individuals concerned are working for more than one employer or feel they are an entrepreneur. Such factors will dramatically change the expectations of, for example, a freelancer who feels that he or she is marketing personal skills rather than just seeking work. Orthodox notions of the psychological contract may be similarly difficult to apply to temps, who may well be unsure as to who, precisely, their employer is – is it the agency's client or the agency that pays them? Consequently, they may well be confused as to who their primary loyalty and duties should be towards. Such may also be the case with staff for outsourcing companies. Where they wear the client's uniform, eat in the client's canteen and obey the client's health and safety rules, they are likely to see the client as 'their' employer. Importantly, what do the individuals see as a 'good' or 'bad' employer?

The individuals that make up the non-employee workforce are by no means a homogeneous group. The self-employed can be highly skilled, very demanding and well-paid people. They can also be employed in manual work and for low pay as 'casual' or seasonal workers, perhaps in the hospitality or agriculture sectors, or as homeworkers. Agency temps can also range from highly paid and highly sought-after medical, IT and engineering staff through to lower-paid cleaning and catering staff. It goes without saying that outsourcing companies also operate in widely different skills areas. Sometimes the traditions of an employ-ment sector are important, with strong notions of culture and loyalty, often concerning the skill involved – such as in health care. Such features appear to be common across countries.

There is another important reason for this book. It is not simply that non-employees are an important and often increasing feature of many employing organizations across the developed and developing world; rather, it is that questions of efficiency, productivity and competitive-ness have become especially urgent. The EU has formally addressed this through its European Employment Strategy. With the spotlight increasingly falling on efficiency savings, improved productivity and enhanced quality, the effective management of non-employees has a critical role to play.

The structure of the book

The book relies on some thirty-six case studies of organizations and individuals that have relevance to the topic. The research methodology of triangulation provided for case studies of employing organizations, the providers of skills such as agencies, organizations that support or have a role in the development of non-employees and a few individuals who work as non-employees.

The case studies, details of which appear in Annex A, were undertaken in 2005 and 2006, and include studies from the UK, Australia, France and Belgium. These countries were selected because of their distinctive employment, regulatory and cultural features. The quotations in the book are generally from experienced and often front-line managers, some of whom are HR managers. It is recognized that the case studies cannot provide a representational or systematic view of such managers or others involved in the development and management of non-employees; nonetheless, we believe they bring valuable insights and practical experiences. In the text, material from our case studies is presented in a different typeface to that of the main text (Stone Sans). Other material is presented in italics.

The book begins with an overview of the development and key features of the employment of non-employees. It focuses on the characteristics and motivations of non-employees themselves, not least because non-employees are so often the victims of stereotypes, assumptions and misconceptions. It then follows the key HR aspects of employing non-employees, along with the legal issues that need consideration. Questions addressed include:

- How do you decide whether to use non-employees?
- How do you select skills providers and successfully integrate non-employees into the organization?
- What are the key HR issues for non-employees?
- What is the nature and impact of the regulatory framework applying to non-employees, including health and safety, employee relations and wider social and welfare issues?
- What are the key issues for the successful use and skills maximization of non-employees?

Summary and some challenges

This chapter has introduced a number of issues, including the contrast between the management of non-employees and that of standard

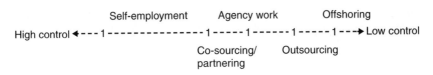

Figure 1.1 The control spectrum

employees. The topic is a complex and fast-changing one. At its heart is the question of ensuring skills maximization whilst not jeopardizing quality. In this process, control is critical. This presents particular problems when staff are off-site, are with the employer for a short time, or want their priorities and expectations to be responded to as self-employed people. It is possible to develop a very simple spectrum of control. High control is easier where non-employees are on-site and do not have other employers. Clearly the management challenges are increased where work is, say, off-shored or the non-employee has strong loyalties to an agency. Figure 1.1 provides a diagrammatic representation of this spectrum.

The challenges for the effective use of non-employees are considerable. Examples include:

- How to control work quality where you are not the employer
- How to be cost efficient without sacrificing the company's business reputation
- How to ensure efficient working and appropriate levels of loyalty and commitment where you are not the employer
- How to ensure consistency of service
- How to have different groups of non-employees working for you without it leading to confusions and conflict
- How to ensure training and upskilling of non-employees takes place
- How to bring in flexibility and diversity to the workforce without alienating employees
- How to bring in diversity and flexibility without alienating customers and stakeholders
- How to define a role for HRM when the training has all been geared to managing employees.

13

Not all of these challenges are considered within the confines of this book, but they can nonetheless be usefully considered.

A postscript: the question of nomenclature

At the start of this project, we engaged in a certain amount of hand-wringing about what collective phrase to use to describe the mix of self-employed professionals, agency staff and outsourced workers that the book encompasses.

The current vocabulary used by both managers and lawyers is now twenty years old. It originated in the mid-1980s in the wake of the 1980–1982 recession, when employers – traumatized by the unprecedented number of redundancies they had made – did not re-staff to pre-recession levels and started using a broader range of part-time and temporary workers.

The trend was captured by the employment researcher John Atkinson, of the Institute for Employment Studies (then the Institute of Manpower Studies), in a widely read report on 'the flexible firm' (Atkinson, 1984b). Atkinson argued that in order to deal with the resourcing dilemmas of a volatile economy, employers were restricting conventional full-time employment – with all of its security and ancillary benefits – to a 'core' of 'permanent' workers who performed services linked to the organization's key aims and goals. Ancillary and support tasks (catering, security, pay administration, etc.) were being devolved to a polyglot mix of part-time agency and contract staff at the 'periphery' of the firm.

Atkinson also distinguished 'functional' from 'numerical' flexibility. 'Core' workers would secure long-term employment by being open to redeployment and retraining in line with changing skill needs. 'Peripheral' staff would provide the firm with numerical flexibility (whether they liked it or not!) by being recruited and dispensed with in line with changing economic conditions.

European lawyers and labour market researchers termed the same workers 'marginal' or 'atypical'. These terms were accepted by the majority of trades unions which, in the 1980s, sought to resist the expansion of peripheral workers – partly to protect the employment rights and status of their existing members, but also because they recognized that 'core' staff were easier to recruit and represent.

By the time two of the contributors to this book wrote its precursor, *New Work Patterns: Putting Policy in Practice* (Leighton and Syrett, 1989), the veracity of these terms was already in question. Fifteen years on, they are wholly inappropriate.

The outsourcing of functions previously regarded as central to the firm's activities – financial administration, human resources, IT, PR and marketing – has created real difficulties in defining what remaining activities are truly 'core' to the organization. Moreover, if the term 'core' denotes services that are essential to the organization's main goals and to sustaining its reputation and 'brand' among key stakeholders – customers, investors, the media, etc. – then the experiences of the case study organizations in this book illustrate that self-employed, agency and outsourced workers are as 'core' to most firms as are their colleagues in full-time employment. They are therefore also hardly 'marginal' – if indeed they ever were. Additionally, with anything between one-third and one-half of the workforce in most organizations now in these categories, it is patently absurd to term them 'atypical'.

Attempts to update these terms have often provoked more confusion than clarity. Some firms term self-employed, agency and outsourced workers 'contract staff', on the grounds that they are usually performing their work under a contract to perform specific services. Others – for example the Royal Mail (see Chapter 4) – term these workers 'non-contract staff', on the grounds that they are not working under a permanent contract of employment.

After much head-scratching, we have plumped for the collective term 'non-employees'. The one common denominator of all these workers is that they perform their work for the 'user' organization under a contract to supply specific services (whether in their own right or on behalf of an intermediary employer) rather than a permanent contract of employment.

The distinction is important not just in legal terms but because, as Chapter 2 demonstrates, 'non-employees' do not necessarily have the same motivations, aspirations or expectations as their colleagues in permanent employment. Although some do see this kind of work as a pragmatic 'second best', others have chosen it willingly because it brings specific benefits in terms of flexibility and work/life balance that they can 'trade off' against the security and long-term benefits of a full-time job.

2

Context and evidence: the rise of the non-employee

Pattie Pierce has worked as a temp in the UK high-skilled secretarial/PA occupations for over twenty years. She chose to work in this way for health reasons. Several of Pattie's relatives have bi-polar affective disorder (manic depression). While Pattie's symptoms have been controlled by drugs, her life has nonetheless been difficult, with bouts of severe depression alternating with periods of damaging hyperactivity. Temporary work lets her take breaks to care for family – and also herself – without needing to take sick or compassionate leave:

> As long as you have reasonable references, and can give an account of any gaps, you can get work, take time off, and return to work – in my case, I have been able to continue working at this level despite chronic [drug-controlled] fast cycling symptoms. This is mostly due to choosing to work at a level I know I can cope with whichever phase I am in.

In her early years as a temp, Pattie worked primarily on a self-employed basis directly for client organizations, only using work through agencies as a means of 'filling in' during lax periods. Because temps were not granted Schedule D – self-employed – tax status, she worked through her own limited company, bought 'off-the shelf' for €150:

> I had my own calling cards and stationery, my books were audited annually by an accountant and I invoiced clients directly for my work. I found myself in secretarial work because my illness had interrupted my higher education. I was nonetheless able to specialize in specific sectors – investment banking mostly, but also legal secretarial work and public sector administration.

At that time there was a variety of word processing and other software used in these fields. I kept competitive by keeping up to date with the latest versions. Ringing up potential clients 'on the off-chance' to see what new systems they were using proved a good way of getting new clients.

I much preferred operating as an independent. I could play on my track record effectively, there was no shortage of work, and I could position myself for the assignments I wanted.

The stock market crash in 1987 brought this period of prosperity to an end:

Investment banks took much of the work in-house and were corporately forbidden to use freelancers, having established cost-saving contracts with large agencies. I had to harden myself to marketing in a depression.

Pattie eventually accepted the inevitable and signed on regularly with a leading employment agency and work contractor, Manpower. She worked for Manpower for eight years as a temporary worker, including two years on a permanent basis. Having lived in West London for most of her life, she then moved to the Sussex coast and has worked for the same agency since. Her assignments have been for a much wider variety of employers, including local government, a major defence contractor and a regional regeneration programme.

Aims of this chapter

- To cover changes in the composition of labour markets and the composition of workforces at individual employing organizations
- To explore the developments and features of the key groups of suppliers of non-employees – outsourcing companies, employment agencies – along with the emerging features of self-employment
- To consider the motivation, expectations and aspirations of non-employees
- To analyse any unifying features of non-employees.

The context, and the impact on the worker 'individualism' employment relationship

The rise in non-traditional work patterns has gone hand-in-hand with an emerging individualism among young adults entering the labour market following two decades of headcount reductions, industry restructure and cost-based management policies.

In part, this is a natural response to the failure of the post-war employment 'contract'. In his book *The Individualised Corporation*, Sumantra Ghoshal, London Business School Professor of Strategy, argues that business has totally failed to engage millennial-era youngsters in conventional corporate work (Ghoshal and Bartlett, 1998). Of 140 students on a management course he taught in 1998, only six wanted anything to do with careers in large companies. It was as much to do with quality of life and relationships as with the work itself. 'Most of their parents had worked for big companies – quite a few had reached senior management level – and these guys had seen what their life was like from inside the home', he said in an interview at the start of the decade. Their answer was: 'not us, no way' (Kennedy, 2001).

From this disillusionment with the past has emerged a new social culture less dependent on sustained contact with a single workplace. A recent book based on extensive interviews with young workers (Lammiman and Syrett, 2004) suggests that eighteen- to twenty-five-year-olds born after 1980 are the first generation that wholly lacks the psychological baggage of a post-Second World War social contract based on a guaranteed job for life and pension.

Inspired by hit television series like *Friends* and *Buffy The Vampire Slayer*, these 'millennials' stick together as a group far more than their Generation-X predecessors, whose key characteristic was ironic detachment. This presents both employers and brand managers with a distinct challenge. The social networks built up by most millennials by the time they are young adults owe far less to mainstream corporate culture than did those of their parents or elder siblings at the same age. A far higher proportion of these networks are likely to made up of peers who are home-based free agents, who regard old-fashioned brand image building with suspicion and whose social (as well as professional) lives do not revolve around a constant, all-encompassing workplace.

This is having a direct impact on their relationship with employers. New opportunities for the freestanding individual have emerged from the breakdown. As labour markets in a number of developed countries have become more deregulated and fragmented, pockets of opportunity exist for those workers with skills in high demand. Taking advantage of these 'hot' labour markets, such workers – termed 'gold-collar' in Australia

(Holland *et al.*, 2002) – are able to attract large salaries for their specialist skills. These workers are being included for consideration in this book, for although technically they may well be employees for an employing organization, they have such quasi-entrepreneurial features that they present similar challenges to an organization as do genuine self-employed workers.

The most notable of these workers are the information and communications technology (ICT) sector workers, such as programmers and systems analysts. In the USA they are generally seen as attracting annual salaries of at least €63 000. What also appears different about these workers is their attitude or psychological contract (explored in more detail later in this book) with regard to the employee–employer relationship (Holland *et al.*, 2002). As the Australian Centre in Industrial Relations Research and Training (ACIRRT, 1999: 3) explains:

Often found at the cutting edge of computer technology in banking or in publishing, 'gold-collar workers' have found high-paying jobs which stimulate and challenge them. They often spend extremely long hours at their job, they are young, ambitious and very well paid. Their loyalty, however, is owed less to their employer than it is to their career. As a result they are highly mobile, lured by new jobs which offer technical challenges or opportunities for self-development.

This reflects the dominant view of most ICT workers – highly qualified, relatively young individuals (over half in the UK are under thirty-five). However, the cyclical nature of this industry can be problematic. On the other hand, in biotechnology companies, which typically escape cyclical moves in national economies, it is the older workers with their intellectual and job experiences that are considered to be gold-collar workers, with average salaries of €60 000 plus benefits.

In China it is the senior business professionals who are known as gold-collar workers, with 342 000 of them in the developed cities of Beijing, Shanghai, Guangzhou and Shenzhen (China Staff, 2004/2005). Of these professionals, 12 per cent have disposable incomes of more than one million yuan (about €132 000) per year, and 68 per cent are executive managers in the fields of marketing, financial, executive and business planning. In conjunction with other gold-collar workers in other markets, they work hard – more than 11 per cent work over twelve hours per day, and 19 per cent work an average of ten to twelve hours daily.

The 'gold-collar' term is more widely spread than it would seem from the previous examples. Workers like electrical power-line installers, mechanical engineering technicians, plumbers and pipe-fitters, tool- and die-makers, mould makers and machinists are paid up to €63 000 a year on average. These jobs do not require a bachelor's degree, but workers earn high wages, have advanced skill levels and enjoy stagger-ing opportunities for employment.

Such workers may well be employees in an employing organization, but, as considered earlier, they have such quasi-entrepreneurial features that they present similar challenges to an organization as do genuine self-employed workers. These workers are thinking and acting differ-ently from traditional employees, who often held job security, working conditions, internal advancement and organizational loyalty as key employment values. Job-hopping, self-managed careers and loyalty to their profession are their priorities.

These trends are causing many managers and others to reflect on the implications of the rise of the gold-collar worker:

A director with the recruitment agency Talent2, in Australia, commented that: 'Employers are now having to offer greater and greater rewards to attract and retain staff. They also offer less-tangible benefits, such as flexible working and help with career management'.
Despite these efforts, another director said: 'There is going to be a – I don't know if it's a revolution or a strong evolution – in the whole way organizations manage the workplace. It's a question of how long these things take, but I reckon work as we define it today will be a very different thing in ten years time'.

(Adams, 2005)

Innovation in skills supply for nursing – USA style

In the USA, just as with many developed and developing economies, there are major skills shortages for nurses. Employment agencies are often used to supply needs. More recently, shift-bidding is being used to attract nurses. Nurses can log on to a hospital's website, view the empty nursing shifts and make a bid to work shifts at a rate of pay within a range posted by the hospital. All things being equal, the lowest bidder wins. The consequence is that the average hourly rate for those bidding is higher than that for standard employees but lower than for temps. The system allows nurses who are self-employed or work for an agency to exercise more control over their working conditions. Other bidders are standard part-timers who want to increase their hours or full-timers who want to earn overtime pay.

(Anonymous 2004)

An example such as this clearly challenges assumptions about traditional ways of working and presents new issues for HRM, especially when responding to skills shortages. Importantly, it also illustrates changing aspirations on the part of workers, and their need to develop new skills. The skill of bidding for a shift introduces direct notions of entrepreneurism to an occupation few would normally consider entrepreneurial.

This fundamental shift in the employment relationship will put further pressure on employers regarding how to manage the relationship. Many workers in these relationships lack organizational commitment, and this, combined with an increasing shortage of skilled labour (particularly in the information, communication and technologies (ICT) industries) is creating growing concern for employers. As a result, employers are having to review their own perceptions of the employment contract.

The evidence: what do we know about non-employees?

Despite considerable debate regarding the changing nature of employment relationships and the new issues that are emerging, has there been, for example, a growth in self-employment and agency working?

There are many sources of data on the composition of the labour market. Several are international, such as the International Labour Office (ILO), or multinational, such as the OECD. Others cover a specific geographical area – such as Eurostat, which provides data on EU member states but also on applicant and associated states. There are also well-developed data sources for other countries, such as the USA, Australia and Japan. Sometimes data that are focused on flexible working, such as the incidence of and trends in part-time, home-working and fixed-term work, will also cover, for example, agency/interim working and self-employment.

Self-employment

Many management writers and specialists in the 'future of work' discourse had predicted that by the turn of the twenty-first century there would be a number of distinct labour market changes. Included would be a move to the casualization of work, with an increasing incidence of precarious employment, such as fixed-term and standby/on-call work. This, though, would be in contrast to the predicted 'rise' of the portfolio career and to various forms of self-employment. Such changes, it was predicted, would be most marked in higher-skilled and mobile workers (Bridges, 1994). All this would be aided by IT and the ability to work at home or at a variety of locations. Such workers would sell their skills to organizations and would need to have honed their marketing and negotiating skills. They would have a high degree of discretion and autonomy and the work performed would provide high levels of reward and job satisfaction. It was often postulated that women facing problems with access to equal pay or faced with a 'glass ceiling' would turn to self-employment to avoid the obstacles they faced within traditional employing organizations.

What do data reveal? Before considering some key indicators, a note of caution needs to be sounded. The data are rarely collected on a consistent basis, and it is difficult to make cross-country or cross-sector comparisons. Some countries do not record data for self-employment, and there is anyway considerable confusion as to how to differentiate the employed from the self-employed. In the UK, it is estimated that up to one-third of the workforce may have an ambiguous categorization (DTI, 2002) – a matter that is also a feature of other countries, though perhaps not to such an extreme extent (Perulli, 2003). The law has struggled in virtually every developed economy to provide workable 'tests' to differentiate the employed from the self-employed. This is a matter that will be returned to later, as the category into which a worker fits is so often critical for legal and other purposes.

In the UK, some 12.5 per cent of workers are reported as being self-employed. This represents a slight decline since 1992, despite this period being one of considerable government and other activity to promote entrepreneurism and small business development.

Within the EU's twenty-five member states, in 2004 self-employed workers constituted some 15 per cent of workers (EC, 2005a). However, it must be borne in mind that many self-employed persons act as 'sole traders' in professional services, retail and construction work, etc. They deal directly with clients and consumers, and do not work for other employers. They are not therefore part of the topic of this book.

In the EU labour market, 15 per cent of workers are self-employed. Men account for 18 per cent, and women 15 per cent. The overall percentage of self-employed persons has remained relatively stable in recent years, though there has been a slight decline in female self-employment. There are, though, major variations in the percentage self-employed between countries. For example, Denmark and Sweden have only 5 per cent and 4 per cent, respectively; by contrast, Portugal has 27 per cent and Greece 42 per cent, suggesting major cultural, economic and legal factors at play.

Data for the new EU member states, many of which are post-Communist and have only recently embraced a market economy, are also of interest. In some of these countries – for example, the Czech Republic – self-employed numbers have grown considerably. Mostly, however, after rising until the late 1990s, they have more recently declined.

Beyond the EU, a similarly mixed picture emerges. There are higher numbers of self-employed in most South American states and in many parts of Asia. In developing countries, the self-employed can constitute over half of the labour market. By contrast, the percentage is around 10 per cent in Japan and 15 per cent in Canada, but only 7 per cent in the USA. The point made about complex factors appearing to impact on the proportion of self-employed can be made with reference to Australia and New Zealand. For Australia, the percentage is around 13 per cent, while for New Zealand there is a significantly higher rate of 18.6 per cent – not much less than one fifth of the total labour market (World Employment Report, 2005). Amongst the likely explanations for these variations are economic, educational, regulatory and cultural factors. Perhaps important, too, is the willingness and effectiveness of employing organizations in using the skills of non-employees.

Overall, self-employment is very variable in its contribution to labour markets and has seen a slight increase in some states but slight decline in others, indicating relative stability.

Are different types of people becoming self-employed?

If there has been no dramatic increase in the EU and elsewhere regarding the overall numbers of self-employed, has there, nonetheless, been a change in the type of people who are becoming self-employed? Are the highly qualified and skilled moving disproportionately towards self-employment? Are older people turning to self-employment? Are women turning against it? Although the evidence is not well developed, there are some indicators that changes have taken place.

Those who have analysed the rise in self-employment in the 1990s tend to have very different standpoints. Some argue for the impact of the 'portfolio career', especially for younger workers (Cannon, 1995; Crainer and Dearlove, 2000). Others argue that the change has been largely towards marginalized, precarious forms of work (Mangan, 2000), sometimes through the 'eviction' of staff from large employing organizations. The organizations provide them with a certain amount of work initially – sometimes called 'sweetheart' deals – but this often dries up.

Recent figures from the Australian Bureau of Statistics (ABS) have shown an increase of 79 per cent over a two-year period in those that 'have thrown in the corporate grind and are going solo'. These are predominately men. Many value the flexibility, being 'opposed to the old model of having to work like a dog at the expense of family time to earn it'. People have had enough of this, and rightly so (Toomey 2005).

A recent review of the research evidence in Britain (the UK excluding Northern Ireland) provides useful insights into the characteristics of the self-employed (Smeaton, 2003). This explored the occupations, age, gender, earnings, motivations and employment preferences of people defining themselves as self-employed. The review reveals that although younger people do indeed increasingly enter self-employment, they typically fail to remain self-employed. This finding is mirrored in other EU states. Older workers form the largest percentage of new entrants, and are often invited or required by their current employer to move to self-employed status. Mostly such workers are professionals, and they appear to move to self-employment with varying degrees of enthusiasm.

For the purposes of this book, although the evidence does not appear necessarily to support the widespread development of a distinctive portfolio or entrepreneurial model of self-employment, it does raise some relevant points. First, the self-employed tend to report higher levels of job satisfaction than do employees. Second, although initially many were reluctant self-employed workers, around 40 per cent stated that they 'wanted to be their own boss', a growing percentage (up to 21 per cent) saw self-employment as a dimension of a specific occupation, and 26 per cent considered self-employment as a better way to earn more money.

Issues of security, occupational benefits, etc., tended not to be cited. Thus, although the picture painted by the work 'futurologists' has not been fully confirmed, at least for the UK and for most other parts of the EU, there are some major conclusions that might be drawn by the employers of such workers. These are the different priorities and preferences that self-employed people appear to have when compared with 'ordinary' employees (Smeaton, 2003). These issues are considered more fully in Chapter 3.

The following comments taken from interviews with self-employed people illustrate some of their typical characteristics and attitudes (Leighton, 1998):

To be self-employed, you have to be risk tolerant. If you can't sleep at night because you worry about the mortgage payments or booking your next package holiday, don't even contemplate self-employment. When I went solo as a musician and music teacher, I barely broke even for three years. It's OK now, but it has been tough.

A lot of the things you take for granted as an employee go out of the window when you are self-employed. Its not just regular earnings, but simple things like not getting feedback on your performance. It's as if paying you is the only feedback the employer thinks you need.

In a funny sort of way you have to be so much more disciplined as a freelancer than as an employee. The freedom and flexibility can be your undoing. You really do have to self-manage big time, or it will all go wrong.

I never thought of myself as an entrepreneur or freelancer. I had a regular job for many years and did a little 'private' work in my spare time. As retirement loomed, it seemed a good idea to build up the consultancy work and develop contacts and new skills. Even so, it can be quite scary moving to the world of self-employment.

A case study undertaken for this book develops several of these ideas:

Dominic Brender has been a self-employed journalist, researcher and management consultant since 1982. When considering his reasons for being self-employed, he said:

Like a lot of people I became self-employed because the company I worked for went bust. I had caring responsibilities and chose the flexibility that I think self-employment provides. My father was self-employed, so I knew what was involved. However, I have never seen myself as an entrepreneur. I think there is a big distinction between those who consider they have a business to run and people like me. I see it more as a lifestyle choice. I want choice to see friends and to achieve a kind of work–life balance that suits me.

He thinks, though, that ideas of why and how people work have not really changed that much despite the growth in flexible working, etc. Management thinking still focuses on employees, and

Managers still tend to work in that frame, and this drives the agenda of what it is assumed people want from work. Today, the first generation is challenging these approaches. If you start from a mindset that security is all, it does not resonate with me. Take pensions. I take it for granted that I will have to work on. Notions of careers and retirement are therefore alien to me.

Agency work

Agency work is variously described as interim working, temporary work, temporary help work and, more popularly, temping. Whatever the label, the common feature of such work is the supply of labour for a limited period to an employing organization by an intermediary (the agency). The supply may be to cover employee sickness or maternity leave, or perhaps to deal with a specific short-term project. Temps might stay a few days or for years, though they typically remain a worker for the agency during these periods.

Agency work has often been highly controversial in many parts of the world. Until recently, several EU states considered the operation of an agency an unlawful activity. The opposition largely came from trade unions which considered that agency working would undermine working conditions for permanent staff and could be used to weaken industrial action by the supply of alternative ('blackleg') labour. Opposition also came from supporters of public employment services – labour exchanges, job centres, etc. – which considered that their role would be challenged by the private sector. Other groups expressed concern for the working conditions of the temporary workers themselves, as their vulnerable position, in terms of relying on agencies for work, made them open to exploitation. Individual agencies also had very bad reputations regarding such matters as paying the temps, and the failure to provide any benefits beyond pay.

The notion of an agent providing labour for another is not a new idea. It has been common for many years in sectors such as construction, agriculture, and other forms of manual work, for contract labour to be provided. Today, we can note the impact of so-called 'gang-masters' in supplying (often migrant) labour to other organizations. Their record has been particularly poor.

However, in recent years the image has generally improved. Many multinational organizations have achieved a higher profile, with some (such as Adecco and Randstadt, and longer-established companies such as Manpower and Kelly Services) being household names. The numbers working for agencies have dramatically increased. Most importantly, there has been a major revision of the role that agencies can play in transitional labour markets and in terms of dealing with employment restructuring. Although opposition remains in some quarters, agencies have become a well-recognized feature of developed economies. The temporary workers themselves have become regular topics for research and analysis, not least regarding their motivation and experiences of working for agencies (*Personnel Review*, 2006).

How established is agency working?

Agency work is longest established in North America, with many of the multinationals being based there. Outside North America, agency working is most highly developed in the UK, France, Switzerland and the Netherlands. Many of the most successful agencies are European multinationals. Agencies can belong to an international body – the CIETT – which acts as a lobbying organization as well as setting good-practice standards.

Identifying the numbers involved in temporary agency work is notoriously difficult. Do you count the number of workers 'on the books' of an agency, who may or may not be in work at any given time? Do you count the number of assignments undertaken? This is also unreliable, as the same person may be working for fifty-two weeks a year and account for, say, thirty assignments. Do you rely on business data regarding the agencies, and household or similar surveys of the staff? The latter is probably the most reliable.

Globally, the industry has variable impact in different countries. A recent report for CIETT by Goldman Sachs reveals that 39 per cent of the agency market is in the USA, 21 per cent in the UK, 13 per cent in Japan and 11 per cent in France. Only 16 per cent of the market is accounted for by other countries. For example, although growing, Australia accounts for only 2 per cent of the global market. In terms of labour market contribution, this is highest in the UK, at almost 4 per cent, compared to only 2.2 per cent in the USA. In other parts of the EU, the comparable percentages are 3.2 per cent (though rapidly increasing) in the Netherlands and 0.7 per cent in Germany, despite the presence of several major agencies. In some EU states, especially the new member states, agency work is barely developed (Goldman Sachs, 2003).

There has been recent and significant growth in Japan – a country renowned for its traditional 'jobs-for-life' culture. Major employment restructuring in 2002 and 2003 initially led to growth in outplacement services. Now, skill shortages have led to increased demand for agency workers, helped by deregulation in March 2004. Pasona Inc., established in 1976, is the largest staffing business in Japan. It has developed a particular market for older (50+) workers who:

> are tired of commuting in packed trains and gruelling workloads
> and want part-time rather than full time jobs. Their use of agencies
> to obtain work is a growing trend and business is booming.
>
> (*The Economist*, 2004)

A study that mapped the development of agency working concludes that 'The global market for temporary labour is not emerging spontaneously; it is being constructed' (Peck *et al.*, 2005). It notes growth in Japan and China, largely driven by the major global agencies. There is also rapid growth in countries, such as Italy and Spain, which had traditionally

29

banned agency work. Nonetheless, there are many countries that remain agency-free zones.

The type of work performed by temps varies considerably, although for men it is well developed in IT, engineering and manual work, and for women in medical, secretarial and administrative work. Some employment sectors have been more recently entered by agencies; these include management and teaching, and a growing range of professional services such as law and accountancy. Increasingly, agencies are specialized. Many are very large but, typically, agencies are small or confined to a limited geographical area.

The temporary agency work industry in the UK is subject to annual market intelligence reports, and it is likely that many of the broad findings are valid for the industry in, say, the Netherlands, France and Switzerland. In the UK, in 2003 the industry was worth over €30 billion, although this represented a 5 per cent decrease on 2002. The decline was caused by pressure on fee rates and increased competition generally. The decline was most marked in IT, financial services and medical services, following dramatic growth in 1997–2002. It appears that the industry has matured in the UK and is reflecting on its future. Some of the possible changes are considered later in this book and in our case studies. They have considerable relevance for the clients of agencies.

In Australia, agency employment grew at 7.5 per cent per annum through the 1990s, compared with 1.6 per cent growth in standard employment. However, there was a decline in the percentage working for an agency from 1998 to 2004. Currently, Australia represents some 2 per cent of the global agency market.

In New Zealand, agency work has benefited from major labour market deregulation. For example, there are three global agencies in cleaning – Spotless (Australian), OCS (British) and ISS-Tempo (Danish). There is evidence of fierce competition in the sector, leading to pay undercutting.

Although the peak for profitability may have passed, several interesting trends are worth noting. The public sector's demand for agency temps appears to be holding up well and, interestingly, there has been growth in 'preferred supplier agreements'. These are agreements whereby one agency supplies the temporary needs of, generally, large organizations. This development is illustrative of the desire by many employing organizations to bring more structure and stability to the process of using temps.

Amongst the leading EU-based agencies are Adecco, Hays, Manpower, Nestor Healthcare, Spring Group, Capita Business Services, Kelly Services, the Corporate Services Group (which includes Blue Arrow) and Randstadt. Some of these are the subjects of our case studies. The fact that some of these well-known organizations have suffered recent losses has caused the industry to undertake a SWOT analysis of its own position, and the conclusions seem highly relevant for this book.

1. The *strengths* of the industry include:
   - expertise and access to skilled resources
   - provision of an essential or shortage service
   - the ability to offer an integrated advice package to clients
   - a proven track record with many clients.
2. The *weaknesses* of the industry include:
   - a poor image and concerns over standards
   - difficulty in retaining good staff.
3. The *opportunities* of the industry include:
   - new leadership in the UK's professional body for agencies
   - the move to 'partnering' with clients.
4. The *threats* to the industry include:
   - the increased use of client company websites to themselves recruit temporary staff
   - off-shoring
   - skills shortages experienced by the agencies themselves
   - regulation adding to costs.

(KeyNote, 2003)

Are agencies changing?

Our case studies confirmed some of the major changes in the way agencies are working and, relevantly, are relating to their temps. The competitive challenges identified by the SWOT analysis above have caused several of the leading agencies to rethink or amend their employment policies for the temps. A contentious issue has been the nature of the employment contract between the agency and the temp. Many agencies, particularly in the UK, do not provide employee status, and this makes access to employment rights and other benefits highly problematic. Some agencies provide low pay, and this is one of the factors that have led to the 'poor image' identified above.

Two of our case study agencies – Manpower (France) and Kelly Services (UK and Ireland) offer employee status or, in the case of Kelly, are moving to provide such status to more and more temps. Both consider that they need to build up a cadre of reliable and well-rewarded temps. In highly skilled and specialized areas there may still be pressure from temps to be self-employed to, as they see it, safeguard high earnings. This is so with RSA Ltd, the UK-based case study organization that provides staff to the pharmaceutical and IT industries.

This trend is also observable in Australia, as another of our case study organizations shows:

Frank Hargrave founded the SKILLED Group Ltd, an agency, in Melbourne, Australia in 1964. Publicly listed since 1994, the company has seventy-three offices in Australia and New Zealand and employs people in every employment sector. Its business philosophy is to provide 'good quality people and systems, flexible work practices and the delivery of excellent customer services'. The agency has always seen itself as providing a career for people [not just work]. Jessica Schauble, Manager, Corporate Strategy, says, 'We give our people a range of benefits they might have only got if they were working in the core [of the client firm], and SKILLED, with a focus on partnerships with client firms, sees itself as having a competitive advantage in managing these "core" employees'. If SKILLED's objective is to be the employer of choice in the markets in which it operates, its success appears to be borne out by a survey it undertook with 1000 trades people in 2005. This showed that what SKILLED people valued was not just good pay but also 'workplace relationships, job satisfaction, opportunities to learn and progress, location, security and flexibility'. Somewhat ironically, a growing selling point for the agency is that: 'The employment table has turned in terms of employment . . . no secure jobs, so working with SKILLED is no less secure than anyone else and does provide benefits that are valued'.

The situation generally was summed up by CEO Greg Hargrave, son of SKILLED's founder:

Essentially we have two key customers – our client base and our employee base. We understand we have to meet the skill needs of the first group and satisfy the career aspirations of the second group. Our clients are looking for flexible workplace solutions and our employees are seeking flexibility in their working hours and structures. Managing the needs of both clients and employees is our means of creating a strong competitive advantage. To achieve this in an environment where skills are in short supply, we need to actively focus on attraction and retention of staff and being an employer of choice. This means investing in the people side of our business.

Why do people become temps?

Clearly, if agencies conform to the philosophy and model set out above, the agencies can become employers of choice and provide workers with rewarding work and careers. However, it is possible that the picture is more mixed than that set out in our case studies. The Goldman Sachs report referred to earlier also explored this question. It found that although 40 per cent of temps were temping because they could not find a permanent job, 26 per cent were gaining work experience and 13 per cent stated they were 'between jobs', some 21 per cent wanted to 'work flexibly, work for different employers and have different experiences'. The Pattie Pierce account at the head of this chapter illustrates the value of temping for those with health issues.

Across the EU, there is a 43 per cent conversion rate from agency work to permanent work with the agency's client employer. Clearly, some use agencies to seek permanent jobs. Their time at the client organization may, in effect, be a probationary period for the client/employer, as well as for the worker. The worker will have clear aspirations and expectations. These can be of value to the client/employer, especially where the temporary worker has relevant prior varied experience. However, the data also reveal that a significant percentage of temporary workers enjoy the different experiences and flexibility that agency work can provide. They appear to enjoy working for different employers, and can use agency work to fit in with their own priorities. Such workers present a different set of aspirations and expectations to the client employer.

A less usual reason for temping emerged from one of our case studies. This, in part, dealt with the increasing tendency within the UK for teachers and lecturers to be provided to education employers by agencies:

Chris Sharp works as a senior manager for Capita (Learning and Development), part of the Capita Group that provides staff and undertakes many major outsourcing contracts. Commenting on the increasing role of agencies in the education sector in the UK, he said: 'a lot of temporary teachers are people who are retired from senior posts. They like temping because it allows them to teach but frees them from responsibility and all the paperwork. You can get really good people working this way.'

Recent studies taken from the UK (Drucker and Stanworth, 2005) and from New Zealand (Casey and Alach, 2004) indicate higher than might be expected levels of job satisfaction. A respondent to the former research, who expressed herself happy with temping, said that her main reason was that: 'They are selling my skills and as a person. Without them there is an age discrimination barrier. There is no age discrimination at the agency. They push my skills and experience.' A typical respondent to the latter research, which only covered women, said: 'There's a lot of freedom to just up and go – its like being your own boss. Would I go back permanent? I don't think so.'

Another of our case studies confirmed the typical reasons for temping:

Jean-François Denoy, Director of Human Resources Development at Manpower, France, reflects on the reasons people work for his agency. He thinks there are four main groups of temps:

1. Young people who want to find out about jobs and different companies. This, he thinks, builds confidence. A high percentage of Manpower's temps are aged between twenty and twenty-six. This partially explains Manpower's investment in training (see Chapter 5).
2. Specialists, i.e. those with high skill levels but who do not want to be in one company all their life. They want to focus on their skills. M. Denoy said: 'We have a big relationship with them. They often stay with us for fifteen years or more.' Typically they are in construction or specialized engineering, such as aviation engineering. 'We treat them well and they are very loyal to us.'
3. Older workers.
4. Those who do not want to work regularly all year. There are many reasons for this, but M. Denoy said: 'They are not always easy to accommodate'.

Another reason was identified:

Darren Cox, Director of Human Resources at Kelly Services, UK, says that, for many on a permanent contract, 'The psychological contract has been dismantled.' Many highly skilled people are disillusioned, so:

> We will tap into them. At the least, we give them a learning and development opportunity. For such people there is a temp/permanent continuum and no longer a clear divide. It is something we debate and something that is evolving.

Kelly Services has created a special contract for these highly skilled 'Kelly people', who typically work on a series of projects and are well rewarded.

The overall position with intermediation via an employment agency appears to be that, generally, the very significant growth in countries familiar with agency work in the 1990s has slowed, though there has been a recent upturn. The industry is now reflecting more closely on its role and how it works with client organizations.

The industry is also reflecting on the impact of regulation. Although in many countries (for example, Italy, Spain, Japan and the Netherlands) there has been a general move towards less regulation and growing opportunities for agencies to develop, there are also fiscal and other legal changes that are making matters more difficult in other countries.

On the positive side, many observers see the 'war for talent' as being helpful to agencies. The industry sees that in the near future it must:

- remove the stigma that still attaches to agency work in some contexts
- improve public relations
- establish better links with trade unions
- make temporary agency work more attractive to individuals through, perhaps improved training and development opportunities, as well as improved employment terms and more secure contracts with agencies
- bring more coherence to the industry through more conscious development of niche sectors – which might be in terms of skills but also geographical factors
- restructure through more mergers and acquisitions, creating more efficient 'big players'
- demonstrate more effectively the 'value added' that high quality and usually specialist agencies can bring
- identify the new emerging markets, such as for 'HR solutions' (Goldman Sachs, 2003).

To these ends, the industry is also developing new ways of working with clients and in partnership with both public and private bodies. It has already played a major role in job creation initiatives, has acted in partnership with public bodies responding to long-term unemployment or mass redundancies, and has generally made an important contribution across the EU to skills development and deployment.

The industry, using a number of initiatives, is responding to some of its perceived problems through a process of self-regulation and standard setting. In some countries, this best practice has already been translated into legislation that regulates the day-to-day activities of agencies. This is the situation in the UK, where the Conduct of Employment Agencies and Businesses Regulations 2003 have sought to improve dramatically the communication and vetting systems between client/employer and agency. In effect, these regulations require agencies to be the 'guarantor' of agency temps. For their part, clients have to be much more precise regarding the skills and other needs of temps, and ensure basic standards for them regarding, for example, the unambiguous definition of skills accreditation and health and safety requirements.

The process of intermediation, therefore, can be far more than simply responding to short-term skills needs. It can play a key role in restructuring and, according to the OECD, some agencies can be 'the host vehicle for people's careers' (OECD, 2002). It is this creative dimension to agency work that is explored in Chapter 3.

The position appears to be that as the industry has matured, the role it plays has also changed. Importantly and relevantly, as the case studies on Manpower (France) and Kelly Services and RSA (UK) have shown, economic and other pressures have caused the industry to reflect on whether it continues to make business sense to employ transient workers, perhaps keen to finance their backpacking trip round the world or looking for short assignments while they decide on their careers, or rather to employ a trained and committed cadre of temps with wide work experience who offer skills and adaptability to a client and who take pride in their versatility. It is self-evident that the latter workers will provide different benefits for and make different demands on a client organization than do the more stereotypical transient temps.

Outsourcing

Human problems are generally underestimated when it comes to outsourcing procedures. One explanation for this is that the focus is usually on technique, on the service concept or on the legal, without taking into account the full dimension of the impact of change on human beings.

(MEDEF, 2002)

Along with neglect of the human dimension of outsourcing, its development has been attended in many countries by controversy and opposition. Where outsourcing involves off-shoring, the controversy is heightened. The OECD (2005), in its *Employment Outlook*, has recently stated:

15–20 per cent of total employment in Australia, Canada, the EU and USA correspond to service activities that potentially could be subject to international sourcing.

The threat posed by outsourcing to, say, the Indian subcontinent, Africa or Eastern Europe has provoked many expressions of concern, though there is some evidence that for skilled workers, at least, the impact is not so drastic (OECD, 2005). Nonetheless, trade unions, professional bodies and many politicians and policymakers remain very anxious.

Many also see the loss of standard jobs within countries and within employing organizations as unacceptable. Others consider the impact of the 'dual workforce' at the workplace a source of apprehension and practical problems. These are, of course, important matters that will be addressed in Chapters 4, 8 and 9. The problems are not insurmountable, but they can be major and, if handled poorly, can also undermine the many tangible benefits that outsourcing is capable of providing.

An example taken from Australia illustrates well the controversy that can be engendered by outsourcing, especially where it also involves off-shoring:

Coles Myer Ltd operates more than 1900 stores in Australia and New Zealand under the brand names of Target, Coles Supermarkets, Bi-Lo, Myers and Grace Bros. It is Australia's largest non-government employer, with over 165 000 staff. Following a decade of difficult trading, the CEO decided in 2002 to consolidate all its credit card brands and the call centre business was outsourced to GE Capital. GE Capital then off-shored call-centre work to Delhi. It was unclear how much Coles Myer was a part of the off-shoring decision, but there was a storm of protest. There were radio and television programmes, including a documentary, *Diverted to Delhi*. The trade unions were to the fore in this protest. Belinda Tkalcevic, from the Australian Council of Trade Unions (ACTU), said, 'It is great for big multinationals who can get cheap labour from India, but what about Australian workers?'

The core issue uniting the Coles Myers stakeholders was the export of Australian jobs: 'The low cost advantage needed to be reassessed against the moral and/or other concerns of stakeholders which say that an "icon" company which accounts for 40 cents of every retail dollar was exporting home-grown, skilled local jobs.' One critic said, 'I think the part that annoyed me most is that I see this as exporting jobs. Myer does not have stores in India, so their customers are not in Delhi. The customers are here, and I think that sort of employment should be here in Australia.'

It is important to note that the opposition to the off-shoring focused on Coles Myer, not GE Capital. It aimed to damage the brand. Late in 2003, the call centre work was brought back in-house. Coles Myer itself refused an invitation to participate in the research.

As with agency work, there are many names that are given to the practice of outsourcing. A useful definition of outsourcing is as follows:

> *Outsourcing consists of confiding the entirety of a function or service to a specialized outside service provider for the duration of several years. This provider then supplies the service in conformity with the specified level of service, performance and responsibility.*
>
> (MEDEF, 2002)

'Outsourcing' is the term that has recently become prominent; previously, subcontracting was the more usual label. Many argue, though, that outsourcing is generically different from subcontracting, the latter being characterized by contracting for 'a business activity that does not affect business strategy' – such as cleaning and maintenance – whereas outsourcing 'signifies an actual process of re-examining the strategy and specialization of the enterprise' (Guerre, 2000).

Some refer to outsourcing as 'insourcing'; others call it 'co-contracting' or 'co-sourcing'. The different labels do have significance as, to a greater or lesser extent, they shape management and other practices that impact on or drive outsourcing. Increasingly, the emphasis is on partnership arrangements and on greater integration of the management and delivery of the service in question between the outsourcing company and the employer/client.

Outsourcing, of course, is not new. The manufacturing industry has long outsourced for components and production. Service sectors have also long outsourced for, for example, suppliers of food, business equipment and vehicles. The more recent change has been to outsource a growing variety of services, from catering, cleaning and maintenance through to ICT, payroll, recruitment services, outplacement, customer services and quality management. This development has brought workers for the outsourcing companies into direct contact with the client organization and its staff. This has been an important change.

The industry that provides these services is becoming mature and increasingly multinational. Although the small cleaning company, the local IT firm and HR consultancies are a feature of outsourcing, large companies are of growing importance.

For a number of reasons the UK is a global leader in outsourcing: first, the labour market has been comparatively unregulated; secondly, trade unions have been relatively ineffective in challenging outsourcing; and thirdly, since the 1980s, so-called 'market testing' for efficient and cost-effective services provided to the public sector has led to massive growth in the practice and a commensurate decline in directly employed cleaners, caterers, maintenance staff, etc.

More recently in the UK, the Public Finance Initiative (PFI) introduced a novel form of outsourcing whereby an outsourcing company built new schools, hospitals, etc., for the public sector in return for lengthy service delivery contracts to provide security, cleaning, catering, maintenance and the like to the occupiers of the new building. The service contracts typically last for twenty or more years. The intention is to provide investment for the public sector, underwritten by an outsourcing company. The reason for this type of outsourcing is therefore distinctive, and its success or otherwise is judged differently. Other countries, in particular Ireland, have adopted this approach to public investment. Again, though, the matter has proved very controversial.

The political drivers for change towards outsourcing remain significant and of lasting importance in the UK, despite the change of government in 1997.

How developed is outsourcing?

Within the EU, over 90 per cent of all UK employers outsource for at least one service. In Switzerland this is 74 per cent and in Germany 70 per cent. By contrast, only 32 per cent of employers in Spain and 28 per cent in France outsource for at least one service. It is clear that patterns of outsourcing vary from country to country. For example, there are major differences in the extent to which the public sector in different countries outsources for services. There are also variations in terms of the services typically outsourced. In Italy, these tend to be highly specialized technical services such as IT, legal and financial services. In Germany, the pressure following reunification led to a need for rapid service development. However, opposition from the public and trade unions meant that outsourcing was frequently undertaken through the creation of subsidiary companies that then provided the relevant service.

In the UK, the greater opportunity to outsource, combined with government support, has led to outsourcing for services across the board. Thus, in 1991 BP Exploration (BPX) broke new ground in the oil industry by outsourcing its accounting function and staff, plus the associated accounting software and support groups. This was not a one-off decision but part of long-term strategic focus on core activities.

The decision affected the entire accounting services of the UK Continental Shelf operations. It was taken against the background of maturing oil fields and rising costs of BPX in the North Sea. In the previous decade production costs per barrel had tripled, while in real terms the selling price had slumped to one-third of what it had been in 1980.

To remain profitable, BPX had to reduce its spending substantially – and strategic outsourcing was top of its list to achieve this. Accordingly, it divided its accountancy function into the following categories:

- Accountancy policy (based on professional judgment)
- Interpretation of financial information
- Production of financial information
- Processing of input transactions
- Software support for the accounting systems
- Provision and maintenance of computer hardware.

The top two functions were considered to be 'core', and required an internal knowledge that would be hard for any supplier to acquire unless they had a detailed knowledge of the oil industry. The remaining functions (which represented 90 per cent of the accounting function) were seen as being handled just as easily from the outside.

In the move, over three hundred BPX staff from six locations were transferred to a single site in Aberdeen run by the chosen supplier, Andersen Consulting. The operation, Accounting Services Aberdeen, was tasked with handling all BPX accounting functions, while BPX retained control over developing policy, and interpreting and using the information to manage the business.

At the time of the relocation, the Control and Planning Manager at BPX, Tom Wright, commented:

> *the real effect of this arrangement is that we have turned a fixed cost into a variable, or at least a semi-variable, cost. As the service expands – say, drilling increases or new fields come on line, or we dispose of other assets – so the cost varies. Now we can concentrate on the core business. It allows us to focus on exploration and production. We do not have to worry about training, developing and motivating 300 accounting and support staff to be concerned with replacement systems.*
>
> (Syrett, 2003)

Nor was this rationale confined to the private sector. At the same time as BPX launched its outsourced operation in Aberdeen, Berkshire County Council was engaged in a similar exercise. It contracted out its entire range of financial services, including those that would previously have been seen as core functions – such as the provision of technical and corporate financial advice – as well as more routine services such as payroll, pensions and creditor payments.

Tony Allen, Berkshire County Council's Chief Executive, used the same rationale as BPX's Tom Wright:

> *I see great merit in having a much smaller, cohesive local government, concentrating on its strategic activities, accounting to its public more effectively; and not being distracted by employing tens of thousands of staff. If you have a bureaucratic, monolithic type of organization, outsourcing is one way of slimming it down to get a grip on the core business.*
>
> (Syrett, 2003)

The data regarding outsourcing are limited in terms of not yet reflecting the extent of what might be called 'multiple' outsourcing. This is where a wide range of services is outsourced. Where the services are cleaning,

building and vehicle maintenance, security and possibly the so-called
'hotel' services of reception, catering and housekeeping, they are often
provided by one company that describes itself as a facilities management
company. This 'facilities management' is backed up in the UK by professional bodies, training organizations, voluntary industry standards
and journals.

An important (though often overlooked) dimension of outsourcing is
the extent to which the outsourcing companies themselves outsource for
skills – or, indeed, use employment agencies. This is especially marked in
building and equipment maintenance work, where it is possible that the
people actually working on the client's/employer's premises are working
for an organization with whom it has no legal relationship and, indeed,
the people maybe several 'contracts' down the line. The implications for
security, health and safety, and work performance are self-evident, and
are explored in Chapters 6 and 8.

A number of market intelligence bodies provide data on the outsourcing organizations for the UK and other parts of the EU. These
include Mintel and KeyNote, primarily covering the UK. Turning first
to outsourcing for cleaning, the KeyNote Report for 2004 on Contract
Cleaning reported a recent slight decline in the value of the industry.
This was the result, it postulated, of health and safety and employment
law concerns, major skills shortages and high labour turnover, combined with intense competition for contracts. Nonetheless, in 2002 the
industry was worth over €6 billion.

There has been continuing consolidation of companies. Mowlem,
a major UK construction company, has bought a number of leading
cleaning companies, such as Compass and Carlisle. Perhaps the best-
known UK cleaning company, RCO, was acquired by ISS A/S, a Danish
company, in 2000. ISS now has sixteen specialist cleaning companies in
the UK. OCS operates in 40 countries and has 44 000 employees world-
wide. Rentokil/Initial, which merged in 1996 to create a company that
employed 140 000 employees, also operates in 40 countries; its profits
and sales dramatically increased up to 2002, although the climate has
been more difficult since.

Possibly the largest outsourcing company in the world is Sodexho,
a French-based company that, throughout the 1990s, acquired many of
the leading European catering and facilities management companies. It
operates in 74 countries and employed over 315 000 employees in 2004.

Catering has traditionally been one of the leading outsourced services. Major companies include Aramak (a US company which made further acquisitions in 2004), Compass, and the UK company that was Granada plc. It now has Moto, Leiths and Roux Fine Dining in its group. Initial Catering's main business is in the public sector, especially schools and hospitals.

Despite the presence of several well-known and large companies, since 2002 there has been an increasingly difficult trading position. The causes appear to include health concerns, the impact of food handling and environmental regulation and pressure on margins. This has led to major reassessment of the strengths and opportunities for the industry, but also the problems and threats. A number of proposals for improvement are being explored. The way the industry now sees itself and how it can both improve its image and develop more effective working partnerships with clients is very relevant for this book. It appears that the days of assured growth, consolidation of companies and new markets in the public sector easily opening up are over. New approaches are required.

Management consultancy and outsourcing for HRM services has been a more recent development. Many of the major companies in this sector are household names. They provide a range of services ranging from IT and business processing through to HRM. IBM Global Systems employs 70 000 consultants world-wide, including staff from PriceWaterhouseCoopers, which it recently acquired. Accenture, which is USA-based, operates in 47 countries and continues to expand. Fast-growing in the UK is Capita; PA Consulting is the largest UK company. Atos, a French company, acquired KPMG Consulting in 2002; Cap Gemini, also a French company, operates with Ernst and Young. Xansa, formally FI, maintains a large market share. Other familiar names, all based in the UK, are Mercer, WatsonWyatt and TowersPerrinTillinghurst.

Just as with other sectors within the outsourcing industry, management consultancy has been facing difficult trading conditions, with even some of the largest companies issuing profits warnings. By way of further illustration of economic pressures, a daily fee of around €1800 per consultant was the average in 2001; by 2003 this had fallen to around €1150. Despite various problems, management consultancy nonetheless saw 4 per cent growth in the UK. Globally, IT companies are challenging some of the major management consultancies, and some speculate that the Enron and other scandals have badly damaged the reputation of the sector.

Management consultancies are inevitably reviewing their markets and their structures and processes. They, along with outsourcing companies in other sectors, are aware that clients are becoming more hard-nosed about their demands and about the quality of delivery through outsourcing. Mostly, these reviews are focusing on the strategic and financial aspects. The 'people issues' are only slowly being addressed, and often only as a consequence of a major problem or disaster.

Changes to employing organizations

The data presented above note both the increase in outsourcing for skills by employers and the growth in the outsourcing market itself. However, it is extremely important to reflect on the impact of such developments on the employing organizations themselves. The rhetoric may be of the 'virtual organization' – i.e. the supply of goods or services by an organization where the bulk of the work is undertaken by people other than those employed by the organization – but clearly the role of the people who *do* work for it, especially HRM professionals, becomes very different.

We know from our case studies that so many employers have embraced outsourcing and the use of agencies that over 50 per cent of their skill needs may be provided by non-employees. The impact on communication systems, quality assurance processes, employment relations and health and safety, for example, is considerable. Most importantly, it raises issues around the role and nature of employment relationships themselves.

Drivers of change

If there are changes in the ways in which people are working for employing organizations, it is important to understand what is driving the changes. It has been noted that much research data is not confirming universal radical change. The standard employee on an open-ended employment contract is by no means an endangered species. We cannot say, therefore, that standard employment contracts have failed and the growth in agency work and outsourcing is a direct response to failure. Rather, we are arguing that there are several issues that have made change in employment policies viable and attractive. Secondly, we are arguing that there are many practical and organizational reasons for reviewing labour-use strategies. These are almost invariably linked with skills, and their most effective supply and deployment.

Some of the changes have been driven by the following:

1. *The opportunities provided by ICT.* It is a truism, but it now matters less when and where much work, especially services such as customer and financial services work, is undertaken. Work can be outsourced or provided by an agency within the employer's own country or elsewhere. As some of the case studies in this book illustrate, there can be real choice for employers – especially those faced with pressure on margins or aiming to expand – between directly recruiting extra staff, using agency staff to provide additional staff, or outsourcing to another and cheaper country.

2. *Government and other policies.* There has been a boost in some countries to the employment of non-employees through government policies to encourage outsourcing in particular. In the UK, the obvious examples are compulsory competitive tendering/market value programmes since 1984, and the PFI programme. The relaxation of regulatory provisions has also encouraged the employment of non-employees. These policy changes have sometimes been aided by weak political and industrial opposition.

3. *Economic drivers.* These have played an important role. The pressure on labour costs has been a major driver for outsourcing, especially where there are particular current features. If overheads are high, if fiscal regimes impose high demands or if the work is relatively straightforward, the incentive to outsource is great. Conversely, if there are skills shortages, if the work is highly specialized or if it is short term, using an employment agency can appear attractive. Self-employed people who do not attract employment protective rights, do not seek a career within the organization and will move on to the next client, can often be preferable to a directly employed person.

4. *The relaxation of regulatory regimes.* Generally, regulatory barriers or obstacles to, say, the use of private employment agencies and outsourcing have been weakened or abolished. The activity may still

be regulated, but it is possible to do it. At the same time, there has been explicit governmental encouragement of flexible and innovative working.

5. *Attitudinal changes*. Younger and typically highly educated and skilled people increasingly report their rejection of normal, standard employment. They dislike bureaucratic organizations (Parker, 2002), the constraints imposed by such work, the 'new managerialism' and the lack of variety (Lammiman and Syrett, 2004).

Although the research data do not suggest that the numbers who want to be self-employed or want a more open-ended relationship with the employer are great, if they are the 'brightest and best', are in skills shortage areas or are otherwise highly sought after, the issue is a real one. They may accept a contract of employment, but, as research shows, they tend to be 'technically core but psychologically peripheral', and will present particular challenges to the employer (Holland and Hecker, 2003).

Conclusion: what unites the non-employees?

This chapter has sketched in the nature and characteristics of the provision of skills other than in a standard employment relationship. Self-employment takes various forms, and there have been major developments in the provision of skills through intermediaries. This presents employing organizations with a wide range of management challenges. The self-employed and those provided through an intermediary present different demands to employing organizations. They may be there for a very short period of time or for many years; they may work with teams that include standard employees, or comprise a distinct project or function group. They may have differing degrees of integration with the organization.

Despite these differences, it is important to reflect on whether they share any characteristics. If so; their management may be simplified as a consequence of this process of analysis. It is suggested that that many will share the following features:

- They will tend to accept that they are different from standard employees and will be subject to different expectations. Unfortunately, they may well consider themselves to be 'marginal' or 'secondary', and some will consider themselves to be 'victims'.

- Their primary loyalty will tend to be to their skill, profession or occupation, as opposed to an individual employer. Their notions of a 'career' will be similarly distinctive.

- They will tend to be conscious that they may lack the protective and social security rights of the standard employee. This is especially so for the self-employed and agency staff; workers for outsourcing companies may well receive some benefits. Questions regarding pensions will tend to loom large, and they will attach greater importance to direct rewards, personal development and transactional skills.

- They may not share the same sense of ownership of work and quality assurance as the standard employees they may be working alongside. This might be because they are transient or short term, or because they are focused on a very specialized project or area of work.

- They will be subject to different control and performance management processes than standard employees. Greater emphasis will be placed on the contract and the detailed specification/schedule/output, etc. The focus will tend to be on output rather than overall contribution to the employer. Control/management may well be through the intermediary – i.e. the agency or outsourcing company.

- There will be central ambiguities and uncertainties over the nature of the employment relationship and the notion of the psychological contract as applied to non-employees. There will tend to be problems over mutual expectations, and the likelihood of misunderstandings. Very little can be 'taken for granted'.

- Even where people are technically employees, such as in the case of gold-collar workers, they will tend not to regard themselves as 'core' workers but will be mentally 'peripheral'/entrepreneurial.

Summary points

- There has been significant global growth in outsourcing and agency work along with growth in some types of self-employment.
- Outsourcing and agency work has seen structural changes in the organizations providing skills. There is a move to specialization, through growing competitive pressures.

- The motivations and aspirations of those working for outsourcing companies and, to a greater extent, those working for agencies or who are self-employed, tend to be different and distinctive from those of standard employees.
- Non-employees tend to have key features that unite them. These have considerable relevance for their management.

3

Matching strategic and employment needs

An exchange between senior HR practitioners published in the UK journal *People Management* at the turn of the decade illustrates how very similar organizations in the same industry reached different solutions when exploring choices of working arrangements.

Peter Whalley, HR Outsource Relationship Leader at BP, looks after the outsourced relationship with Exult, which now handles the corporation's HR administration from service centres in Glasgow and Texas:

> *Outsourcing was chosen because we recognized the transformation we were seeking would be enabled by technology that we needed help with. We felt that a different HR model was required as people's expectations were changing, fed by the internet. Line managers now expect answers to questions much faster. And there are changes in the employment environment generally, such as globalization . . . The decision was also strongly influenced by our history and culture of outsourcing. Cost-cutting was not our primary goal; it was about transforming the company and creating the capability to do this. The people who didn't transfer to Exult have found other roles and some have since left BP.*

Lisa Carlson is Global Business Department and Customer Relationship Manager at Shell People Services, Shell International:

We went through similar discussions in the latter half of 1999 and formed Shell People Services [an internal shared services centre] in January 2000. We decided not to outsource because we felt the Shell people processes were essential to our business success. The knowledge of Shell business and strategy was core to our organization and we wanted to deliver the services through Shell people . . . We had a commitment to reduce costs and felt that savings should accrue to Shell and our shareholders and not to an external provider. We also felt that outsourcing would disrupt the delivery of our HR services and affect our process improvements.
(*People Management*, 11 July 2000)

In February 2006, the Post Office, UK, was fined around €16 million by its regulatory body, PostComm, for major failures in its management and delivery of the mail. Specifically, considerable amounts of mail had been lost or stolen. It appears that, following restructuring and considerable staff redundancies, many skills shortages were met through the supply of agency temps. The temps were blamed in the media for the failures. Indeed, some staff could not read English, and one had a criminal conviction for an armed robbery on a post office. There were poor quality standards, including poor screening of temps and weak management of their work.

An emergency (skills shortages) had turned into a crisis for the Post Office through the fines and adverse publicity.
(*Evening Standard*, 9 February 2006), p. 6

This chapter is about options and making these choices. It covers fundamental HRM issues, and focuses on:

- Who is working for an organization and on what basis, and how do you decide what is best?
- When might it be preferable only to use employees to perform certain roles?
- Are there some situations or circumstances where outsourcing is too problematic to be contemplated?

- When can using a consultant rather than an employee make business sense?
- When might it make sense to pull back from using agencies, outsourcing or freelancers/consultants?

The agenda has long moved on from a position where it is assumed that organizations will only use employees on standard contracts for all their skill needs. Indeed, the assumption that even core skill needs will be performed only by those on standard employment contracts is widely challenged. Some argue that, potentially, all skills can be provided by non-employees, creating a 'virtual' employing organization. By this criterion, it is possible for core strategic roles in finance, product development and delivery, business services and even HRM itself to be undertaken by non-employees. All of these approaches, including that of retaining most or all skill needs on standard contracts of employment, have their devotees. However, employing organizations recognize that the decision to employ skills on a different basis from that hitherto is a critical one.

Aims of this chapter

- To explore the typical reasons for employing people on one basis rather than another, including matters of cost, efficiency and short-term skills shortages
- To consider and analyse the issues and factors that might influence that decision, including possible constraints
- To draw on the experience of many employing organizations that have experienced and reflected on this process of change and different forms of skills supply
- To consider different approaches to using non-employees in the organization; specifically the 'hands-off', 'integration' and 'partnership' models.

Choosing work patterns: what the case studies tell us

The case studies carried out specifically for the book were especially useful for this chapter. Subjects include organizations that provide non-employees, as well as employers that use them. The people interviewed tended to be 'hands-on' practitioners with long experience of dealing with either the provision or the use of non-employees (see Chapter 1). The case studies also feature accounts of discussions with organizations that support employers, workers and the self-employed. Some of these discussions took place with organizations outside the UK, and most took place in 2005, with a few in 2006.

The case studies also contain information about the organizations themselves, and legal and other instruments used in the process of setting up and managing the employment relationships. The documents include promotional material, annual reports, and the results of relevant internal or commissioned research. Often the material was explicit in terms of the opportunity to provide skills by an intermediary or, alternatively, the reasons for using externally provided skills or consultants/ freelance staff.

Other sources include case studies undertaken by the authors for earlier relevant projects and research reports. These include material providing guidance on outsourcing to employers contemplating or using non-employees at the workplace.

The case studies confirm that the processes by which it is decided to move to the employment of non-employees or make changes to current arrangements are frequently unclear, ambiguous or unarticulated. The role of HR itself is carefully explored here. Some of the individuals interviewed are highly critical of this role, seeing HR practitioners as missing opportunities to improve business performance through more innovative employment strategies. One such critic is Nick Stephens, CEO of RSA, the largest recruitment specialist for the pharmaceutical industry in the EU. It is based in the UK. He says:

> Human resource management has become a risk reduction department, rather than aiming to maximize what people bring to the business. Do you want to jump out of bed in the morning, or are you staying under the duvet? HR should be about fitting individuals into organizations and understanding the balance between people performance and management.

Not all our respondents share this view of HRM. However, one of the major issues that surfaced through the case studies was not only some confusion about decisions regarding whether and why to use a temporary work agency or outsource a function, but also the lack of involvement by HR in the process itself. Often, the decision to outsource and its implementation is undertaken by the purchasing/procurement function in the organization without reference to HR. Sometimes, decisions to use temporary agency or self-employed consultants etc., are undertaken by line managers without consultation or guidance from HR. This can happen even where the function itself is an aspect of HR, such as training or recruitment.

This absence of HR input is lamented by several writers who specialize in the topic, some of whom emphasize the vital distinction between buying in people skills and buying goods. It appears often to be unclear where and why decision-making regarding, say, employing consultants or using an agency is located in a particular department or job role. The reasons for the decision itself are also often unclear or ambiguous.

One of our respondents emphasizes the practical implications of this. Rehman Noormohamed is a highly experienced lawyer, at the time of the case-study working for Morgan-Cole Solicitors, based in Cardiff, Wales, and specializes in the legal issues surrounding outsourcing. He says:

I find, when discussing matters with clients, that it is often not clear what the strategic reasons for outsourcing are. Sometimes the decision has been made by others and all the client I am dealing with does is to implement it. This lack of understanding can make the outsourcing process more difficult than it need be.

The 'invisibility' of HR in many of our case studies is a matter we probed in discussions, but no clearly or consistently articulated reason for this was put forward. It is not just that the HR function appears often not to be involved in the 'people' dimension of decision-making about using non-employees; it does not have an ongoing role either.

The BA/Gate Gourmet problems that hit the headlines in the summer and autumn of 2005 highlighted the consequences:

Andy Cook, who only took over as HR Director at Gate Gourmet eight weeks before the dispute broke out over the outsourcing contract for in-flight meals with BA, described his experience in dealing with the dispute as 'walking into a storm of the brown stuff'. He admitted, 'If there have been mistakes, it is only as a consequence of it being new territory for everyone involved'. It was a surprise to many that the people issues beyond simply the ones of employment relations had been perhaps neglected and then had become so fraught. This led many commentators to call for a close involvement by HR in outsourcing, etc.

(Berry, 2005)

The case studies also confirmed other conundrums – managers who report that they use non-employees to save costs, but then pay large daily fees to consultants who appear to be on rolling contracts for months; and those who also pay high fees, sometimes for years, to an employment agency for routine skill needs. Clearly, other arguments, such as ones based on head-count reductions, have a role to play in decision-making. However, if basic economic tests are applied to some of these decisions, they simply do not stack up.

Why change to using non-employees?

This has to be the first question. However, it remains the case that most employers in most countries continue to rely on standard employees on contracts of employment for their skill needs. Some employers who have outsourced for service needs have decided to revert to standard employment contracts. Others have reduced their reliance on agencies or consultants. This tends to be approached in a more strategic way than the original decision to outsource or use consultants. It may also reflect a renewed appreciation of what employees (as opposed to non-employees) bring to the organization.

What advantages do standard employees bring? Although under attack, the European Social Model continues to see secure, well-rewarded and stable employees as the most effective way to provide high quality work, albeit now in the context of being more flexible. Such stability is, many argue, most likely to ensure that the EU remains productive and competitive. Insofar as there have been policy interventions to support non-employees within the EU, it has been on the basis of providing as many 'employee-like' benefits to non-employees as appropriate. This is rather than viewing non-employees as having distinctive features and distinctive needs. The employee remains the 'gold standard'.

This assumption is reflected in the comments of another of our respondents, Stefan Clauwaert.

Stefan Clauwaert, Senior Researcher at the European Trade Union Institute for Research, Education and Health and Safety, a part of the European Trades Union Confederation (ETUC), expresses his support for the model as follows:

> *The European Social Model, itself now based on the 'flexicurity' model of employment and backed up by law, is still the preferred way to protect the economy.*

Although he recognizes that, for example, outsourcing can make sense for some functions, and especially for small- and medium-sized firms, it is clear that he sees standard employees as the strongly preferred and dominant option. He is concerned that policy changes in the EU towards further liberalization of employment practices should not jeopardize either employees or non-employees. Policy changes should be genuine and not a 'façade or window-dressing', he says.

It is unsurprising that trade unions have a preference for employees, as they are easier to organize and represent. Some unions have targeted 'flexible' workers such as part-timers. Relatively few initiatives to recruit non-employees into trade-union membership go beyond those employment sectors such as the media, where freelance work is endemic. The employee relations aspects of employing non-employees are considered more fully in Chapter 8.

What are the views of employing organizations?

Given that most HRM literature is based on the assumption of employees, there is relatively little written on the relative value of employees and non-employees. However, many would regard the following as the major advantages of employees:

- Contracts of employment can be used to express obligations that are firm-specific and can protect the commercial and other interests of the employer.
- If contract terms are broken or employee performance is unacceptable, employees can be dealt with by the employer through internal (including disciplinary) procedures.

- The terms included by law in employment contracts in most countries apply to the key issues of performance, discipline, confidentiality, loyalty, etc. These are reinforced by notions of the 'psychological contract', which emphasize the synergy and commitment between the employee and the employing organization and shared values. Although in EU states aside from the UK and Ireland and in many other countries employers may not be familiar with the concept of the psychological contract, they will nonetheless see the standard employment relationship as giving rise to obligations for human capital investment and mutual support.
- The 'human capital investment' by the employer can be used for the benefit of that organization, and training and development measures can be firm-specific and directly beneficial.
- HRM can focus on career management of employees and workforce development more generally.
- The culture and identity of an employer can inform HR practices, and these in turn can be reflected in the performance and attitudes of individual employees.
- Secure employees will be more committed to the organization and enhance its performance – 'You get what you pay for!'
- Although few people now expect a 'job for life', most are attracted by a job that offers security and prospects rather than by work that is more precarious or intermittent. Research has shown that, given a choice, some agency temps would prefer a permanent job – though this may now be changing. Most people appreciate the value of regular training and development, typically available from a standard employee contract. Employee contracts aid recruitment and retention of staff.

Research for this book confirms that many employers continue to see the greater value of employees. Some have increased rewards to them as well as more clearly differentiating the situation between them and non-employees.

John Raywood of GlaxoSmithKline, the pharmaceutical giant, reflected on the dramatically different reward systems for those who are employees and those who are not. The company employs many staff through employment agencies, uses consultants, outsources for many services and employs people on fixed-term contracts. Employees have access to a wide range of benefits, including a package named 'Total care: Total

Reward'. This offers extensive health-care/well-being facilities, employee assistance schemes, and family, legal and financial support services. These are not available to non-employees. When asked 'Why not?' he replied: 'Well, not involving them (in benefits, etc.) goes with the territory. They want the biggest cash benefit they can lay their hands on. They condition themselves to a certain lifestyle. They have different needs [from employees].

This discussion highlights the 'differentness' many feel between the employee and the non-employee. Many reflect that self-employed people and agency temps have their own 'personal balance sheet'. They trade-in security, employee benefits and other aspects of employee status for high cash earnings, variety and flexibility as to whether, when and where they work. The 'differentness', however, does not prevent many of our respondents from having non-employees performing core roles – a matter to be considered later.

Some respondents emphasize the cultural and sector-specific factors that lead to the employment of employees – for example, Brian Kultschar.

Brian Kultschar, HR Director of the Principality Building Society in Wales, a medium-sized building society operating as a mutual society (i.e. owned by its members) rather than as a bank, says:

> *In Wales there is a strong feeling that the people we employ must be honest. If we handle people's money we have to ensure we minimize the risk [of dishonesty].We have a feeling of comfort if we use employees. We like to carefully recruit them and we recognize someone as a 'Principality person'. We also like continuity. We must reflect the fact that our business is about relationships and we need to nurture customers. We see ourselves as strongly community-based, and recognize the expectations of our customers, who are typically in small local communities.*

In the last few years the Society has moved cautiously towards the limited employment of non-employees, but clearly continues to see standard employees as its preferred option.

Although some of the people interviewed clearly prefer employing employees – so as to ensure loyalty, honesty, continuity, etc. – many others are not so sure. Some reflect on the 'gold-collar' workers considered in Chapter 2, who highlight the 'shifting sands' within standard employment contracts. These highly skilled, highly paid professionals move from job to job, albeit on a contract of employment. However, as considered earlier, such workers' loyalties tend to be to their profession and to their own careers, and in many ways they exhibit characteristics more typical of freelance/self-employed people or even some agency temps. The employer may consider that employing them on a standard contract will provide benefits and ensure loyalty, etc., but the reality is otherwise. Gold-collar workers will move to where the opportunities are, and create new forms of employment relationships with a different set of expect-ations. These workers will not want the rewards provided for employees, many of which can be utilized only on a long-term basis. Such rewards include an occupational pension, a share option scheme, health insur-ance, and facilities such as employee assistance programmes and child-care support. Such benefits are very costly to the employer and operate as the *quid pro quo* for commitment and a career at the particular orga-nization. One must question their provision for people who do not want them but would prefer higher basic pay.

Gold-collar workers provide only one indicator of the shifting sands within standard employment relationships. Another is the rise of flex-ible working across developed economies, such as flexi-hours, time account working and home-working. This is dramatically changing the shape, workings and management of employment contracts (WF, 2005).

Although there are still major differences between employees and non-employees, the standard employment contract itself is undergoing change and itself placing new demands on managers and management.

Several of our respondents are 'employee enthusiasts', while many others are more sanguine about the benefits of non-employees to the organization. Based on their own experience, they argue that non-employees can bring equal (at least) benefits. They suggest that using employees is simply the traditional way of working, and that sometimes the assumed benefits of employees are not there in reality. At the same time, they suspect there may be assumptions made about what non-employees cannot or do not provide. Laura Sykes (not her real name) is an experienced manager who worked in many firms before joining the Regulatory Body. She reflects on her own experience of working previ-ously as an employee in a large insurance company. She says:

Although employees, I felt the field staff were not part of our organization. There was no real sense of interdependence, said to be a key aspect of a contract of employment. There was no bond between the staff. When I moved to a smaller company we used self-employed 'consultants'. Employment status was not critical. It was just as easy to develop a relationship with a consultant as an employee. The company was US-owned, and fast-moving with lots of business pressures. What mattered was to get to know an individual and provide the right support. We became interdependent. The 'label' on the relationship was unimportant.

One of four respondents may be expressing the views of many managers on using agency staff when he says:

If they are temping, especially for secretarial work, they are probably not very good.

These assumptions may need to be challenged, even at the level of assuming that self-employed people are less reliable, out to make money quickly and save on tax; and perhaps that agency temps are inevitably people who have failed to get a 'proper' job or who are generally feckless and unmotivated. Chapter 2 considers research findings that indicate the typical reasons why people turn to self-employment or become temps. These findings suggest an emerging and increasing coherence concerning the motives and expectations of many non-employees.

Where are you now?

In making a decision to change and settling on what type of change to make to the workplace and skill needs more generally, the first stage is to assess the current position. For example, it may be that the organization faces one or more of the following:

1. High/increasing premises costs, perhaps with low or fluctuating usage
2. High labour costs, especially non-wage labour costs
3. Skills shortages and recruitment difficulties
4. Pressure from a parent company or from a public body/government to reduce costs, improve competitiveness, etc.
5. A need to improve service or product delivery
6. A high level of investment in time by managers on non-core service support such as cleaning, catering or security

7. Inflexibility or complacency of staff in performing non core service functions and/or lack of energy and enthusiasm
8. High levels of employee absence/sickness/demotivation, etc.
9. High insurance costs
10. A high incidence of short-term projects for clients
11. Fluctuating or seasonal demand for services or goods or particular skills, leading to some staff being underemployed for significant periods.

Some of the items listed suggest that outsourcing and agency working should be options and carefully considered – particularly in terms of the first seven items. The need to improve service or product and/or a need for staff for project or diagnostic work might suggest employing consultants or freelancers. The last item might suggest use of an agency to supply skills. For some of the items, all options could be 'put on the table' and the merits of each carefully analysed.

Many other matters could be added to this list. However, several of those set down are often cited as the major drivers for change to employing non-employees.

The prevailing conclusion of respondents in our case studies is to caution against hasty, under-researched or ill-considered changes – or unrealistic expectations.

One respondent urged a long, hard examination of the reasons for change. He says:

> There is a danger of doing things for reasons of fashion or just because someone else is outsourcing lots of services. You have to make changes for the right reasons, for example, that you gain access to greater expertise at a good cost.

All the people we spoke to emphasized the need for careful risk analysis and the danger of 'throwing the baby out with the bathwater'. To do so might be putting the key marketing strength or the culture of the organization at risk. Where an organization is, for example, in the not-for-profit sector, or has built up high levels of trust from customers/clients, this should not be jeopardized. It is important to have a broad overview when contemplating change. The motivation for change might well be to save costs, but if non-employees damage the business reputation or cause disruption and disputes, the decision will be essentially a bad one.

The HR function should be at the heart of assessing where an organization is at any given time. The 'people issues' must be on the change agenda. It is essential that HR professionals are consulted and involved in any skill needs assessment and are able to supply the relevant data and experience. HR managers may or may not be the major drivers for change. This depends on the situation in each employing organization. However, if ever the mantra 'Harnessing HR to the strategic needs of the business' had direct and practical meaning, this is it.

It is also essential that the data and other material are robust – and that costings are calculated accurately and fairly. It may be cheaper to outsource cleaning, but if the cost of redundancy payments for several hundred long-serving employees is taken into account, the savings may not look so dramatic.

One of the long-running issues of using non-employees is that of transactional management costs. The costs of devising a specification, job role, information for an agency, legal costs, etc., may well be recognized. However, the induction/orientation for people who may not stay long and the day-to-day issues of communication, problem-solving and handling possible disputes must also be taken on board. The fact that such costs are notoriously hard to estimate should not imply that they are unimportant.

The costs may be borne, or even hidden, at different levels within the organization. Regarding the use of temporary workers, John Raywood, of GlaxoSmithKline, comments:

> The real 'victims' [of using non-employees] are the permanent employees who have to induct and train the temps. There is no allowance or recognition for these managers who undertake this work. We have to think of these types of less obvious costs.

Using non-employees: the benefits

The following are the typical reasons put forward for using non-employees. They are generally confirmed by our cases studies as conditioning decision-making.

Cost savings

Many of the advantages most commonly cited for moving to use non-employees centre on cost savings. The savings are largely because key costs are borne by someone else, though it must always be borne in mind that there are some irreducible costs – for example, those concerned with health and safety requirements, and the costs of documentation and communication more generally. It must also be remembered that some employment protective rights across the EU (which many critics argue are a major cause of higher labour costs) are also open to some non-employees. These include the right to paid holidays and protection from anti-discrimination laws.

Cost savings, it is argued, can be made through:

1. Lower recruitment costs – the costs are either 'one-off' costs when outsourcing, or are more limited when obtaining agency temps or consultants/freelancers, etc. Savings can also be made through using less formal 'recruitment' processes (although the legal requirements will still have to be met, especially in terms of discrimination law). In the case of temporary agency work, the costs of screening, reference-raising, etc., are increasingly being borne by the agency in the UK and in many other states.
2. Lower non-wage/non-fee costs and lack of or lower level of provision of welfare and other benefits.
3. Fewer costs associated with legal responsibilities, such as for dismissal and maternity rights, and those generally associated with the regulation of the employment relationship.
4. Ease of termination, and savings on internal disciplinary and other procedures and costs associated with dispute resolution.

The impact of costs as a driver for change is illustrated below.

The Children's Mutual is probably the largest provider of insurance and other services specifically designed for children. A key recent development was the launch of the Baby Bond scheme, whereby the UK Government provides £250 for all newborn babies, to be invested on their behalf. Unfortunately, the profit margin for organizations providing the investment opportunities is extremely low. Children's Mutual considered it could only provide the service through outsourcing the customer services function to a provider that could make economies of scale.

In May 2005 it was announced that Boots plc, the major health and beauty retailer based in the UK, had outsourced its HR services to Xchanging. The contract is for seven years and for £400 million.

The functions to be outsourced had an annual spend of several hundred millions. The contract provides a guaranteed price reduction over the life of the contract. Julian Coles, Director of Sourcing and Purchasing, said: 'We have partnered with Xchanging in order to benefit from its proven methodology and procurement skills, to deliver efficiencies that allow us to offer our customers even better value.'

(Anonymous, 2005)

Another of our case study organizations, RWA Ltd, had given the question of costs very careful consideration.

Rob Wortham of RWA Ltd, a specialist software company based in South Wales, was faced with a pressing need for more staff in order to undertake an important contract. Originally RWA had used contract (self-employed) staff, who were 'hugely expensive'. They had then outsourced to an EU company.

Following the ending of that relationship and the securing of a new, important contract for a major travel company, Rob Wortham said he could not afford to use either contractors or employees, so he had to explore any route other than, as he saw it, the 'expensive options'. This led him to outsource to an Indian company. He appreciated that 'there was an element of risk' in the decision; however, he thought this was offset by:

- major savings on labour costs, especially non-wage costs
- access to non-chargeable resources – 'staff in India were already trained up'
- RWA only being billed for work actually performed.

Despite these attractions, Rob was keen to stress the criteria he applied before finally deciding to outsource to the Indian company. These were:

- ensuring that staff in India could do a 'reasonable job'
- careful testing of information and communication systems
- ensuring that staff were 'developing and showing potential'
- applying these criteria through a carefully monitored three-month pilot scheme.

However, it is not simply a matter of costs. Respondents from the case studies generally argue that if cost were the only motivation, using non-employees would be unlikely to prove successful. Nick Stephens of RSA, the pharmaceutical agency, recognizes the cost argument, but adds that the flexibility of the relationship is a more persuasive factor from the perspective of the client/employer. He says:

> If you've made a mistake [with a temp] you can get rid of them quickly and rectify the mistake. But this can be done without major cost and, importantly, without loss of respect. Getting rid of employees can be very acrimonious and stressful for managers. When you have a more flexible relationship, it is transactional rather than emotional.

Bottom line cost savings are clearly a key driver for many organizations, and where the service provider is a specialist in the skill area(s) the solution of outsourcing or partnering with an agency is an attractive one. It does always depend on the quality of the service provider's staff. Many in our case studies reported that work standards declined and there were other problems. Sally Worsley-Speck used to be a senior administrator in a further education college in the east of England and, following the outsourcing of cleaning services, reported:

> There was a definite decline in standards – I was always having to deal with complaints from staff. There was also constant friction with our directly employed caretaker – though he was rather feisty anyway! We only noticed an improvement in standards when the cleaning contract was up for renewal.

Furthermore, many respondents argue that not only should cost savings not be achieved at the expense of quality of work; there must also be a plus factor in the change. They say that there should be improvements in services and benefits to the client in terms of business performance, improved reputation, etc.

Rehman Noormohamed, of Morgan-Cole Solicitors, who specializes in advising on outsourcing and its legal issues, makes the very simple point that:

> It is essential to have clear expectations of outsourcing. This means what you will gain and over what period. You don't outsource to simply stay still. You must enhance the service you provide.

Organizational needs

Many needs in our case studies were not cost-dependent, but a response to other organizational imperatives. Skill shortages or recruitment problems might lead to the use of an agency because it would have access to a wider range of skills. For short-term absences (such as for illness or maternity leave), there are advantages in using an agency or a self-employed person. This applies equally where the self-employed person is an interim manager with high status, as well as using a 'contract worker' to fill a short-term technical or professional post. There are also additional attractions in using a skills supplier that has access to many people.

Chris Sharp, of Capita Learning and Development – part of Capita plc, UK, a very large and fast-growing service provider – comments on why organizations use Capita's consultants for training, etc. He says:

> We can provide consultants to organizations for various HR functions. We can supply them 'on a package'. We have hundreds or even thousands on our books. They all work for other organizations, so they offer a wide range of experiences, and we provide the quality assurance.

Where the need is less urgent but the skills required are very specific, outsourcing is a preferred option. The argument here is that it is not always efficient to employ a specialist directly, especially where the skill needed is a non-core one. Where the numbers required are low, many use consultants/freelance workers. Phrases such as 'We simply did not have the skills in-house' or 'It would have been hugely complicated to recruit an employee for such a short, specialist task' are typical. Reports of increasing skills shortages in many countries and many sectors will likely make non-employees sourced this way an increasingly attractive option.

Service improvement

Many referred to drivers for change that are driven by neither cost nor recruitment needs. David Bornor, CEO of the Children's Mutual, a specialist provider of financial services based in southeast England, accepts that costs were an important aspect of the decision to outsource their customer services function (as considered earlier), but says the main driver was:

> *The desire to separate organizational strategy from operational matters. This process frees up key staff in our headquarters.*

Other practitioners focus on ideas for service enhancement, often delivered through a partnership with the skill providers. This partnership model can potentially be applied to outsourcing, agency work and the employment of consultants, although using some types of consultants has often traditionally followed this approach anyway. It can also be formal or informal. These matters are considered more fully at p. 81.

The enhancement of the service provided by the client/employer through using non-employees tends to focus on two issues. The first is that, through outsourcing or otherwise, and using some types of non-employees, the organization can concentrate on its core activities and not spend time and energy on peripheral matters such as cleaning, reception/hotel services or IT support. In any case, those providing the peripheral services are experts in that work, will do it to a higher level and will probably be able to make economies of scale and provide the service at a highly competitive rate.

Secondly, the service provided by non-employees will be enhanced because, especially where the service is peripheral to the client, the individuals performing it will do it on the basis of 'back of office service provided in a front of office way'. In effect, what is peripheral to the client is core to the service provider, and the people who perform those tasks focus on specific skills rather than the nature of employing organizations, and achieve improved levels of job satisfaction. They have a career within, say, the IT or cleaning company, and are not 'just' the cleaners/security staff/catering staff.

Thirdly, many non-employees working for themselves or for an agency or outsourcing company tend to be skilled or highly skilled, often in skills shortage areas such as medicine and aspects of IT. They are looking for increased variety and opportunity in their work, and see the agencies or outsourcing companies as the intermediaries in their careers. Agencies and outsourcing companies may well provide training and development opportunities. We have already noted in Chapter 2 the changing nature and role of many of the leading agencies in the training and career management of temps.

Temps and self-employed people work for a client using their professional skills, but also provide 'added value'. This is because they have experience of many employing organizations and work systems, they will tend to have strong interpersonal skills and, by their nature, be adaptable and flexible. They can be a very useful resource for the client employer, but are often not fully recognized as being a quasi-internal consultant or specialist.

John Raywood, of GlaxoSmithKline, which employs significant numbers of staff on non-standard contracts (including through agencies), comments:

> *Temps know their place and quickly establish rapport with the company and colleagues. They know they often need the support of the company to get a reference for another assignment. However, sometimes by contrast permanent employees can seem complacent. Sometimes the temps run the place! We ought to value them more!*

Raywood's observations apply to long-service temps like Pattie Pierce (see Chapter 2). Twenty years of working in this way have made Pattie an expert in what can make or break an assignment. She highlights poor induction, lack of support and a general unwillingness to recognize her skills.

Perhaps the questions ought then to be posed:

- Why is it that temps appear to 'run the place' but often have their skills undervalued?
- Why is an agency temp in engineering, finance or administration 'just a temp', but an agency temp on a short-term assignment as a manager considered to be a valuable property because he or she is referred to as an 'interim manager?' The latter may bring different (managerial and diagnostic) skills and experience to the former group, but many of the skills will be comparable. The skills of the interim manager will often be valued in terms of project or change management. The engineer, accountant or administrator may well have skills to offer and a contribution to make in terms of service improvement, but may not be appreciated also as a change agent or service enhancer.

The conclusion, applying a balanced scorecard model, is that the value that non-employees bring to the organization, its customer/clients and its stakeholders might be better appreciated.

Employing non-employees: the constraints

In approaching this important consideration, it should be borne in mind that the longer a contract is for the supply of skill needs, the more problematic it will be if there are difficulties, or if a mismatch occurs between the supplier and the client. There are so many banana skins that the greatest care must be taken not only in selecting an outsourcing company or agency (see Chapter 4) but also in deciding whether to use non-employees at all. At the same time, the benefits that can accrue from the right sort of relationship with the skills provider or self-employed persons must be put on the table.

Our case study organizations have a wide variety of characteristics, in terms of size, location, whether they are public, private or not-for profit, and, importantly, sector. All are conscious of the need to assess any risks to the business through the use of non-employees. This is especially the case where the non-employees work on the premises of the client/employer. There is also recognition that providing services to the organization off the premises or, indeed, outside the country raises other risk factors, along with cultural, linguistic, managerial and quality concerns. Nobody in our case studies uses non-employees as an unthinking, knee-jerk response to a problem – though, for many, skills shortages are a marked imperative.

Possible constraints are varied, and range from legal constraints through to sector-specific issues and matters of organizational culture and ethical concerns. How they impact on any particular organization will clearly depend on individual circumstances, as will their relative importance as a determining factor.

Legal and regulatory restraints

These might derive from the legal system in terms of 'hard' law (i.e. law that can give rise directly to a penalty or other remedy) or 'soft' law (i.e. law that is not of direct effect but is taken from codes, guidance and recommendations) – see Chapter 6. Failure to comply with codes, etc., can have relevance for professional and business accreditation. Soft law might be drawn from the legal system of the particular country or, more likely, from professional or regulatory bodies. In terms of the former, there is legislation in many countries that regulates the use of employment agencies and outsourcing.

Within the UK and in other parts of the EU, managers blanch at the thought of the complexities of the legislation that regulates outsourcing. In the UK this is known as TUPE (Transfer of Undertakings and Protection of Employment Regulations, 2006), and in the rest of the EU as the Acquired Rights Directives as transposed into national law. Any managers dealing with the employment of non-employees need to be familiar with the demands of the law in this area and ensure they are up-to-date. Specialist advice is generally required on these points.

In some countries there remain 'hard' law constraints on employing temps or outsourcing, in that such employment must be for a purpose that the law recognizes as legitimate. It should not be assumed that because the employment of non-employees is viewed favourably or encouraged in one country that this is the position in all countries. National legislation must always be checked, along with EU laws.

Increasingly and globally, business (as opposed to employment) activities are subject to regulation. Policy objectives regarding ensuring protection for, say, consumers, patients and investors, and for the embedding of standards to ensure quality of service delivery are having increased impact. The standards affect employing organizations in that the requirements of accreditation or benchmarks have to be met. These are especially features of financial services, manufacturing and retailing, health care and education, and in sectors where there are particular health and safety risks.

Many of the case study organizations operate within these sectors, and are especially mindful of the need to ensure there are no risks in terms of accreditation or the regulatory framework. In management literature such regulatory issues tend to be neglected, and yet they are vital for the success of so many organizations. It is not so much the loss of accreditation or court proceedings that are the problem (although they can be painful and damaging); it is the impact on reputation through adverse publicity.

A contemporary issue of growing importance is the increased regulation applying to migrant workers. The sheer numbers of asylum seekers and family members moving to other states to join relatives has caused concern in many countries, though employers often welcome the skills they provide. The growth in terrorism has heightened calls either to limit or to rigorously control entry to various states. Employers employing people without a right to be in a country are running the risk of criminal penalties, and the imposition of penalties is becoming more common. The regulations generally apply whether the individual concerned is an employee, is self-employed or is supplied by an intermediary.

Regulations such as those setting environmental or financial standards apply to the employing organization such that anyone delivering services for it will be required to comply with the standards. If agency nurses are employed, or IT systems within the financial services sector are outsourced, the client/employer has still, nonetheless, to comply with the regulations. The regulations discount the fact that non-employees are delivering the service, and expect the relevant standards to be met regardless.

Interestingly, few of our respondents specifically referred to regulation. This may well have been because it was a 'given' of their sector. An exception was the Principality Building Society, which operates within the very tightly regulated financial services sector in the UK. Their core activities are clearly regulated by legislation and codes:

> We always have to do a risk assessment of any change in the basis upon which we employ people. If non-employees are performing 'core' activities, there must be regulatory risks. We must audit and monitor very closely. Our Code tells us that we must apply due diligence processes to 'material' outsourcing because of the regulatory demands. We find the definition of 'material' quite difficult. However, even if the function is not 'material', we still have to ensure proper controls are in place.

The other important dimension is the regulation of individuals. They may need to hold particular professional qualifications in order to work. There is an increased emphasis on qualifications within the EU, where the intention is not only to ensure that there is recognition of those qualifications within all member states but also to prevent cowboy operations and individuals. In some parts of the EU, the requirement for specific qualifications tends to be more demanding. These apply to jobs such as public service vehicle drivers, care workers, personal services and most types of manual work. Qualifications are not just something of extra value – they are essential.

A related and emerging issue is that of professional regulatory bodies requiring formal updating of skills through continuing professional development (CPD) schemes. Failure to undertake such activities can prevent an individual from undertaking work in their profession. This clearly has direct impact on skills and supply. It also raises the question of where and how such CPD programmes are arranged for non-employees, and how they are financed.

The implication for employing non-employees to perform these professional, craft and other roles is that the individuals must hold the qualifications required and, if necessary, have successfully undertaken skills updating. As regards agency temps, the law in the UK has recently tightened up requirements on agencies to ensure that temps do hold the relevant qualifications and capabilities for the job they are being asked to perform. The agency must check the qualifications and also carry out other screening activities (Conduct of Employment Agencies and Businesses Regulations, 2003). This provides some reassurance for the client/employer, but the system may not be foolproof. Professional and specialist employment agencies will undertake this task efficiently and provide considerable assurance to the client. The best agencies are well aware of the need for professional and quality assurance. At RSA, the employment agency specializing in the pharmaceutical sector, Nick Stephens, the CEO comments:

> We accept that interims [temps] have to be accredited and re-accredited. We provide the specialist training here, on our premises, through face-to-face delivery, provided through a fund to which we and the interims contribute. Of course, we must maintain the highest professional standards and we cannot tolerate weak staff unless there is a short-term reason for it. We say 'The wounded we carry, the strugglers we shoot' (in a manner of speaking)!

This 2003 law only applies to UK employment agencies, although there are similar provisions in many other countries. Where the skills are provided by self-employed people as contractors/freelancers/consultants, etc., the client/employer has no such protection. There have to be rigorous checks, which can increase the recruitment costs considerably. Where skills are provided by an outsourcing company, the client/employer is very much in the hands of the company. Where contracts are to last for many years, it is essential that the contract itself deals with the question of worker qualifications, and that the client/employer carefully monitors the situation.

A right to check qualifications should be reserved by the client/employer. Where there are many staffing changes at the outsourcing company, this may be a considerable burden. It may also suggest that outsourcing poses unacceptable risks to both quality and compliance with the relevant regulatory framework. In common with health and safety rules, professional regulations are a 'bottom line' issue that cannot be ignored. The permit-to-work system used in the construction industry so as to ensure only known individuals with the right qualifications are working on a building site has often been criticized, but it is a useful model to note.

Another related issue is the possible need to protect quality 'kite marks', such as awarded by government and professional and other bodies. ISO standards are an example, and in the UK 'Investors in People' accreditation can be hard earned and highly prized. These kite marks cannot afford to be jeopardized by non-employees (or employees).

However, it should be noted that research (including the case studies for this book) does not reveal a correlation between highly regulated sectors and a reluctance to use non-employees. For example:

Laura Sykes from a Regulatory Body, itself concerned with compliance and high professional standards, has a workforce with up to 40 per cent of skill needs provided by non-employees. These include consultants and agency temps. She says:

> The temps are at least as good as our employees. They adhere to the same rules and go through the normal induction process. Many are non-UK nationals. However, we recruit them through an agency that is in the same building as us. We know the agency well and we rely on their processes and judgments. The temps anyway earn good money and we want the best out of them. We do not seem to have had any disasters.

It should be added that the Regulatory Body has a very clear philosophy and clear practices regarding the employment and management of non-employees. In part, this is derived from the fact that they employ so many non-employees and have aimed to identify the factors that ensure success. This matter is considered more fully in Chapter 5, and a more detailed summary of hard and soft laws as they relate to non-employees is provided in Chapter 6.

Security and confidentiality

This is an important consideration for many organizations. The leaking of confidential or market-sensitive information is a major risk for employers in particular sectors. In particular, these include high-tech industries, global companies, and research and development activities, although, potentially, all organizations have data they need to protect. This is as true of the public as the private sector. It is also important to bear in mind that leakage of certain types of data, regardless of who was actually responsible, is an infringement of the increasingly demanding regulations regarding data protection and privacy (for example, in the UK, the Data Protection Act, 1995 and the Human Rights Act, 1998). This has particular application to personal data.

Several organizations that have specific issues of confidential information are included in our case studies. Employees can have inserted in their employment contracts terms that deal with the matters of confidentiality and security. This will not, of course, necessarily protect the organization from loss, but will provide for redress, and failures will typically be covered by insurance policies. As referred to earlier, the essence of the employee contract is mutual trust and support, so complying with rules applying to confidential matters will be at the heart of those provisions.

Sally Worsley-Speck, the manager in a further education college, reflects on the issue of confidentiality and security. She said:

We feel we have more control over permanent employees. Disciplinary procedures are, indeed, useful. With lecturing staff supplied through an agency, you can, of course, simply ask the agency to take them back. This, though, in our area of work can be very disruptive and it can be problematic to deal with the consequences.

Experienced temp Pattie Pierce adds:

As the invisible eye in the office, the scope for temps to act as corporate spies is immense. Clients think nothing of using someone who has

73

temped for a competitor. This is being tightened up these days   I have been asked to sign confidentiality agreements, have twice signed the Officials Secrets Act, and have been security-vetted – a good reference for future work. But in some companies, security as regards temps is very lax, many being expected to use borrowed computer passwords.

There will be risks to market-sensitive or confidential information whether non-employees are employed on the premises of the client/employer or work a long way away. This will be the situation where services are off-shored or are performed at a shared service centre where staff have access to information from several organizations. Already scare stories have emerged from off-shoring operations in financial services that are not only costly but also very damaging to business reputation.

The reality and level of risk is notoriously hard to estimate in any given situation. This is compounded by the fact that several respondents in the UK case studies tell us that most companies are more lax about loss of sensitive material than might be thought. Nonetheless, where data loss affects clients, customers, patients and the like, or concerns data on criminals or terrorists, the business can be fatally damaged. All this suggests that great care must be taken about the decision to use non-employees unless they can be carefully controlled or there are adequate systems in place to prevent loss or damage. Again, long contracts with intermediaries or with self-employed people will need to be even more carefully considered, not least because of the likely change of personnel who will typically not have been screened by the client/employer.

Although our respondents in the case studies reported that they had robust systems in place to prevent loss of confidential or market-sensitive data, there were occasional comments such as 'There have been a few instances of leaked information [by agency temps]'. Another comment was that: 'In truth, when recruiting agency temps, we do not go through all the tests we should. When you employ them [non-employees] it does tend to lead to a relaxation of attitudes.'

A dramatic instance of the problems that can arise through inadequate screening and/or monitoring of non-employees is the massive fine imposed on the UK Post Office considered at the beginning of this chapter.

No foolproof system can be applied, but there is no logic in an assumption that because an individual is with you for a short while or has only limited access to sensitive data there will be no or fewer risks.

It is important to apply rigorous vetting procedures to everyone who works for the organization.

Quality assurance issues

For many, this is the central concern. Can service delivery standards be maintained or, ideally, enhanced by using non-employees? The absence of direct performance management facilities and the need to operate through an intermediary or rely on someone who is self-employed generally makes quality assurance a challenge. It requires new systems and new techniques. Are there circumstances when the risks to quality are so significant that using non-employees should not be an option? Anecdotally, there are many examples of irritated customers/clients/patients, etc., who resent 'their' company/hospital/etc., using 'other people' to provide for them – but is there a reality behind these scare stories?

Most of the concern about the quality provided by non-employees has focused on outsourcing, especially off-shoring, although temps too are often blamed for poor standards in, say, hospitals, schools and other service sectors. Recently, the Chartered Institute of Personnel and Development (CIPD) in the UK undertook a survey of 600 senior HR practitioners from a range of industries. It explored the impact of different types of outsourcing, including through off-shoring. This was typically to India, although China, Poland, the Czech Republic, Malaysia and South Africa were, respectively, the most popular countries to outsource to.

The CIPD research illustrated, much as evidence from our case studies, that HRM does not play a dominant role in the strategic decisions to outsource, although most respondents considered the role of HR critical. The findings regarding the experience of outsourcing through off-shoring indicate that there can be some major problems. Over half of the respondents noted the negative impact on staff morale, but, more relevantly, half considered that management control was difficult, over a third considered there were major language problems, and around a quarter reported interruptions to supply. There were many mentions of reduced quality of service. As a consequence, over 15 per cent of respondents reported that off-shored services had been brought back to the UK (CIPD, 2006).

Clearly, many of the points referred to are a reflection of the particular problems of off-shoring. Nonetheless, there may well be some messages to note that have relevance to outsourcing within the UK, and in the use of non-employees more generally. Much may depend on an effective role being played by HR to ensure that, say, poor morale does not impact on the quality of service delivery, and that there are effective communications and other systems and processes to ensure that business risks are minimized.

Ethical and cultural issues

Some organizations operate in intrinsically sensitive and difficult employment sectors. They work with vulnerable adults or with children, for example, or in medical research; in environmentally sensitive areas, such as nuclear power, and extractive industries; or in governmental bodies where there are obvious political sensitivities. In all of these there are particular risks if a worker behaves in a manner that damages the activity or the client/employer's reputation.

An increasing number of employers globally are signing up to the ideas of corporate social responsibility (CSR) or to organizations that promote fair trade or ethical policies more generally. Their membership and commitment is often prominent on marketing literature, recruitment information, websites, etc.

It is self-evident that if the use of non-employees is contemplated, those non-employees need to share – or, at the very least, recognize – these concerns and priorities. It is important that the organization can precisely articulate the relevant concerns, so there is no risk of ambiguity or uncertainty on the part of the skills supplier or self-employed person. There must be an obligation on them to select and screen appropriate staff. It may well be that so central are the ethical concerns, there is an unacceptable risk in using non-employees at all. This might apply to many organizations in the not-for-profit sector, and to some public services – such as aspects of the prison service.

Where there is a strong organizational culture, such as strong family-friendly measures, strong links with local communities or even a strong religious orientation, similar considerations can apply. This will, of course, be subject to anti-discrimination law, but, on the assumption that the rules are complied with, the question of whether non-employees will 'fit in' might be considered.

Off-shoring raises another set of concerns. Some of the issues of BPO outsourcing are succinctly expressed as follows:

The negotiation of these cross-border contracts with Indian service providers raises cultural as well as legal issues. Gaining a strategic advantage is important, and fraught with communication problems with legal implications. With the facility that Indians have with the English language, their familiarity with Western culture and their sharp business acumen, they are able in many cases to gain strategic advantage over their EU and American counterparts. Westerners usually do not have the benefit of the same type of familiarity with Eastern culture, where bargaining is part of everyday life. Although English is widely used as a second language in India, inherent difficulties arise in arriving at a common understanding of a concept such as 'data privacy'. True communication does not take place without a full understanding of the culture and background of the language spoken. Thus, it is not hard to imagine that there are probably opposite reactions between an American in Washington DC, who shudders upon hearing the word 'identity theft', and an Indian living in New Delhi, who may shrug upon hearing the same term.

(Crutchfield-George and Gaut, 2006)

Time constraints

This is not exactly a constraint; rather it is a cautionary matter, as in many of the case studies non-employees started off being employed for a very specific reason (skills shortages, maternity leave, short-term project, etc.) but were still there long after the original need had expired. This can lead to high costs. One respondent comments:

The relationships tend to be longer than we had anticipated, but sometimes this is because managers like the individuals concerned and want to hang on to them – though generally not as employees!

Anecdotally, and in case law, there are reports of people recruited ten years earlier to deal with an emergency and who are still employed today. In most legal jurisdictions there can be risks. A long unbroken relationship with a consultant – or, occasionally, a temp – can (legally) evolve into an employee relationship, with different expectations and legal duties. It is not just a question of cost or possibly increased risks through the application of less rigorous selection processes; the whole relationship can change simply through the passage of time and, gradually, increased responsibility for the individual occurs (see Chapter 6).

Impact on the workforce

We have previously considered that there might be repercussions in terms of clients/patients/customers. However, there is also the host workforce to consider. This is not problematic where the employment of non-employees adds to numbers or is for a short period of time – indeed, most employees welcome an agency temp when another employee is off on long-term sickness or maternity leave; the alternative may be work overload. However, where outsourcing, off-shoring or even a very systematic use of an employment agency is in prospect, there will tend to be anxieties – especially regarding job losses or a transfer to another employer under the application of legal rules on business transfers. The prospective employer may not be attractive, and even though a job is secured there may be fewer career opportunities, few non-wage benefits or a generally poor employment reputation.

Management of these anxieties can be time-consuming and stressful. There may be concerns over what function is next to be outsourced or contracted out. In the EU, there are often uncertainties over whether the legal protection provided by the Acquired Rights directives will cover the given situation. The uncertainties can often last a long time, leading to reduced morale and increased disruption.

One of our respondents in the financial services sector preparing to outsource a function says:

Yes, the staff were upset. Over the years they had won awards, enjoyed working here and lots of them had not worked anywhere else. We had to work hard to deal with their concerns. No-one left the organization at this time.

What type of employment arrangement with a skills supplier is the best for you?

This question is linked to the issue of why an organization chose to use non-employees in the first place. If reducing labour and other costs was the prime mover, there is no point in forming a relationship with a skills supplier that is expensive and adds to management costs within the organization.

If the decision was driven by the intention to enhance the delivery of services and do that in a manner that does not compromise the value and culture of the organization, it may not make sense to relinquish the entire control of staff to the skills provider.

This section suggests that there are three main models that characterize the relationship between client/employer and skills provider, and this seems to apply equally whether the skills are provided by individuals on self-employed contracts or whether work is outsourced. Inevitably, the edges of each model are blurred, and some organizations may combine the models.

Although it is likely that many arrangements for the use of non-employees will combine elements of more than one model, the three models are:

1. *The hands-off model* (Figure 3.1). This is where the client/employer leaves the supplier to make the key HR decisions and manage the contract and the people involved with relatively little interference by the former. This model can only really apply to some types of out-sourcing, to the supply of contract labour by an intermediary and to some types of work by self-employed people. What unites these groups is the fact that contact with the client/employer is minimal, or

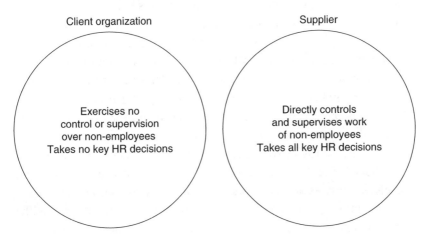

Figure 3.1   The hands-off model

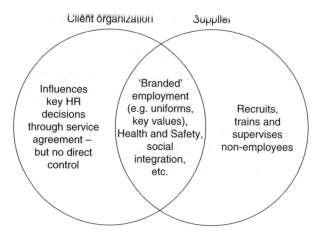

Figure 3.2   The integrated model

a specific piece of work or project is being undertaken. It is also most likely to be the case where the skills are provided beyond the client/employer's premises (or maybe off-shore). The objective is to push the HR issues away from the client/employer and to achieve 'commodification' of the work involved. There may be other reasons involved – for example, associated with avoiding legal employment responsibilities by aiming to pass them to the service supplier.

2. *The integrated model* (Figure 3.2). This is where the intention of the client/employer is to complement the skills supplied by others with its own workforce. Hypothetical customers/clients/patients, etc., will not know that the individual looking after them is not an employee of the client/employer organization. The individual might wear the uniform of the organization, follow all of its procedures, attend meetings, be invited to social functions and use social facilities at the workplace. The intention here is to substitute labour to perform skills that could have been undertaken by directly employed staff or to provide skills where they are not available in-house. The legal and organizational arrangements provide for some key tasks to be undertaken together by the client and skills supplier. Areas that are susceptible are health and safety, security, provision of social facilities and organizational events. The intention is also to ensure recognition and worth by integrating the non-employees and treating them in a comparable manner to the treatment of the client. This is to ensure an appropriate level of engagement

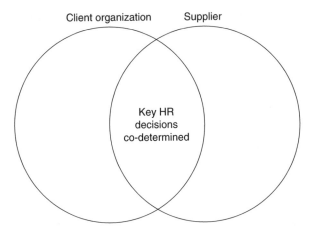

Figure 3.3   The partnership model

between the non-employees and the client. However, differences will remain in terms of the workings of the employment relationship, especially regarding performance management and employment benefits, and there will likely be concerns that the relationship between the client and non-employees does not become 'too close'.

3. *The partnership model* (Figure 3.3). This is where there is a conscious attempt to create a new kind of relationship whereby both the client/employer and the skills supplier have a vision of where they both want the service delivery to be. Each will benefit from the skills and experience of the other, and the relationship has strong elements of trust and confidence. Perhaps the best way to sum this is up is to rely on the policy documents produced by the L'Institute Esprit des Service (IES), a department of the Mouvement des Enterprise de France (MEDEF) – the French equivalent of the UK's Confederation of Industry (CBI). Interestingly, outsourcing is referred to as 'l'externalisation' – a more neutral phrase than outsourcing (or perhaps subcontracting). Their advice to French employers is to use the partnership model, referred to as co-sourcing. The implication is that the service levels and quality issues are agreed between the parties, as is the position of the staff that deliver them. Within IES, there is a working group comprising representatives of outsourcing, agencies and self-employed groups, as well as users. The group has the objective of developing and disseminating good practice in the employment of

non-employees. The details of their work will be considered later. Adopting a partnership model clearly requires major changes of thinking, though there are several examples, drawn from the UK and elsewhere, that have successfully partnered in this way. It might be added that MEDEF has a committee, with membership from leading multinational companies, that meets regularly to discuss the nature and content of contracts with agencies and for outsourcing. These include contracts for co-sourcing.

What might suit you best?

When considering what type of employment relationship with the skills supplier might be the most effective, a first step is to assess the type of your own organization. Is it, for example:

- hierarchical rather than 'flat'?
- traditional rather than innovative?
- an organization with formal performance management systems rather than informal ones?
- committed to team-working, rather than individualism?
- effective in terms of communication systems?
- an organization with a high level of autonomy despite having a parent company?
- in the public sector?
- an organization where HRM has a strategic role, partnered with business strategy, or does it primarily tend systems and monitor performance?
- experienced in partnerships with other organizations, or not?
- effective in change management?

Few of our respondents reflected on the type of their own organization. This was in contrast to their often strongly expressed sense of their market position and of their competition. An example of an organization that had given the matter thought is provided by Children's Mutual:

We chose our service provider on the basis of the synergy between them and us. They were familiar with mutual societies and were already providing services for a mutual society that we knew. Although the provider is an acquisitional conglomerate, we felt they knew our type of work and we could work with them. It was important that our systems and values would continue and we set up a system where this could happen.

It is equally significant for the client/employer to have a good sense of the characteristics of the service provider. This is just as important whether employing a consultant or selecting an outsourcing company. Agencies also need to respond to an organization and complement the way in which they do things. Many of the problems associated with using non-employees at work derive from a clash of cultures and systems. Having decided to use non-employees, it is vital to select a supplier (including a self-employed individual) that will enhance rather than reduce efficiency.

Few of our respondents knew much about the organizations that supplied their skills needs, in terms of what type of employing organization they were. They checked out (often very informally) the reputation of the potential skills supplier, and were frequently conscious of the level of skills or skills sets provided. Some undertook a formal benchmarking exercise. However, generally the emphasis was on ensuring that the client/employer did not take undue risks and could plan to avoid disputes and resolve problems; 'matching' of types of organizations (and self-employed people) did not appear high on the agenda.

From our case studies some useful practice emerged, especially where the supplier of skills was integrated closely or worked on a partnership model. Two of our examples, Avon Cosmetics and South West Water, were from Kelly Services. They reveal high levels of joint working and can probably be classified as examples of the partnership model.

Avon Cosmetics is a large UK manufacturer and distributor of cosmetics, toiletries, lingerie and toys. Demand is fluctuating and seasonal. Kelly Services provides all its needs for temporary staff through a type of contract called Master Vendor. There is a Kelly Services coordinator permanently on site at Avon. One of their tasks is to administer tests for Avon on potential temps, and Avon and Kelly jointly undertake a half-day induction programme. Kelly is now well known to local people who may want work at Avon. Its Contract Manager reports:

I spend every morning at Avon, so have close contact with the client as well as our temps. I walk around the production area speaking to supervisors and temporaries – essential to staff retention.

The HR advisor at Avon commented:

> Having an on-site coordinator has been brilliant. We have a good relationship that has been built up over the last few years and can now leave [staffing] to them.

Kelly also has an even closer relationship in supplying skills to South West Water, UK:

Again, Kelly has a business presence at South West Water, where the recruitment, induction and supervision of temps takes place. Kelly comments:

> Working closely with a client brings about a better understanding of its culture and philosophy. We have fostered a partnership which has resulted in a Joint Business Plan with shared goals.

Some of our respondents reported on less-collaborative relationships more typical of the hands-off model:

Chris Sharp, from Capita Learning and Development, Capita plc, UK, attached considerable importance to the amount of time and effort a client requiring training by Capita's consultants would spend on explaining their organization and its culture. He says:

> Some clients are very unhelpful; they are not prepared to give the time to see the best way forward. For example, if we are developing a training programme for an organization to improve its sales performance the client may rush into it and simply want a programme developed in an 'off the peg' way. They just hand it over. In fact, it is often the case that the client's real needs are different than those assumed – for example, the real problem is failing to close deals rather than selling itself. Negotiation rather than selling skills needed to be developed. The rush to offload the problem means that the underlying problem is not identified.

Another example of the hands-off model came from a further education college in East England which outsourced its cleaning services:

The cleaning was outsourced several years ago, but many of the cleaners working for the college had been former employees of the college. They had then been subject to the disciplinary procedures of the caretaker and of the college itself. The outsourcing contract was deliberately designed to mark a real shift away from both the employment situation and the culture of the prior situation. Efforts were made to differentiate the in-house from the outsourcing staff. For example, car-parking and social/welfare facilities were not available to outsourcing staff. The college caretaker specifically had no role in the cleaning work.

The case study above illustrates that, where a hands-off model is adopted but the people performing the service are former employees of the client, ambiguities and tensions can arise.

Summary points

- The process of making changes to or expanding the use of non-employees requires very careful research and analysis. It has to be the right decision for the right reasons!
- The relative advantages of using employees as opposed to non-employees should be weighed up in a dispassionate and pragmatic way.
- The drivers for and constraints on using non-employees need assessment in the context of your organizational sector, structures and culture.
- All risks need identification and coherent policies must be adopted to minimize them.
- Change should only be made where it will enhance quality and service.
- The suggested models for employing non-employees should be opted for on the basis that the choice complements organizational practices and HRM.

4

Recruiting and preparing for non-employees

Prescient tale

In 2003, the US insurance and financial services company, Alpha Corp, off-shored and outsourced several of its customer retention services. When the company found that some of its customers seemed likely to switch to rival competitors, it provided data on them to its outsourcing call-centre firm in India. The firm contacted the customers and, on Alpha Corp's behalf, offered them waivers, upgrades and free financial products as incentives to remain with Alpha.

The Indian staff were enthusiastic but lacked the experience needed to sell sophisticated financial products such as disability and loss-of-income insurance policies. They did not know now to interpret customers' responses. Unable to respond, they often placed people 'on hold' over the telephone line while they frantically tried to contact Alpha staff. The result was that the demands made on Alpha's marketing managers was as great (or greater) than if they had continued to supervise the service in-house and they retained fewer customers.

(*Harvard Business Review*, December, 2005)

It is clear that mistakes made in the selection of, say, a consultant, or an agency for the supply of staff, are highlighted throughout this book. The consequences of mistakes can include:

■ poor work standards
■ adverse publicity

- loss of business reputation
- loss of key customers
- declining profitability or performance
- negative impact on employment relations at the workplace
- failure to comply with legal requirements and the imposition of fines or other legal consequences
- increasing incidence of accidents and injuries
- damage in terms of loss of confidential data or damage to intellectual property rights
- becoming, as a client, embroiled in problems of consultants or other suppliers of skills.

There are, of course, other more subtle problems if the skills supplier or consultant/self-employed person is 'wrong'. There may be clashes in terms of working methods or clashes of organizational culture. Often it is very unfair if there are problems, but sayings such as 'mud sticks' or 'there's no smoke without a fire' are capable of damaging the most innocent of clients. It is self-evident that care must be taken in selecting non-employees. However, evidence from some of our case studies and from other sources indicates that often the recruitment of non-employees is undertaken in an unsystematic or informal way. There is a lack of a centrally devised and controlled framework, and the HRM function is either not involved or is bypassed.

On the other hand, several of our case studies reveal a high degree of awareness of the risks involved if rigorous procedures are not applied to the selection of skills suppliers and self-employed people. This is not just in terms of selecting the supplier, but also in introducing individual workers into the employing organization. Many recognize that the risks are just as great, if not greater, when people are working for an organization for a short time or in a highly specialized way.

Contracts and other documents can clearly go some way to protecting the client organizations. However, resorting to litigation is usually slow, costly and divisive and, typically, the damage will have already been done.

Aims of this chapter

- To explore the options for selecting skills suppliers and self-employed people
- To examine the selection process
- To identify good practice

■ To consider, where non-employees are being used for the first time or in a new way, how the organization should be prepared for them
■ To explore effective means of introducing non-employees to the organization.

Introduction

The matters covered in this chapter can be complex. This is particularly so when selection is cross-border or off-shored. There may be language and cultural issues to consider, and the process may be heavily dependent on the effective application of technology.

Some of the familiar selection processes – for example, using assessment centres and executive search – may not seem appropriate or may be too costly for non-employees. At the same time, the completion of an application form and shortlisting, followed by a formal interview, is not often used – even for consultants. Outsourcing and the selection of the outsourcing company tends to focus on the work to be undertaken, rather than the people who will do it. There is not always a role for the client regarding staffing issues in a service-level agreement or an outsourcing contract. The people issues have, therefore, to be dealt with differently.

In agency work, the key issue will be the selection of the agency that will itself select the staff to be deployed to the client. Indeed, the rationale for many using an agency is relieving the client from the staff selection process. The efficiency of the agency, not just in providing a set number of staff for the roles required but also in finding the 'right' staff and preparing them well for their role(s) at the client organization, is critical.

The selection of self-employed is distinctive, in that the client organization will usually itself perform the task. In addition, the variety of work performed by, say, craft or trade people, freelancers and consultants, along with the differing traditions of employment sectors, will likely suggest different ways of selecting people. For some the process will be very informal, with little if anything written down; for others – for example, a highly paid specialist consultant – there will be many formalities within a lengthy process.

Before turning to the recruitment process itself, it should be borne in mind that the selection of staff of any sort is anyway fraught with problems. As regards employees, many employers report misleading information on CVs, or even downright lies. The increasing profession-alism of CV writing appears to have led to some 'career inflation'. References are not always reliable, with a growing tendency for the writers of references to be extremely cautious in what they write – including ignoring or playing down adverse information about an indi-vidual. In some countries references are anyway uncommon, especially from academic institutions. Regulation on data protection, human rights and even equal opportunities are features of most developed economies, and all can lead to reluctance to make statements about job applicants.

As well as problems with documents, many consider that recruiting by using a formal or informal interview is unreliable. People often perform differently at interviews, or have been trained to present a par-ticular impression (Leighton and Proctor, 2006). Employers concerned about using interviews have moved to recruitment processes that emphasize the testing of competences, and formally assess those rather than relying on impressions and recommendations. Alternatively, a combination of various recruitment methods is chosen.

Some preliminary issues

In the light of evidence that recruitment is generally a complex and often risky process, one of the first questions to any organization planning to use non-employees is: to what extent can existing practices be applied to the recruitment of non-employees?

A second (and closely related) question is, even if different methods are used to recruit non-employees, are there some key issues and experiences of the recruitment of employees that can be carried over? For example, where the employer operates in a fast-moving area of technology, or in financial services, or in an area where there are vulnerable people or, more generally, in areas where honesty and ethical issues are at the fore, is there practical experience that could – or indeed must – be applied to the recruit-ment of non-employees? There may be a need for security, health or other screening, along with the need for checks regarding a criminal record or

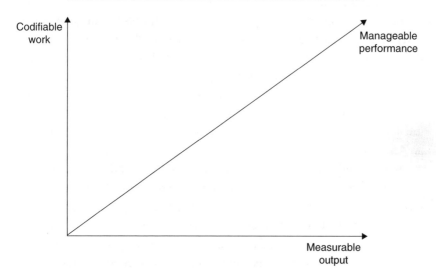

Figure 4.1 The management risk model

antisocial behaviour, where certain types of work are involved. The case study at the beginning of Chapter 3 concerning the Post Office in the UK, which was fined for losing or having had stolen an unacceptably high number of postal items, showed that one of the major causes was the poor screening of temps.

Figure 4.1 shows a management risk model that can be used to assist in assessing the risk of using non-employees for different types of tasks. A full explanation of the model is in Annex B.

Outsourcing and recruitment

In the UK, the process of outsourcing and selecting the provider has long been contentious, as it was sometimes used to market test, within the public sector, the efficiency and value for money of the current in-house provider or Direct Labour Organization (DLO). Even where there was no real intention to outsource, devising a tender and checking the performance of the DLO against outside providers could give rise to great suspicions; it was thought by many to be a cost management device rather than a genuine effort to change the basis of skills provision. Further suspicions arose over the government's requirement from the 1980s that, generally, the lowest tender should be accepted. This put even more pressure on DLOs, heightened by the fact that the selection process specifically banned the consideration of or requirement that outsourcing companies had fair employment practices. Matters have now changed, but it remains the case that outsourcing and the selection of the outsourcing company continues to give rise to concerns.

Once the decision to outsource for skills needs has been made, the selection of the outsourcing company becomes the core task. It usually involves devising the specification (i.e. what has to be done) and a formal tendering process, followed by the selection of the outsourcing company. There is considerable advice available regarding the choice of contractor. With the move to off-shoring and the increasing length of many outsourcing contracts, careful control over the selection process is vital.

Many of the texts and other sources of advice also emphasize the need for synergy between the client and the outsourcing company. Advice is available from organizations such as the International Association of Outsourcing Professionals and the Outsourcing Institute, which in 2005 published its *Buyers' Guide to Outsourcing* and the *Outsourcing Boot Camp*, which deals in part with the question of how you select a supplier. Mostly, publications stress the need to ensure that you select a supplier that provides skills on a cost-effective basis and maintains quality. There is, typically, less emphasis on the human resources issues. However, in 2002 the Australian Government's Public Service Commission produced *Outsourcing – Human Resource Issues*, and the *HRM Kit for Outsourcing*. Sometimes the people issues are subsumed under 'cultural' or 'ethical' concerns, but only rarely are they highlighted as a discrete issue.

One source of advice that does stress the people issues in selecting an outsourcing company is that of MEDEF's Institute Service Esprit in France. MEDEF is the leading employer body in France, and its specialist Institute is well established. It is one of our case studies. Its guide *Pour une externalisation reussie (For Successful Outsourcing)* is helpful. Its emphasis is on confidence, respect and trust between the client and supplier, and the notion of co-sourcing rather than outsourcing. It also deals with the importance of organizational culture and emphasizes the need for appreciation on the side of both the client and the supplier of 'leur culture specifique (traditions, rapports hierarchiques, vie familiale . . .)'. Even the section on 'Outsourcing contracts' reminds us that 'Le success d'une externalisation repose sur les competences des hommes'.

Nonetheless, we know that one of the major concerns about outsourcing is how the workers of the outsourcing company respond and the extent to which they feel committed to the client. Where the outsourcing is off-shored this seems to be a particular issue, and one that has direct bearing on the selection of the outsourcing company.

The Children's Mutual, UK, specializes in providing investment for government-funded baby bonds for newborn babies. It was decided that the company would have to outsource for customer relations staff. Cost was an issue. David Bornor, Chief Executive, said:

We were under enormous pressure in 2003–2004 as the baby bonds provided us with low margins. We needed staff to be quick and efficient to maximize our service. We carefully explored what skills were needed and on what basis we could obtain them. Two companies tendered for the contract. One was based in India. They would have done the work at a third of the UK costs. They were hugely professional and placed great emphasis on learning about our products and were willing to spend time with us. We checked them out but learnt they had little track record in our type of work and became worried about what would happen if things went wrong. We became aware of the major logistical issues, along with ones of culture and synergy. So we selected a large UK company. The selection was made because the outsourcing company already had contracts in specialized financial services sectors and there was synergy between us.

The possible risks of off-shoring to India did not prevent another of our case study organizations from outsourcing in this way:

RWA, the specialist software company based in South Wales, UK, also faced cost pressures. Rob Wortham, a Director of RWA, said:

We knew there were risks in using a company in India and we knew we would have to work hard to get it right. We would have to spend time in India and we would need excellent communication systems. We set these things up.

Some issues for the selection processes

Details about devising the specification, the tendering process and the technicalities of expressing what and when work has to be done, along with quality assurance processes, are beyond the scope of this book. A point that is of concern is that of identifying and responding to the relevant people issues that typically arise in outsourcing. If people are the biggest asset of any employing organization, they are also critical for the decision of how and who to select as a service provider.

Where the outsourced work is performed off-site, such as in the case of BPO, pay-roll and other HR services, IT, legal and accountancy services, the key points for selection are the quality of the staff and their effective management. There will often be a need to ensure that the staff know sufficient about the client and are responsive to its culture and ethics.

Where work is performed on the client's premises, such as with catering, cleaning, security, maintenance and hotel services, the people issues are vital in terms of not just the efficiency of the staff and their management, but also how staff will work alongside or even integrate with the client workforce. The nature of the client's business or activity is also critical, and the outsourcing workers need to be complementary to it. The case of the maintenance and garden maintenance company that worked at a girl's exclusive private school is illustrative. The workers were prone to take off their shirts in hot weather and to use obscene language, as well as playing loud music when they worked. The grass was perfectly cut, but the conduct of the workers caused major problems that were ultimately unresolved – so the contract was ended early (Leighton, 1985).

Where the work is in the not-for-profit sector, health care, care of vulnerable children, etc., similar issues apply. It will not just be a question of ensuring that the outsourcing company only uses staff that have been screened as appropriate for the work, but also that the workers themselves are sensitive to their working environment. It is particularly important to ensure that staff allocated to the contract, as the contract works through, are similarly carefully selected and screened.

Security and safety are also important issues to bear in mind. Jeff House from BP, in the UK, reflected on how they dealt with the matter:

We are clearly in a high risk business. We do outsource for security guards, but we ensure there is thorough vetting. The Royal British Legion put in a very good bid. We chose them because most of the guards they supply are ex-military people and are reliable.

It has been increasingly popular to use one company to supply a range of skill needs. So-called 'facilities management' or 'vendor' contracts appear attractive, as they simplify administration and reflect the fact that there have been mergers and acquisitions in the outsourcing industry generally, making provision of a range of services by one company viable. Despite the attraction of such arrangements, some of which provide for one company (the main outsourcing company) to, in effect, outsource for other services, the people issues remain important and should not be jeopardized in the interests of cost or convenience. The more complex the contractual arrangements, the more effective management structures need to be.

How to select a provider

Most potential providers, even small ones, have websites and other material that provides useful information. There are many professional bodies and trade organizations in most developed economies that can be very useful in the selection process. Public bodies are generally required to provide a tender notice, and, increasingly within the EU, notice has to be given to potential providers across member states.

When devising information about the service(s) to be outsourced, it might be helpful to keep in mind the three suggested models for using non-employees set out at the end of Chapter 3. The people issues where the intention is to have a hands-off relationship are markedly different from those in a partnership model. For example, the quality and sensitivity of managers in the outsourcing company are critical to the success of a partnership or co-sourcing model, along with training and development policies and practices. In a hands-off model, priority is typically given to performance indicators, cost, etc., but with less concern for employment practices and management processes at the outsourcing company. In the integration model, flexibility and adaptability of workers and good communication systems for staff, along with effective liaison skills, are perhaps key. Liaison over induction and training is important for all models.

Although with major contracts the selection process is often formal, detailed and lengthy (usually considerably adding to transactional management costs), many report that it was more useful to ask informally about the reputation and performance of a company. There are commercial organizations that will do this for you, but where there are particular sensitivities or risks it may be best done by the client.

Some questions

In terms of people issues, it might be helpful to pose the following questions regarding a potential skills provider:

- How important in this contract are the people issues? Where will the work be performed? What are the risks if the people supplied are, say, dishonest, violent or inefficient? How long is the contract likely to last, and how central to the contract are the wage and non-wage costs of staff?
- Does the outsourcing company have a reputation for reliability and efficiency? Is it a stable organization? Have informal as well as formal enquiries been carried out? Have you checked with other clients or used market intelligence material? Are you sure that you have been checking on the company's current reputation and efficiency, as opposed to that of a 'past golden era'? Has it lost previous contracts or does it have a bad track record for failed tenders? Why might this be?
- What do you know about employment practices and HRM at the outsourcing company? What are the arrangements for payment of staff and provision of benefits, and what are its practices regarding training and development? What is its current staff turnover, and has there

been significant litigation or other legal action against the company, especially in the area of employment/labour law and employee relations?

■ What experience does the outsourcing company have of your area of work, and has it successfully undertaken similar contracts with other clients? What level of awareness does it have about your organization, its HR policies and practices? Do you consider the company's HR practices to be compatible with yours?

■ Does the outsourcing company have strong supervisory and management structures, including effective communication and liaison procedures? Are they compatible with yours, especially where outsourcing staff are working on your premises? What do you know of its responses to poor performance and misconduct? Do you feel it will be able to suggest improvement and enhance work quality?

■ What are the company's procedures for monitoring the performance of the contract? What are the procedures for responding to complaints? Does it tend to rely on the strict wording of a contract, or is it open to criticism and able to modify practices? Do you get a sense that it really wants the contract to succeed, rather than just making money?

■ Do you think you will feel confident and comfortable with the company providing staff for you? Can you trust it?

Figure 4.2 provides an example of the management risk model as applied to outsourcing or contracting out insurance work.

Selecting an agency

This again is far from straightforward, not least because of the different types of agencies in the marketplace. Although, globally, larger and more specialist agencies are a feature and, in those, distinctive HRM policies are tending to emerge so as to create a cadre of professional temps, there are still many small agencies to choose from. Where the intention is to have a hands-off model of using non-employees the preference may be to use smaller agencies and to focus on skills and output, along with an attractive price.

Again, as with outsourcing, there has been a move not simply to select an agency but also to develop a partnership between client and

Moderate risk	Low risk
Insurance underwriting to cash-flow forecasting Equity research [Easy to codify difficult to measure]	Insurance claim processing Telecollection Technical support [Easy to codify easy to measure]
High risk	Moderate risk
Pricing policies Product design Strategy determination [Difficult to codify difficult to measure]	Supply chain coordination Customer data analysis Customer service [Difficult to codify easy to measure]

Figure 4.2 The management risk model: outsourcing or contracting out insurance work

agency with a high degree of involvement by managers of both parties. In these cases, the agency tends to provide a wide range of skill needs and to have an ongoing and often lengthy relationship with a client.

In many developed economies, agencies, unlike outsourcing companies, tend to be tightly regulated, and in some countries their activities are limited. This is less likely in the common law world, though, for example, in the UK there are duties on agencies regarding the screening of temps. This, of course, is helpful in the selection process. However, in our case studies, few respondents/clients mentioned the regulations but rather spoke of other qualities they looked for in an agency.

Caroline Waters, from BT, UK, who has considerable experience of using agencies, said that the reputation of the agency was important and that they tended to use the larger, well-established agencies. However, she also said:

> We do, of course, have a 'preferred supplier' list, and we check the standards of those on the list. We like large agencies as they can relate to large organizations like ourselves. They must, though, understand what being ready to work with BT means. They must accept the set of values we work to. Our brand is one of the most trusted in Europe; it cannot be jeopardized.

Several of our respondents spoke of their close and productive relationships with an agency:

Laura Sykes, from a Regulatory Body in the UK, spoke of her experience in having consultants supplied through an agency that is closely involved with the Regulatory Body itself:

The agency specializes in providing experienced consultants in business improvement. They have been excellent and well prepared.

Although several organizations report good experience of selecting and using agencies, largely as a result of very systematic management, others report a more 'hit and miss' approach. One said:

We have a staff member who knows the woman at (X) agency. They have a good working relationship and trust each other. I don't know what will happen if one of them leaves!

Another said:

We have an agency on our premises. It seems to work well.

There is a marked contrast in approach between those clients that have a well thought through and often a partnership arrangement with an agency, and those with informal selection methods. The former tend to select through a formal 'beauty parade' involving major agencies. The selection of a smaller agency is still based on word-of-mouth recommendation or random choice. Some (including some in our case studies) seem to have low expectations of both agencies and their temps, and wait for problems to arise. When they do they will move to using another agency.

Some questions

Many of the questions to pose when selecting an agency mirror those for an outsourcing company. However, as the relationship between temp and client is inevitably close and there are particular ambiguities and confusions about the nature of the essentially 'triangular' relationship, particular care has to be taken. At the same time, in most countries where agency working is well developed – and especially where multinational agencies operate – information on the agency should be relatively easy to obtain. The main question then is, which is the best agency for my needs? The questions to pose include:

- Should I use a generalist agency that can offer a wide range of skills or use one that specializes in say, IT staff, catering staff, engineers and technologists, media specialists, etc.? Am I looking for a partnership/ vendor relationship whereby all/most of my short-term needs are dealt with by one or a few agencies, or am I seeking the best agency for particular skills?
- What is known about the reputation of an agency, especially in terms of compliance with regulatory demands, stability, profitability, professional memberships and generally being up-to-date?
- What are the agency's policies on employment? Does it provide employee or similar status whereby employment rights and key occupational benefits are provided by the agency, or is employee status denied and temps, though possibly in receipt of good basic pay, left without rights and benefits? This is a critical issue, especially in the UK, where ambiguity as to employment status has left clients being considered the employer of the temps (see Chapter 6).
- What are the agency's policies and practices regarding HRM and, in particular, training and development of temps? If there is strong human capital investment by the agency in its temps, are you willing to pay what is likely to be a higher fee?
- Does the agency seek to develop or has it developed a cadre of temps that retain loyalty to the agency? Does the agency reward them with reference to their skills and experience? Is this a relevant matter for you?
- How does the agency retain supervision and quality control over temps? What are its performance management processes, and are they effective? What is their reaction to poor performance by temps? Do managers take ownership of these issues and aim to resolve them, or do they just withdraw the temp and not explore the reasons for failure?
- Does the agency have experienced managers who are strong on analysing and responding to clients' people requirements and to organizational culture?
- Do you trust the agency to be professional and ethical, especially in its treatment of temps and in its relationship with you?

- What of price? Why are some agencies apparently more expensive than others? If they provide training, employment benefits and good support structures, how much more is that worth to you? If you go for an agency with low prices, why might this be? Is it more efficient and better managed, etc., or is it cutting corners and likely to send you poorly trained and prepared staff?

From an agency's perspective, this issue is a difficult one. Most are conscious that margins are smaller and reducing, so they have to compete on quality and value added.

Greg Hargrave is the CEO of SKILLED, the Australian agency that specializes in staffing for healthcare, elder and home care, and workforce services. Despite major skills shortages and a generally buoyant marketplace, he says in relation to competing on price for contracts:

> If you are constantly competing on price, it's difficult for service to be your focus.

Selecting a consultant

This process is distinctive, in that the person you select is the one that will provide skills directly to you. You have control over the process and can, of course, apply the same or similar methods as are applied to selecting standard employees. In most organizations, the selection of employees is managed to a greater or lesser extent by the organization's HR department. This ensures that there is central administration, and regulatory matters, especially anti-discrimination requirements, are advised on and fully complied with. It is important to bear in mind that this area of law applies to most non-employees, and so there are particular legal risks if a manager selects a friend, ex-colleague, etc., and arranges for a particularly high fee.

The recruitment of consultants, contractors and the like may or may not be centrally managed. The questions of who undertakes the recruitment process, and how, are critical because, as other chapters of this book have illustrated, contracts with self-employed people are frequently subject to mismatches, misunderstandings and different expectations.

Laura Sykes, from a Regulatory Body in the UK, reports that the way her organization aims to reduce problems is to select consultants in exactly the same way as it does employees:

Given the nature of our work [regulating financial services], we have to have robust systems in place.

All the clients/organizations in our case studies use consultants. For some it is only for one-off or highly specialized projects, while for others consultants are routinely used to supply skill needs. Sometimes consultants are supplied through specialist agencies. This is particularly the case where the skills needed are technical, or research- or IT-based. For example, RSA, the UK-based specialist agency for the pharmaceutical industry, supplies staff to research institutes, manufacturers, etc., on a self-employed basis.

Gaining information about potential consultants is now easier than it was a few years ago. Many have websites and other promotional material, and will often 'cold-call' possible clients. At the same time, other clients, including several in our case studies, report that they make informal enquiries, check out relevant professional associations and academic institutions, and try to match an individual to their needs. Much depends on the numbers of consultants required.

Informal enquiries can focus on:

- whether work by the consultant/contract worker was completed to target or deadline
- whether the quality of work was satisfactory
- whether the work was value for money, and completed within estimate or budget
- how the consultant, etc., worked with in-house staff — was he or she cooperative, responsive to needs and culture?
- whether the person contracted actually undertook the work, or a less experienced person was used
- whether a relationship of professionalism and trust had developed
- whether the client would use them again.

When considering selection processes, it is important to recognize any particular areas or risk or difficulty. A self-employed person, unlike an employee, has different loyalties and ambitions.

A few of our respondents made observations about problems or losses when using consultants:

Yes; a few things did go missing.

or

We did have a suspicion that he ripped us off and 'sold' ideas he got from us to others.

On the other hand, Chris Sharp, from Capita Learning and Development, UK, felt these concerns were not that serious. Capita supplies consultants to many UK clients. When asked whether there were risks in terms of security, confidential information and damage caused, he said:

We have not found this a problem – certainly, it is no more a risk than employing someone else. Our quality assurance processes allow clients to provide detailed feedback on consultants. If there are problems, we deal with them.

Consultants and contract workers, freelancers, etc., will likely bring to you a range of other experiences, but will want to make the most of the experience that you can provide. They may have access to sensitive data, equipment or people. Where the consultant has worked for a rival company or might work for it again, what checks might be put in place?

A particular issue, also considered in Chapter 5, is that of the fee. This is complex, as it reflects prior experience as well as the task to be done. The client may offer a fee during the selection process and wait for a response. Alternatively, the client may await an offer from the potential consultant. The ability to set an appropriate fee on the part of the consultant, freelancer, etc., is seen as an indicator of professional competence and self-awareness. Clearly, where an individual works for a large consultancy, the fee scales will be known to the client. An individual self-employed person tends to be less expensive, but there may be issues regarding training and up-to-date skills and knowledge. Where there are doubts, these should, anyway, be tested in the selection process. For these purposes, it matters not whether the individual is engaged in manual or craft work, is a freelance in, say, the media industry, or is a consultant who specializes in change management.

Where there is an apparent mismatch between what the consultants quote for a role and what the client expects to pay, there may be an explanation. The client may consider that it has a simple matter for the consultant to deal with, such as leading a training programme on flexible working and work–life balance. The client thinks a simple day rate for the training days is adequate. However, the potential consultant considers that for the change to occur there needs to be major cultural change at the organization, a senior management programme and the identification of a 'champion' for the changes proposed. In this case, rather than dismissing a quotation as extortionate, further enquiries may suggest that the potential consultant has spotted some management and other weaknesses and the role he or she has been asked to play will not succeed without these wider changes.

Some questions

Although there are several important variables that will likely affect the way in which self-employed people are selected, such as type of work, length of project, numbers involved, etc., there are some general points that might be raised. Even where there is not a formal selection process, several matters do need to be verified and proper screening processes applied.

- Statements on CVs need to be carefully checked; if there are suspicions, these should be followed up with educational institutions and professional bodies, as well as previous clients. There is a massive difference between studying for an MBA or a professional legal qualification, etc., and actually obtaining it! Dates should be carefully scrutinized and gaps probed.
- The same approach should be applied to references and open documents such as testimonials, letters from grateful clients, awards won, etc. The individual should be asked to explain any gaps or have a chance to answer your worries before telephone and other enquiries are made. It must be remembered that rules on data protection and human rights apply to consultants, along with anti-discrimination laws.
- As consultants are generally working with or alongside client employees, it is vital that their interpersonal skills and style of working are compatible with the organization. What is their style of working? Do they prefer to work standard hours or do they prefer more flexibility

as to hours and location? If the latter, will that matter? Are they team players or more solitary workers?

- Are you able to provide appropriate support for the consultant, including relevant training?
- There should be probing of the consultant's understanding of the nature and strategic objectives of the client organization. If the consultant's experience has been exclusively in the public sector, will he or she work well in a fast-moving area of the private sector? If the consultant's experience has only been in the manufacturing industry, will he or she adapt to working for, say, a mental health charity? If the consultant has worked for very large and multinational companies, will he or she adapt to working for a small software company?
- Is the consultant able to work with appropriate managers at the client organization? If the role is strategic, say, internationally orientated, requires language skills, etc., has the consultant the ability to operate at that level? If the role requires contact with middle or lower management and the consultant's previous experience has been at a strategic level, will he or she be able to adapt? If driving through change, probably resisted by in-house staff, does the consultant have the experience and skills to do it effectively? If a contract worker or freelancer, does the consultant have the ability to adapt to and thrive in different working environments?
- Do you have confidence in, and trust, the consultant?

There will be other points to be pursued where the client organization operates in particular sectors or locations – for example, political or lobbying organizations, controversial areas of research or business activity, or clients with, say, a particular ethnic, religious or environmental focus.

In the selection process there will likely need to be consideration of the contract and terms of work. There should also be a discussion regarding how, if and when problems arise, they can be best resolved.

Preparing for non-employees

This section is concerned with two basic situations. The first is preparing the organization and others for non-employees, given that preconceptions, stereotypes and assumptions can be present when non-employees provide for skill needs. The second is preparing for the non-employees themselves. Both require the application of strong management, especially communication and liaison skills. There is also the management of the expectations of customers, patients, clients and, of course, employees. The last group may be fearful of the move to using non-employees, or the increased use of them.

We have already noted the controversies surrounding decisions to off-shore or move to long outsourcing contracts. There have been instances of prolonged industrial action, customer protests and political interventions. Of course, much outsourcing today is both routine and expected, especially in the UK. Services such as catering, cleaning and security are so commonly outsourced for that moving them in-house is the surprise. This will not be the position in many EU states and elsewhere, where it remains the case that employees are the norm and using non-employees is often considered to be an abnormal working practice. This presents considerable challenges to those who decide to use non-employees and those responsible for their management. This may be especially difficult where the employing organization uses considerable numbers of non-employees and there are many different groups within the non-employee workplace.

Preparing the organization

Given the frequent concerns regarding the use of non-employees, it is essential that senior management is positive about changes and that the benefits for the organization are stressed. One of the constant messages in this book is the need to ensure that using non-employees provides for added value. This can be in terms of cost savings, but is mainly in terms of bringing diversity and critical faculties to the work of the organization so as to enhance its performance. This message is vital for the non-employees themselves, for they should be presented to the client organization and its stakeholders in a positive way. Phrases such as 'We were forced to use an outsourcing company', 'We are sorry, but Mary's maternity cover is going to one of those temps' and 'We need to increase staff numbers so we have bought in a few fly-by-night freelancers' are extremely unhelpful. They set the tone for the whole work experience of non-employees.

All of the respondents in the case studies were clear as regards a number of issues that are relevant to the success of using non-employees. Some mentioned an internal senior 'champion'; others that success requires effective project management techniques to be applied to the use of non-employees and that there be named and accountable individuals performing the key management roles.

Interestingly, few mentioned the role of HRM in this process. However, we feel that, whatever the structures and processes at the organization, the people issues, especially training in the management of non-employees, should be driven by HRM. So-called transactional management skills are distinctive and, for success, need to be developed throughout the organization. Line managers and team members, as well as senior and HR managers, need to have the appropriate skills. These are particularly required for the effective induction of non-employees, for quality assurance processes and communication skills. In doing this, the different motivations, expectations and priorities of non-employees need to be borne in mind. These are more fully considered in Chapter 5.

Thus, preparation for changes in and/or the arrival of non-employees requires a mixture of good management and positive attitudes. The latter includes careful consideration of the extent to which non-employees should be covered by workplace policies and practices. What facilities they should have access to? Car-parking, canteens, desks and lockers are the purely practical matters that, although not seeming important, (unless there is a shortage of space) are in fact very much so, especially to organizations committed to an integrated or partnership model of using non-employees. Some organizations adopt a policy of clearly segregating employees from non-employees. The reasons for this might usefully be explored. Is it because of legal or other risks?

As well as the preparation of managers and management systems, other stakeholders need to be involved in the process. These include trade unions and/or employee representatives. Where the use of non-employees is a new development, the implications of the change must be fully discussed and suggestions sought on the effective use of non-employees. This will need to be done formally within EU member states, following the Information and Consultation Directive, 2002. Even without this, good practice suggests involving as many relevant stakeholders as possible. However, in this process it is important that the right tone is set and that concerns are addressed.

It has also to be recognized that using non-employees can put extra responsibilities on many staff. These are staff who work alongside, say, temps or consultants and who find themselves explaining how machines work, what to do in emergencies and even the character and attitudes of the departmental manager. This is a very different and less formal process than induction. Induction often comes too early, non-employees do not relate to it, and it leaves them with many questions and dilemmas. This is rarely a topic for feedback from the skills suppliers and analysis by organizations, although it is an important matter.

Other stakeholders are outside the organization. They are the people to whom services are supplied – customers, associate companies, and perhaps wider community and social groups. Again, we know that outsourcing, especially to call centres, is proving unpopular with many, and there are complaints about declining standards. Where an organization announces that it has outsourced a key service or facility, especially one with a customer focus, efforts will likely need to be made to explain and reassure people about the development and possibly the reason for it. Temps and consultants tend to 'merge in' from a customer perspective, so the issues here are less stark.

Some questions about preparing the organization include:

- Has the organization fully explored the systems that are likely to be affected by the change to using non-employees? Has the impact on employees and other stakeholders been taken on board? Where there is experience of using non-employees, has there been a systematic review of their impact on the organization and stakeholders? This is totally different from asking whether a particular contract or, say, relationship with an agency, has been a success; rather, it focuses on the whole organization, its staff, its management systems, and people or organizations that it works with.
- Has there been proper costing of the transactional management costs involved in using non-employees?
- What are the management structure and processes for using non-employees? This includes the role of HRM. Are individual managers responsible for individual projects or contracts, or is there a central locus of the management of non-employees? Have these managers been trained and supported in their work?

- What are the risks and fears that the organization needs to address? What is the strategy for reassuring employees and customers, patients, etc.?
- What are the monitoring and evaluation procedures specifically to do with the management of non-employees, as opposed to the contracts?

Preparing for the non-employee

Consultants and freelance workers, along with temps, have, in the nature of their work, to adapt quickly to different work environments. Some are used to spending as little as a few days with a client organization, but in that time they have to learn a lot. The fact that they are generally able to adapt does not mean that efforts should not be made to ease the transition and maximize their skills for the benefit of the client.

This process requires careful planning and preparation. It generally starts at the client organization, with a careful analysis of the work to be done and identification of the support structures needed for it. In the case of agency work, aside from a partnership or vendor arrangement with an agency, where skill needs are jointly discussed, the client will define the need for a temp. Matters of experience and qualifications are usually identified with reference to job descriptions, etc. Broader questions – for example, whether the temp will work in a team or act more autonomously, whether the temp will liaise with outside bodies or customers, whether he or she will have a separate office or share a workstation, and what the management/reporting structure is – may not be always communicated.

In the light of the fact that the temp in our case studies reports that there appear to be many opportunities for misunderstanding that can quickly turn to blame, this is a vital matter. The agency, too, has a vital role to play in effectively communicating key information about both the assignment and the client organization.

Consultants, similarly, may be unsure of important matters when they start work. They, unlike temps, will likely have had an opportunity to meet staff at the client organization and generally get a 'feel' for it. Nonetheless, the broader management structure, organizational culture, etc., may not be clear, along with practical issues such as car-parking and attendance at team briefings.

It is suggested, therefore, that the following matters should be attended to before the arrival of a temp or a consultant/freelance worker/contract worker:

- Ensure that there are clear instructions regarding where the temp or consultant should report to, that the relevant manager is prepared for the arrival and that there is a warm welcome.
- Provide information about the organization and its activities if not previously supplied; website details may have been provided earlier. Relevant organizational rules should be carefully explained, regarding, say, alcohol, personal phone calls or emails, dress code or required dress (such as low heeled shoes if a temp is working in the hotel industry as housekeeping staff). Dress code for a consultant, especially if going out of the building to meet customers, will need to be explained.
- Provide information regarding the department or project the temp or consultant will be involved with, and key personnel.
- Provide information regarding the HR department and function in the organization, and its relevance, if any, to the temp or consultant. In the case of consultants, etc., information about pay systems, expenses claims and the storing of personal data, etc., must be given.
- Clarify the precise duties and expectation of the client organization, including any performance targets that have to be met.
- Provide necessary equipment and practical information, such as a mobile phone, passwords, security procedures, clocking-on/timesheets, breaks and their timing, vouchers for the canteen or to exit the car park, etc.
- Provide information about professional or staff organizations the non-employee can have access to, such as sports clubs and cultural activities, and explain the basis of their access.
- Provide information about who to seek advice or support from if there are problems; however, remember that in the case of temps the matter should be raised with the agency, which will then raise it at the client organization.
- Provide information about regulatory matters such as health and safety, including attendance at fire drills, wearing of safety equipment and following safety and security procedures.

Many of these matters will have relevance to outsourcing, although clearly in this case the workers are employed by the outsourcing company.

Nonetheless, matters of welcome, organizational informati
vant rules (especially for health and safety) have great impo,
induction arrangements will be determined by the client an
cing company, although it is important that if there are regulato
tive or practical matters relevant for work performance, t
reinforced by the client organization.

Summary points

- The need for care in the selection of non-employees is usually greater than for the selection of employees. Risks can be higher, and the fact that the involvement with the client organization is brief is irrelevant.

- There are considerable risks in having little or no central control of the process of selection or using informal or, say, just word-of-mouth recommendations.

- The role of HRM in the selection of non-employees is important. It should not be seen as simply one of being a gatekeeper or appearing to put obstacles in the way. The role should be creative and positive.

- Cost is a key issue and, generally, you get what you pay for. This requires careful consideration of priorities and wider concerns, such as those involving cultural and ethical issues, and business reputation.

- There is always a need to be sceptical about information provided by non-employees themselves or their suppliers. If there are concerns or suspicions, these should always be followed up.

- The attitude of senior managers in the client organization is critical. They need to be providing adequate resources for the selection process and for training, and generally to be emphasizing the positives of using non-employees in terms of organizational performance.

- It is essential to avoid any ambiguities or mismatches during the selection process. Things should not be left to chance.

- Non-employees should not get an impression of second-class status when they arrive at the organization, and they need to have confidence in the management and support structures provided for them.

5

People management and non-employees

Prescient thoughts

In the UK not only has the notion of 'flexibility' never really come to fruition, but the psychological contract has also been dismantled for employees. We want to tap into particularly high-skilled people who view with cynicism the psychological contract. We can give them learning and development opportunities. In any case, today there is not such a divide between temps and permanent staff – it is more a continuum. The key issue is whether you want to follow or shape the market [as an agency]. The problem for HR is that UK employers so often want to get rid of risks. Many risks are simply not off-loadable. So you have to have robust management systems for dealing with the people involved. Some call this co-sourcing, but it can only be successful if HR recognizes and deals with the risks that are inevitably there.

(Darren Cox, Director of Human Resources,
Kelly Services, UK and Ireland)

Richard Crawford, one of the owners of the Henry Jones Art Hotel, states: 'Training in tourism is something I am very passionate about. We look for professional excellence; we want people to develop their professional skills. We have people undergoing traineeships while they are here. We favour well-qualified people; people who use the tertiary education system of Tasmania to good effect. I favour these people because they are saying to me: I'm happy to start at the front desk, but I want to be the marketing manager. Anyway, one way or another you have to look after those people or they will leave and any sort of culture you want to foster in your workplace will go and won't come back. What matters are these attitudes – not the category of worker or their background.

Searson Buck is the largest locally owned employment agency in Tasmania, Australia. It emphasizes local knowledge and community involvement. Their business, 'It is not about hiring people out; it's about how you make this project work. We offer a system approach (HR and IT) not just labour. This needs an element of education in the marketplace. Some people still don't understand the concept of having a temporary on the books fully engaged in their workplace but not working for them. We favour partnering – working with clients to achieve their ends. Nonetheless, there is always an element of risk management.

(M. Simpson, Managing Director, Searson Buck Workforce)

We work actively, as an agency, with government and industry in providing apprenticeships, etc., and training to increase the skills base. We aim to give them [apprentices, etc.] a sense of belonging but not a sense of being owned.

(Julie McBeth, Corporate Affairs Manager,
SKILLED, Australia)

What's important to me as a consultant are a number of things:

- *First, I need reliability of payment. This is more of a priority than level of payment.*
- *Then there is making me feel at home in the organization. I do not want to feel second class. It is, of course, nice to be asked to the office party, but I do not look to the client for my social life.*
- *Getting positive feedback is a great motivator, but so few clients bother with this. Being entirely left to 'get on with it' is OK, but can be very isolating.*
- *Recognition of what I 'bring to the organization'. I do bring reliability of delivery and loyalty to the organization I am currently working for. I am often used as a sounding board, and I need to respect the confidential information I am told. But I can be very useful in this regard.*
- *Dealing sometimes with the resentment of employees who think I am overpaid, but they are generally unaware of what skills and experience I bring 'to the party'.*

(Dominic Brender, self-employed researcher and consultant, UK)

We use many temps but we do not want to create second-class citizens. We do not believe in exploitation! We need to remove the worries of low pay and the temps can then focus on their skills. The agencies we use train temps and they have to meet our labour standards. We want the supplier [agency] to be forward thinking and add value. As there is so little differentiation in the market, marginal improvements in the way people are managed and work will make a huge difference.

(Caroline Waters, BT, UK)

It's more and more a market relationship with our temps. But we also have to give a temp a good manager and good training. Our temps have to have the capacity to adapt to individual clients and their HR structures and culture. This can be very useful if the client is engaged in change management. Nonetheless, we have to focus on the agency/client relationship, particularly regarding the performance of our temps. We want a relationship of proximité with significant integration, but not one of partinaire where the involvement is too close. We need to see that the client and agency have separate roles.

(Jean-François Denoy, Manpower, France)

When you outsource a service, for example cleaning, you think there will be a clear break and the people become the responsibility of someone else. In reality, a lot of people issues can still arise, not least relating to the performance and conduct of the employees of the outsourcing company when they are on our premises. It's often not clear what to do and who has the responsibility for dealing with problems.

(Sally Worsley-Speck, former senior manager in the education sector, UK, currently with Capita Learning and Development)

These thoughts and observations provide a sense of the complexity and the subtlety of employment relationships that go beyond the traditional employer/employee relationship. There are distinctive and often new issues that need to be addressed. These are often dealt with through the combination of experience, intuition and pragmatism. What is generally lacking is the direct application of tried and trusted HR management theory and practices. Few texts and even fewer (though a growing number) academic and other articles deal with the effective management of non-employees.

115

These practices include the language of HR. Notions of engagement, career management, human capital investment and the like do not sit easily with the employment of temps and self-employed staff. Such workers do not see that they have a career with a client, the client of their agency or the client of an outsourcing company. At the same time, they are often confused as to where their own loyalties lie and where their own work and career may be going.

In the case of outsourcing workers and temps, their primary employment relationship is with the outsourcing company or agency. Clearly, matters of reward, occupational benefits, career management, etc., will be the primary responsibility of the company or agency.

With the self-employed, the situation is different. Their employment relationship is with the client, though they may have other employment relationships contemporaneously. Matters of reward, benefits and support clearly do arise and need to be effectively addressed. However, the essence of self-employment is independence and a freely negotiated partnership. The 'glue' that holds the partnership together is distinctive from the glue of contracts of employment. Rewards have to be immediate and project-based; support has to be such as to work effectively, notions of trust and loyalty are different from those in a standard employment relationship, job satisfaction has to be obtained in a direct way, and there needs to be recognition of the intrinsically precarious nature of self-employment.

Although many of the usual HRM topics have no, or limited, relevance to non-employees, there are several different or new HR topics that do have to be dealt with to ensure the effective management of non-employees. Sometimes it is a case of having to adapt existing systems to non-employees; sometimes a whole new approach is needed.

Examples of the need to adapt existing HR practices are reward systems supervision, appraisal, and performance management more generally. Examples of new topics include the particular issues that arise out of having different workforces on the same premises; cultural differences or even clashes; responses to confidential, market-sensitive and other data; and access to or use of social, occupational health and other facilities.

At the heart of these issues is the nature and workings of the psychological contract. This is well developed and understood regarding standard employees (although many argue it is under considerable strain; see Guest and Clinton, 2006), but barely considered in terms of the non-employee.

Aims of this chapter

■ To reflect on the nature of the employment relationship non-employees have with their employing organization

■ To suggest the nature and content of the psychological contract for these groups

■ To explore the application of key aspects of HRM that have particular relevance to the employment of non-employees

■ To examine practice, especially good practice, from our case studies and other research

Employment relationships and the psychological contract

The psychological contract defines the mutual aspirations and expectations that employers and employees have of each other. It is argued that these expectations go beyond the formal legal employment contract. The terms of the psychological contract provide not just a framework for the relationship, but also balance and fairness. Commitment and loyalty are rewarded by recognition, support and development opportunities, for example.

The expectations that these work experiences engender may not be part of a formal contract or workplace agreement, but they are important in understanding and managing behaviour and commitment in organizations. Where standard contracts of employment are being considered the emphasis is on the exchange of socio-emotional elements, broadly based and involving long-term, open-ended obligations, centred on support, loyalty and trust, that may change over time (Arnold, 1996; Millward and Hopkins, 1998; Aselege and Eisenberger, 2003). This relational-type psychological contract can engender feelings of affective involvement or attachment in the employee and can commit the employer to provide more than purely remunerative support to the individual. This typically includes training, personal and career development, and job security. As such, relational contracts generally involve investment and commitment to a common interest, ensuring interdependence such that withdrawal from the relationship is difficult.

If relational forms of psychological contracts are indicative of long-term interdependent relationships, transactional ones are based on ideas of economic exchange that more appropriately characterize the employment relationships considered in this book. Transactional exchanges assume rational and self-interested parties, but not an ongoing interdependence. In them, 'money comes first' and people are more concerned with personal benefit than with being good organizational citizens (Rousseau and McLean Parks, 1993). Indeed, many of our respondents in case studies echoed this view. Rob Wortham of RWA, a software company in South Wales, UK, says:

> Our contractors [self-employed] were hugely expensive and they drove a very hard bargain.

One of our respondents in the UK says of contractors:

> They want the biggest cash benefit they can lay their hands on. They condition themselves to a certain lifestyle.

Others, such as Dominic Brender (considered at the beginning of this chapter), are less concerned about the amount of pay than with speedy and reliable payment. Nonetheless, the emphasis on immediate rewards is a popular conception, and the transactional nature of the relationship confirms this impression.

The dichotomy between the relational psychological contract and the more specific and limited transactional relationship is currently being reconsidered. This process is important for the HRM of non-employees. Many note the change in the typical relational employee contract such that the notion of security in return for loyalty has been replaced with a new concept of employability in return for flexibility. This implies that the new psychological contract sees employees expecting to be looked after in return for loyalty, hard work and commitment, but without long-term security (Millward and Herriot, 2000).

Many are now adding to the debate on the nature of the psychological contract by arguing that it contains moral and ethical considerations. This would imply growing concerns for community issues, human rights and the 'ethical balanced score-card' (Thompson and Bunderson, 2003). How do these concerns impact on the employment relationships of non-employees, if at all?

At the same time, the essentially transactional nature of the contract that is especially appropriate for the self-employed is also coming under review.

This is because the whole notion of a single contractual relationship between the individual and the organization is outmoded in the light of contemporary changes in the forms of work organization (Rousseau, 1995; Millward and Brewerton, 1999a, 2000; Marks, 2001).

Reflecting broader organizational behaviour literature, this view holds that individuals can be involved in more than one contractual relationship within an organization and that there are multiple levels of exchange (e.g. team, department, profession, and maybe your primary employer, such as the agency).

Other recent literature has identified the growing complexity of employment relationships and argues, in the context of 'work fragmentation', that there is an even more pressing need to define and put the employment relationship 'centre stage' (Marchington et al., 2004).

This creates a dilemma. Is change in the nature of employment relationships necessarily a negative development and a decline from the relational form of the psychological contract, or an opportunity to identify and support new forms of psychological contracts? The central theme of this book is that it is the latter.

The practical implications of the growing complexities are that the individual worker defines organizations not as one entity but as a collective, and so individuals have varying numbers of relationships, all with different foci operating at a number of levels and with those agents (senior management, workgroups, procurement function, etc.). In the case of agency work, a key relationship may well be the on-site agency supervisor who works in partnership with the agency's client.

SKILLED provides agency temps to clients in Australia. There is a supervisor who looks after the temp in every circumstance, even if there is a client supervisor present. The SKILLED (Worker) Handbook states, inter alia:

The client supervisors and employees will deal with most safety problems when safety issues arise. When an issue cannot be resolved at this level, you should notify your SKILLED representative immediately.

It goes on to deal with a broader issue – that of temps behaviour. It requires the temps to sign a declaration to the following effect:

I understand that each client may have different policies and procedures to those of SKILLED that dictate behaviour and conduct on their sites. I will ensure I abide by these policies and procedures.

This example of 'multiple loyalties' requires individuals to be very adept and flexible in their responses. It also means that individuals may have apparently conflicting demands on them. There should therefore be some system in place to provide information and guidance and, if required, procedures to resolve doubts and conflicts.

Psychological contracts and non-employees

The previous section has sketched in the nature of the psychological contract, at least so far as employees are concerned, and noted the major changes in labour markets that have provoked a rethink of how psychological contracts can operate.

This discussion takes place in the context of these recent rethinks regarding the psychological contract, which have tended to focus on the duration of the relationship and the performance requirements. The relationships of non-employees display considerable diversity in this respect.

Rousseau describes four types of relationships:

1. *Transactional relationships*, where the terms are primarily economic and short term
2. *Relational relationships*, where the emphasis is on commitment and long-term duration
3. *Transitional relationships*, where there are few guarantees due to intrinsic instability
4. *Balanced relationships*, meaning the blending of transactional and relational aspects.

From the perspective of the employing organization, one of the outcomes of using non-employees is (or should be) specified performance outcomes. This means that the focus of this book is on transactional and balanced psychological contracts. The best HR policies and practices can be used to leverage this awareness into competitive advantage. In general, the basic HR processes of recruiting, selecting, appraising, compensating, training and development can, as regards employees, have the following features:

- They can influence perceptions and expectations of employees (Rousseau and Greller, 1994)

- Understanding of HR policies and practices at the organization is often limited and not fully acted upon (Guzzo and Noonan, 1994)
- The relationship between employees' evaluation of HR practices and their level of commitment is affected by their perceptions of organizational support and procedural justice (Meyer and Smith, 2000).

The challenge within organizations is to manage perceptions or, in other words, to become 'managers of psychological contracts'.

The performance and commitment of non-employees, although different, is no less vital. The success of an organization requires efficiency from all its staff. It is therefore essential to understand the different ways that non-employees perceive both the organization and its HRM practices, along with their understanding of their own contribution.

The employment relationships of non-employees

Before turning to the likely content of the psychological contract for non-employees, some basic points need to be made regarding the three groups of workers focused on in this book:

- Most workers for outsourcing companies are standard employees of an outsourcing company. They may or may not be located in their employer's country, and may or may not work on the client's premises. The basic expectations of the parties will be comparable with those in any standard employment relationship, but there will likely be issues regarding performance of work, supervision, organizational culture, social facilities – even over prosaic matters such as car-parking and access to canteens, etc. Such matters should be managed by the outsourcing company or there will be risks in terms of confusion over loyalty, conduct, etc. However, it is the expectations and aspirations of the parties to the relationship(s) that are critical. How will these be managed?
- Ambiguities often exist regarding the relationships and psychological contracts of agency temps. They may or may not be employees of an agency. On a day-to-day basis, their working relationship is with the agency's client. The client allocates their work, sets their work standards and has a key role in their performance management. However,

rewards are provided by the agency, which may or may not provide support and payments for, say, illness, maternity and holidays. With a long assignment to a particular client, the opportunity for confusion and ambiguities can grow dramatically. The temp is 'in the middle', and the relationship between the temp and the client on the one hand and the temp and the agency on the other need both careful definition and avoidance of conflict.

■ The position of the self-employed appears the most straightforward. They have only one employer and no peripheral employment relationships. Nonetheless, self-employed people cannot be isolated from their work environment. They have expectations of the client and, usually, a well-defined view of their own needs and contribution to the client organization. Research is indicating that the idea that the self-employed freelancer or contractor simply 'takes the money and runs' is wide of the mark. According to some writers, contractors often have a surprisingly high level of identification with the client and are capable of forming a close relationship with it (Millward and Brewerton, 1999b).

The psychological contract of the outsourcing worker

As stated above, the employment relationship between client and outsourcing worker should be, typically, of a limited nature. This will be especially the case where work is off-shored as well as outsourced. The two organizations will, in effect, be separate but with particular attention to be paid to communication systems and quality control. The extent to which workers for the outsourcing companies abroad should receive information about the state of the client's business, future plans, etc., is a matter that might be considered. How much do workers want to know? Does geographical distance imply a lack of interest and difficulties in practice in involving them in the client business?

The evidence from one of our case studies in the IT industry that off-shored from the UK to India is instructive. It suggests that even in the context of off-shoring, there is the possibility of an employment relationship between the workers of the outsourcing company and the client, and meaningful employment relationships can emerge.

RWA Ltd off-shored to India following cost pressures and the need to develop specialist software in a short period of time. Following a piloting of the contract, the Indian company outsourced to set about writing 'twenty man years of software in one year'. Their work practices are different from those in the UK, with a greater likelihood of very close working relationships – for example, covering the work of others when required.

RWA was sure from the outset that success would depend on a close working relationship between the staff of RWA based in South Wales and those in the Indian company. Rob Wortham says:

> *They are an extended part of our team. We went over [to India] and wanted to build the working relationship. We work with staff on the ground. The staff from India regularly visit the office in Wales, and there has been much work done on improving language skills. This itself has been helped by the regular contact between staff in both countries.*

Interestingly, when the current contract for software ends, a number of options are being considered so as to retain the relationship. One is that the employees of the Indian company become employed by RWA as contract/self-employed workers.

This case illustrates that models of employment relationships and psychological contracts that emphasize the purely transactional nature of relationships, especially when applied to non-employees, fail to recognize the subtleties and developmental possibilities. The workers of the Indian company involved with the RWA Ltd example given here clearly had an employment relationship with their own employer. However, the close working and personal relationship with the UK company had created a series of expectations and aspirations, despite the huge geographical distance between them. Furthermore, in a number of ways there had been significant human capital investment by RWA.

It is possible to articulate the nature of the Indian workers' psychological contract with RWA. Clearly, it can only be a psychological relationship, as they have no legal relationship with RWA.

RWA expects:

- that the Indian workers work efficiently and are responsive to the needs and working practices of RWA, as well as being loyal to RWA within the confines of a specific and fairly short contract
- that the Indian workers enhance their skills regarding not just IT but also language, communication and interpersonal skills

- that the Indian workers will, through the work experience, enhance their employability and become both flexible and mobile
- that the relationship with workers may evolve over time and even change into a different form, but at the same time it can be easily and painlessly ended.

The workers of the Indian company expect:

- that RWA will properly remunerate their company and enable them successfully to undertake the work
- to show appropriate loyalty and confidentiality, especially given the nature of the work involved
- that RWA will provide appropriate support, including feedback on their performance, and share with them issues around the project and other possible developments
- they will become more employable, especially within a global and fast-moving economy
- that RWA may be open to developing the business relationship, and therefore employment relationships, to mutual satisfaction.

Where the outsourcing for skills and services involves more proximate working (including on the client's premises), it is even more important to define the nature of the relationship between the client and the workers of the outsourcing company. The workers may well interact with the client organization in a number of ways and with different groups of people. Again, issues of reward and performance management, career development, etc., are the primary responsibility of the outsourcing company employer. However, there are a number of basic issues that can form part of the psychological contract between the client and the workers of the outsourcing company.

From the perspective of the client, the expectations are that:

- the workers of the outsourcing company will use their skills to their best endeavours for the client and contribute to the successful execution of the outsourcing contract
- the workers of the outsourcing company will appreciate the culture and business environment of the client and not conduct themselves so as to jeopardize these – this is especially important where the client is

concerned with the care and management of vulnerable adults or children, is in an environmentally sensitive area, or is a not-for-profit or, perhaps, high-profile enterprise

- the workers will interact successfully with the staff of the client, respect quality control, health and safety procedures and relevant codes of practice, and, if appropriate, participate effectively in training and development activities
- that day-to-day matters of working conditions and contracts of employment will be dealt with by the outsourcing company and not become embroiled with the client's workforce and its managers
- that difficulties and problems regarding the execution of work or the conduct of workers of the outsourcing company are responded to effectively by both parties.

For their part, the workers of the outsourcing company (many of whom may well be former employees of the client) will likely expect that:

- they will be afforded appropriate respect and support by the client's managers and workforce, and they will not be thought of as marginal, second-rate or disinterested in the success of the business
- they will be provided with appropriate support and training at the client's premises so as to discharge their work effectively (this would include training for health, safety and environmental issues more generally)
- if there are problems with their work, they will raise these with their own employer but have confidence in procedures, etc., so that their employer resolves them with the client
- they will gain experience and skills to enhance their employability.

There are, of course, practical implications of these mutual expectations, despite there being no legal relationship between the workers of the outsourcing company and its client. There must, as a minimum, be effective communication channels, dispute resolution processes and a clear view about training and development. 'Normal' employee performance management processes are not open to the client, but they do have to operate through the outsourcing company. The need for regular meetings between the client and outsourcing company, procedures for the outsourcing company to monitor and evaluate the experiences of its workforce, and for regular assessment of the success or otherwise of the contract is vital.

Several of our case studies suggested that often the situation was 'hit and miss' and that there was undue reliance on the outsourcing contract documentation itself. This typically contains data on how matters are resolved if there are problems. Typically, also, there are financial penalties and, ultimately, termination of the contract.

An example from our case studies where there has been attention to the particular sensitivities of the client's business is the Children's Mutual Insurance Company, UK, which specializes in the investment of state-funded 'baby bonds'. The company to which customer relations was outsourced employed staff that had to be sensitive to the particular type of work they were engaged in.

This was not just 'ordinary' call-centre work, but involved contact with new parents, some of who may have suffered the early death of a baby or be suffering from conditions such as post-natal depression. It was implicit that customer relations staff would be alert to these issues, and they had undertaken bereavement awareness training. Nonetheless, part of the psychological contract they had with Children's Mutual was that they would indeed be supportive and alert to the particular business and ethical needs of the client. Managers of Children's Mutual and the outsourcing company had very regular meetings to monitor the performance of the contract and deal with immediate and practical problems that arose.

These more subtle or sensitive issues may well be specified in the formal contract between the client and the outsourcing worker's employer (see Chapter 7). This, though, is a commercial document between the client and outsourcing company. The worker for the latter will almost inevitably be unaware of this document. Nonetheless, sensitivity to the client's business, working practices, priorities and culture will be vital. Management systems of both employers need to respond to these imperatives. This will be in terms of both preparation and training, and of problem-solving and dispute resolution.

The psychological contract between agency temps and the client

Increasing attention is being paid to the nature of this relationship, in part as a dimension of growing academic and business interest in agency work more generally (*Personnel Review*, 2006). It is a highly complex relationship with, typically, a close though different relationship with, respectively, the agency and the agency's client. Research indicates that although many assignments by temps are of short duration, some are long. They can last for several years, leading to a high level of familiarity with the client organization and inevitable integration into its work practices.

Practices also vary at the agency itself, with some agencies (such as those featured in our case studies) offering temps employee status, providing training and holding out the promise of a career with the agency, as opposed to simply sending people on 'assignments'.

Other agencies, especially those supplying less skilled and manual workers, provide less support for temps and are, in effect, simply a conduit through which people are supplied to clients. Inevitably, the experience of temps and their expectations of employment relationships similarly vary. It is impossible, therefore, to generalize about perceptions and expectations of either side of the employment relationship when a temp is working for a client. However, what unites most temps is that they are working alongside the client's ordinary employees, usually at the premises and within the sight and potential control of the client.

Darren Cox, from Kelly Services, UK, sums it up as follow:

> *The industry is still dominated by small independent firms. We need to be dealing with global competition for skills, not just responding to parochial issues. There are different markets and different types of temps. They are also in a hierarchy. At the apex you have the interim managers, well paid and fulfilling responsible roles; then you have the specialist contract staff in IT, etc., with strong professional loyalties. Then you have the temps who work for agencies like ours and who make a career out of temping. At the base of the hierarchy you have the low-paid, often low-skilled and precarious workers. The last group remains significant because procurement managers like to squeeze margins!*

Julie McBeth, from SKILLED, the Australian agency, provides different observations. She says:

> *We aim to be the employer of choice and increasingly we are seen as an employer as skill shortages increase. In line with all employers, SKILLED finds generational differences. Generation X and Generation Y*

are a smaller pool of people not taking up trades. They are much more interested in the quality of life.

Her colleague, J. Schauble, notes that:

The average age of the tradespeople is forty-eight and many baby boomers have been burnt by companies they thought they had a lifetime of employment with. They don't necessarily want to retire, so working for SKILLED is no less secure than anywhere else.

Although an emerging literature is suggesting that temps are increasingly seeing temping as a career (Finegold *et al.*, 2005), other writers remind us that many temps are treated poorly and are often alienated by both agency and client (Neinhuser and Matiaske, 2006). Temps are an extremely heterogeneous group. This fact clearly impacts on their expectations and aspirations, and therefore their experience of the psychological contract.

Similarly, as confirmed by our case studies, attitudes towards and expectations of temps on the part of clients and their managers vary enormously. For some, temps are an unwelcome necessity, and the less involved they are with the client organization the better. They are considered as essentially itinerant workers in whom it would be a waste of time to invest time and energy.

Others spoke more enthusiastically about temps, recognizing the value of their experience and professionalism. Nonetheless, many were unsure as to what is the ideal relationship to have with temps. The following comments are illustrative:

We treat them the same as our own staff, though we have to remember they are not our employees.

Some [temps] are really good. We would like to have them on our books, but we don't know what they want.

We want to get the best out of them, but are not sure whether it would be preferable to have an 'arm's length' relationship or one where we aim to integrate them.

Research is increasingly interested in the HRM dimension of agency work. For example, research into five labour service firms in the Hunter region of New South Wales, Australia which involved interviews with the firms and focus groups with temps, looked at the basic HR functions. This confirmed that, unsurprisingly, recruitment of temps is undertaken by the agency. Temps do not integrate and identify with the agency, and integration with the clients depends on length of assignment. Irrespective, temps feel insecure in their position. They are not committed to either agency or client; their commitment is to themselves. They are expected to come to the client appropriately trained. HR administration is solely with the agency (Connell and Burgess, 2002).

Many from the UK, mindful of recent case-law that has recognized an 'implied' employee relationship between the client and the temp (see Chapter 6), see another dimension to the relationship they have with the temp. They are concerned to keep a very clear distance between them and the temp so as to minimize this legal 'risk'. This means that their policies and practices aim to create a boundary between the HR practices of the client and the temp. This clearly militates against integration and commitment on the part of temps. This is not, of course, the situation in all countries, where regulation provides clearer guidance on the nature of the (legal) employment relationships of temps.

Therefore, the nature and content of the psychological contract between client and temp is very much open to debate and is dependent on a number of variables. These include:

- the level of skill, qualifications, professional accreditation, etc., of the temp
- the nature of the work to be performed and the extent to which integration with personnel and facilities is essential
- the length and purpose of the assignment – is it short term and/or very specific, such as to participate in a project or cover illness, or is it open-ended and prone to 'drift'?
- the perceptions and expectations of the parties
- HR practices at the client organization, such as the extent to which the recruitment and management of temps is controlled by HR or devolved to line management, and the development or otherwise of specific policies regarding temps
- the degree of reliance on temps and whether a 'critical mass' has developed over time; this implies the 'normalization' of temping and organizational reliance on the temps themselves.

The last point is summed up by Caroline Waters of BT, UK. She says:

Temps are part of our family of workers, along with freelance and other staff. Almost a third of our staff are non-employees. We have a very clear view as to how we treat and manage temps. It's a way of life for us after all these years.

The psychological contract will hinge almost totally on the extent to which temps are valued and respected, and the extent to which this is directly or indirectly communicated to the temps themselves. If temps are made to feel unwelcome or like an interloper, or lacking skills, etc., expectations will be correspondingly low.

Where there is no formal legal relationship, matters of trust and support have to be built quickly and must be delivered by all at the client organization. A receptionist who greets a temp by saying 'Oh, you are Mary's maternity cover; go to Room 25 and I expect someone will know you are coming and give you something to do – I expect you do a lot of this type of thing as you can't get a proper job' will have conveyed negative attitudes and expectations immediately.

Conversely, a greeting that not only reflects a welcome but also mentions specific skills or experience from the temp's CVs that are thought to be especially useful to the client will set a completely different tone. If backed up by an induction or orientation programme (see Chapter 4) that makes it relatively easy for the temp to fit in, this will again shape the psychological contract in a positive way.

The triangular nature of the temporary agency work employment relationship implies that the policies, practices and attitudes of the agency will also shape the expectations of temps. The extent to which they are trained and prepared for projects and clients will also have considerable bearing. It will have the ability to materially change what could be a purely transactional form of psychological contract into a balanced and more rewarding one. Critical is the extent to which the agency goes to ensure that a temp is sent to a good client and the right processes are put in place to support an effective working relationship.

Good agencies want to send temps to good clients. Their retention of effective temps depends to an extent on positive experiences at the clients to which the agency has assigned them. Thus, the agency has a vested interest in the quality of the psychological contract and the employment experience at the client organization. What makes a good client?

Darren Cox, of Kelly Services, has very clear views on this. For him:

a good client is one:

- *where HR makes the decisions, not procurement*
- *where the organization appreciates the complexities of temporary working and does not see temping in black and white terms*
- *where there is a good understanding of legal obligations, in the context of increasingly flexible labour markets*
- *that has established a good 'relations map' with the agency*
- *that is involved in the vital two-way feed-back process, based on agreed criteria.*

This is much clearer than broader notions of partnership. The feed-back from the temp on the experience of working for the client is also invaluable.

In terms of the psychological contract, the client of an agency can expect that the temp:

- will have the skills and experience required for the work in question
- will have been suitably prepared for the work and will adapt quickly to the client organization
- will deploy his or her skills professionally for the client – ideally, the experience of working for many organizations can be drawn on
- will respect the culture and ethics, etc., of the client organization
- will be able to draw a boundary around the extent to which they want to be integrated or identified with the client organization
- accepts that the client will provide feedback to the agency and that there is no security of employment
- will be provided with the required legal protections regarding, for example, health and safety, and with appropriate support so as to undertake his or her work effectively.

The temp can expect from the client:

- to be treated with respect regarding his or her role as a temp
- to be provided with feedback on performance by the client
- the required legal and other protections
- that situations likely to give rise to uncertainty or ambiguity will be anticipated and dealt with – for example, line management structures

must be clear, as must relevant disciplinary rules, such as no-smoking rules or a dress code

- that if there are problems, these will be reported by the temp to the agency and, ideally, resolved
- that HRM is provided by the agency, not the client, but that there are effective communication systems between the client and agency given that the agency is physically separate from the client.

Many of these matters are the subject of reflection by Pattie Pierce, an experienced temp, in one of our case studies:

> *Many of the problems I encountered were due to procurement mistakes by the HR department at the client organization. But it was far easier to sweep me under the carpet than confront this. Even had I been aware that I had legal rights I would not have protested because I might have wanted to work elsewhere in the organization and did not want to get a bad name. Nonetheless, I did feel bad about what happened.*
>
> *Working for an agency, there are at least formal review procedures. I learnt that your controller at the agency is your best friend. Good agencies ask your boss [at the client organization] for a report. Really good agencies ask you for a report on your boss. Being able to keep the controller informed at all times, especially if there is a problem, is a comfort.*

Her comments illustrate how the relationship with the client can be both enhanced and damaged. If there are misunderstandings or mismatches, they can quickly get out of hand and result in a humiliating departure by the temp from the premises and unfair allocations of blame. Pattie Pierce identifies one typical source of misunderstanding as being the fact that:

> *Although most clients use job specifications when dealing with the agency, they frequently fail to keep them up-to-date.*

Pierce's comments also highlight the vulnerability intrinsic to the temp relationship. This can arise out of the difficulty in complaining if there are problems at the client workplace, and the fear of not being given further assignments. Much of the case-law on temporary agency work, especially from the UK, shows how often temps are despatched from a client workplace following little or no investigation of an incident or problem (see Dacas v. Brook Street (2004), and Franks v. Reuters, 2003, UK). The contrast with the typical treatment of employees is often stark. Legal requirements in the UK and most other EU states and developed economies demand that statutory or contractual disciplinary procedures are followed assiduously. The time taken to dismiss an employee can be very lengthy, and the resources applied considerable.

The sudden dispatch of an individual can occur even where a temp has worked with a particular client for many years and is well known within the client organization. The risk of this happening is clearly very much part of the expectation of temps, and inevitably this impacts on their understanding of the psychological contract.

The relationship of the temp with a client organization is complex and difficult to analyse. Nonetheless, the fact of a temp's presence in the client organization's workforce makes identification and analysis of the nature of the employment relationship and psychological contract a pressing issue. It is easy to identify errors and damaging situations. What is required is a clear understanding of what temps can bring to organizations, and what policies and strategies need to be in place to ensure an effective client/temp relationship – specifically, what needs to be done to ensure that the expectations of the temp and the client are compatible and positive.

The psychological contract of the self-employed

This is of particular importance because it is the only employment relationship for self-employed people. They are literally 'on their own'.

The self-employed workforce covers a very wide range of skills and income, with some achieving considerable success but many others suffering from low pay, poor working conditions and considerable levels of insecurity. As discussed in Chapter 2, the experience of self-employment tends to be conditioned by whether working in that way is voluntary or involuntary – i.e. whether it is the only viable alternative to unemployment, or following redundancy.

Recent research is showing that even so-called elite forms of self-employment, such as IT contracting, can leave people marginalized and disadvantaged. Recent survey results from Australia have revealed a continuum of arrangement for elite professionals. Experiences are conditioned by whether self-employment is perceived as being:

- a trap associated with job insecurity, low earnings and periods of unemployment, or
- a transitional form of employment leading to a more permanent form of work, or
- a career option for the most able and ambitious.

Overall, experiences are more positive where self-employment is in types of work where self-employment is a standard form of working. Importantly, entering self-employment is sometimes a response to negative employee relations, and often people cite reasons of health or child-care as their reason for being self-employed (McKeown, 2005).

What of the mutual expectations of the client and self-employed? These are clearly, from the client perspective, linked to the reasons for using a self-employed person rather than an employee. Clients with short-term or highly specific needs will see self-employed people as attractive. Research indicates that they will be perceived as more flexible, more affordable (lower non-wage costs) and providing instant knowledge. Some express reservations about older self-employed people as being complacent, out-of-date or bringing too much 'baggage' with them.

Self-employed people often mirror these expectations. They are able to market themselves as being 'amoeba-like', flexible and opportunistic, and aware of the demands of project delivery. They also express caution about setting a fee and want to avoid being considered greedy, difficult or inconvenient. Importantly, most self-employed people see themselves as weak and vulnerable, not least because of the problems in obtaining training. Both clients and self-employed consider that employment relationships are created through networks and informally (Platman, 2004).

One of our case studies, the consultant Dominic Brender, confirmed much of this research, although he was even more sanguine about the essential vulnerability of much freelance and similar work:

> I am lucky that I am able to put into the employment relationship what I want. I can shape it. I get a sense of what the budget is and rationalize my role. However, if something goes wrong, there is little you can do and they expect you to go away. There is generally a

honeymoon period, but often little real attention is paid to what you are required to do and how you will do it. You have to second-guess what they want. If it doesn't work out, you have to take the blame.

Your experience all centres on the quality of the client manager. They are rarely trained for the role, and much is to do with personality. They need empathy to anticipate your needs. It is also about loyalty and where the manager's loyalty lies. You are left to pick up vibes and respond accordingly.

Dominic Brender identifies a number of important HR issues, and how they are responded to has a major impact on the experience of the self-employed. Assumptions are often made regarding the self-management skills and self-reliance of self-employed workers. These can detract from the need to provide an appropriate support structure and effectively respond to needs. Many of Brender's comments concern failure and blame, along with the sense of unfairness and impotence felt by the worker. They also echo comments made by agency temps, who often express the view that where there is, for example, a mismatch of needs and skills, or where things don't work out, it is the worker that is despatched or takes the blame.

Although self-employment is very varied and the experiences of the workers can range from precarious and poorly-rewarded work to highly-esteemed and very well-rewarded work, it is possible to construct some general elements of the psychological contract.

The client can expect:

■ that a warranty of competence and specific skills given by the self-employed worker will be matched by performance
■ that the self-employed will respect the structures, culture and ethics of the client
■ that the self-employed will be loyal and committed to the client, consistent with the nature and length of the contract
■ that the self-employed will cooperate with the client's managers and management systems
■ that the self-employed will be able to voice concerns, contribute to developments and otherwise deploy experience for the client's benefit, again consistent with the nature and length of the contract
■ that, where appropriate, the self-employed worker will 'add value' to the workplace.

The self-employed worker can expect from the client:

- respect for their professional skills, experience and self-management skills
- appropriate facilities, support and responses to needs
- feedback on performance and the opportunity to improve, if necessary
- a positive attitude from managers and other staff, especially where the self-employed person works as part of a team ('getting the best out of you')
- a willingness to provide training – at least, training needed for the successful execution of the contract
- that, where there are problems, these will be formally and constructively addressed – where employees have problems there are grievance or complaints procedures than can be used; the response to the self-employed should not just be immediate termination of the contract
- a willingness to provide an 'exit interview', assistance in seeking other work and a generally favourable ending of the relationship (on the assumption that the contract has been successful).

Several of the respondents to our case studies have had considerable experience of using self-employed workers. In a few organizations, the numbers employed are considerable. Some are conscious that the self-employed are differently motivated and have different expectations of employment, and they see their role as one of managing these expectations and differences. Others viewed the self-employed in a more routine way. Laura Sykes, of the Regulatory Body, UK, has considerable experience of managing large numbers of consultants. She says:

> Some have a specific role concerned with business improvement. Generally, they are very good and bring lots of experience to us. They are hands-on; they work alongside us as members of our team. We treat them as our employees (though they do not want to be!). We simply apply sound project management techniques and have few problems.
>
> We also have to manage our own employees regarding the consultants. They understand that [the consultants] do not get the occupational benefits that they get, and are more insecure. That explains their apparently higher pay.

When asked what structures were put in place to ensure the Regulatory Body successfully employed self-employed staff, Laura Sykes says:

We have good communication systems of all sorts. We also have a nominated manager for each project [on which self-employed people are working]. We also have to apply standard operating procedures. The nature of our work [regulation of the financial services industry] means that we have to apply rules consistently, regardless of the employment status of people doing the work. We also apply project management techniques. We have Project Boards, Risk Management Teams and Steering Groups. These methods are very focused and tried and tested.

Specific aspects of HRM and non-employees

Many traditional areas of HRM will have little or no application to non-employees. Recruitment and selection (aspects of which have been considered in Chapter 4) only have relevance to selecting self-employed people. The evidence suggests that this is usually done through networks and informally, although consultants and freelancers are increasingly marketing themselves. There is also often a key role to be played by professional associations and bodies.

Formal recruitment structures and facilities are very limited, as both public and private bodies focus on employees. There are specialist support organizations developing, and many agencies, including several of those forming our case studies, supply staff on a self-employed basis.

This section deals with two key issues for the management of HRM:

1. Reward
2. Performance management

In addition, some wider issues of social integration and organizational support are considered at the end of the chapter.

Reward and recognition systems

One of the central arguments of this book is that, although there is a focus on non-employees, rather than these non-employees being seen in contrast to employees, employment relationships generally are on a

137

complex continuum. There are many changes taking place in standard employment contracts, especially regarding increased demands from both sides for flexibility, work–life balance and human capital investment. The flexibility echoes what are said to be some of the attractions of being a temp or self-employed. However, one of the matters that also unites temps and the self-employed is the importance of pay, in a context where there are few non-pay rewards, and training and personal development has usually to be self-funded.

The increase in the use of agencies, outsourcing and off-shoring, along with some growth in self-employment, is in part the consequence of skills shortages. Those with high-demand skills in tight labour markets have been big winners. As previously described, these workers are often termed 'gold-collar' because their specialist skills attract large salaries.

The term is applied to IT workers, but also to skilled tool- and die-makers, mould makers, machinists, electrical power-line installers and mechanical engineers, although it is the knowledge workers that have attracted most attention. Although the concept is often applied to younger workers, in some sectors (such as biotech) older workers are more valuable because of their intellectual experience.

Gold-collar workers are a feature of most labour markets, including the emerging markets of China and India. Their rewards are considerable. This is generally because it is in management's interest to develop organizing templates that are considered attractive to knowledge workers. Despite these high rewards, it is noted by the Australian Centre for Industrial Research and Training (ACIRRT, 1999) that:

> gold-collar workers have found high paying jobs which stimulate and challenge them. They often spend extremely long hours at their job, they are young, ambitious and very well paid. Their loyalty is owed less to their employer than it is to their career. As a result, they are highly mobile, lured by new jobs which offer technical challenges or opportunities for self-development.

Unaware of the fact that gold-collar workers are typically standard employees, it might be thought that the above quotation is referring to consultants, freelance staff, etc. Indeed, the skills needed to define and manage rewards for gold-collar staff will have one major difference. In the case of gold-collar staff, the employer's reward policies are motivated by the need to recruit and retain them. With the self-employed, the issue of 'retention' is rarely on the table. It might well have relevance when recruiting a consultant, but the nature of the self-employed relationship is generally one of impermanence.

Rewards and outsourcing

Strictly, reward and its management has no relevance as regards outsourcing. The responsibility for setting pay levels, providing non-wage benefits, etc., is with the outsourcing company. However, there are two possible areas of relevance. The first is that in the EU, through the operation of the transfer of undertakings legislation and case law, many of the employees of the outsourcing company will be former employees of the client. The legislation requires the outsourcing company to retain the affected staff. Although many will have retained their previous reward package, they may well fear that, as time goes on, they will have pay and benefits reduced. Where they work alongside their former colleagues who have retained their reward packages, this can be a source of resentment.

The second issue is closely related to the first. This is that many outsourcing companies have a poor reputation for reward. They often pay low basic wages and do not provide pay when the employee is ill or injured. Access (or lack thereof) to occupational pension schemes has been a particular cause for concern. Where the outsourcing staff work on the client's premises, we know there is often confusion regarding to whom they owe loyalty and commitment and to whom they take complaints, etc.

Client managers can sometimes get involved in disputes, including over rewards that, strictly, are nothing to do with them. This can be difficult and time consuming. The process of tendering for and selection of the outsourcing company should pay particular attention to their reward (and other HR) systems. The BA/Gate Gourmet dispute of 2005–2006, referred to extensively in this book, provides evidence for the fact that it is not easy to keep matters of pay and benefits at the outsourcing company separate from the client's business and interests.

Rewards and temps

Once again, this is strictly not a matter of concern for the client. However, reward systems for temps do vary enormously. In some areas of work (typically low-paid or unskilled) basic pay is very low and occupational benefits negligible. The temp will then be earning less than a comparable worker at the client organization. This, coupled with the precarious nature of work and the temp's uncertainty regarding the nature of his or her employment status with the agency, will not tend to make the temp committed and enthusiastic.

On the other hand, some areas of temping provide very high rewards – including IT, health care, some parts of education and training, and engineering.

Nick Stevens of RSA, the agency that provides specialist staff in the pharmaceutical industry, says:

> Good staff can command over €130 000 a year. Our daily rates for contract staff are €1500. They are good, though. If they are not, we don't keep them.

These higher rates of pay, for example in nursing, teaching and other professional areas of work, can be a source of envy for employees. They may think that the temps have an easy ride, as they do not have to engage in the sort of activities that indicate loyalty and commitment.

Traditionally, the rewards paid to the temp have been a percentage of the cost charged to the client. These rates have recently become more and more competitive. Although this reward system has the attraction of simplicity and certainty, for the temp there has been little incentive to work effectively. The opportunity to earn higher pay has been determined by what the market for temporary labour will tolerate.

Many agencies still work on this basis. However, in agencies where there is an intention to attract skilled people to a career with the agency, the policy is to match the reward to the performance of the individual, rather than the price to the client.

Darren Cox, of Kelly Services, UK, says:

> We are aiming to break the link between the temps' pay and billing clients. We need to reward temps on personal factors. This policy will also protect us from anti-discrimination, especially equal pay claims!

This policy clearly has implications for the development of performance management systems at the agency and, with it, the quality of the temps themselves.

Manpower, France, has similar policies and practices, although within the context of the particular *collaborateurs* contract between an agency and temps. At Manpower, this provides them with non-pay benefits that increase with the time they have been working for the company.

Jean-François Denoy, Director of Human Resource Development at Manpower, France, says:

> *We want to attract the best. We put benefits on the table. In any case, it's more a market relationship today with temps. Nonetheless, many staff, typically technical and high skilled staff, have worked with us for many years. We reward them well.*

Where an agency has policies such those described above, it will impact on the client. This is because rewards from the agency will be based not just on the skills and other personal factors of the temp, but also on feedback from the client itself.

Rewards and the self-employed

Although this is clearly one of the key issues for both client and self-employed workers, relatively little is known about how rewards are determined. Linked to this is the question, what happens when, say, a consultant becomes ill, suffers stress or has personal problems? What happens if the project will be late or perhaps not completed at all?

Many of these issues are likely to be in the contract, although our case studies reveal that the employment terms of self-employed workers are often unclear. This can even apply to rewards. A phrase such as 'Usual professional rates' or 'Pay on the same basis as last time' are clearly open to different interpretations. The first statement is extremely vague, and the second may or may not include an inflation element.

Much self-employed work has a 'going rate'. This will obviously vary from country to country, as well as for different occupational groups. Obviously, the rate will depend on how effectively the parties negotiate and, in particular, on the reputation of the self-employed worker. This can be problematic for many as, according to Dominic Brender:

> *Clients do like a hard sell. They like to be in control. It's hard to promote yourself and many, especially women, people with disabilities and members of ethnic minority groups, find it especially hard. They may settle for a lower fee, but they know they have been driven down on price and feel resentful.*

There appear to be two basic payment systems for the self-employed. The first is based on an agreement about how long work will take, with a fee based on that. Alternatively, a fee is fixed for the completion of a project, regardless of time. From then on, the completion of the work is all that matters, and the fact that it took longer than anticipated is irrelevant. A project may have several phases, and payment can then be staged.

The other common reward system is based on time – say, €850 per day. The client is billed for the number of days the self-employed worker spends on the project/activity. If this system is used, it must be plain that the individual who is engaged to do the work is actually doing it and cannot delegate it to, perhaps, a less qualified person. It is also important to have an idea of how long the work should take.

With employees, pay is increasingly related to experience, skills and work quality. Most organizations have performance management systems, and many include performance-related pay. Few apply these systems to the self-employed (see below). In essence, the management of self-employed reward occurs before work starts, and if there are difficulties or unforeseen problems these can easily turn into a crisis.

The contract should have dealt with likely problems, such as illness. Does payment continue through illness where the fee is based on a daily rate? Can someone else cover the work? If illness is serious, does the contract end? Is there to be any compensation? Delays should also have been anticipated and consequences spelt out. However, what if the work quality is considered to be poor? Is that also going to lead to a reduced fee? Who decides, and on what basis is quality judged? Are there opportunities for re-negotiation?

A key issue for a continuing and positive relationship is the promptness of payment. One of the biggest moans of the self-employed is the time it takes to be paid. A high-quality consultant will not take on further work if he or she has to wait months for a fee.

Performance management

Several of the issues here have been previously touched on. The topic covers a wide range of issues, from day-to-day supervision, discipline, motivation, loyalty, etc., through to career management. The issues regarding the workers of an outsourcing company and agency temps are restricted, as the client is not the employer. Nonetheless, matters of communication, supervision and discipline remain extremely important. As regards self-employed workers, performance management is clearly of considerable importance.

Performance management and outsourcing

There is a need at the outset to contrast the performance of the contract, where there will be specific activities to undertake and targets to meet, with the performance of the workers of the outsourcing company. The better their performance, the better the performance of the contract. However, the responsibility for ensuring this rests with the company. The client is only involved at the margins. There are issues, though, especially where the workers work on the premises of the client.

Most of the literature on outsourcing is concerned with the development of the service-level agreement, the process of outsourcing the work, and getting the contract right. Few deal with the people management issues, although many in our case studies spoke of their importance and the need for day-to-day systems to be in place to respond to them. Some spoke of the particular need to protect intellectual property rights and confidential or sensitive material. There are, though, few sources of advice that specifically deal with the people issues and good practice (MEDEF, 2004, 2006).

Most saw, as a minimum requirement, good communication systems between managers of the client and managers of the outsourcing company. Contracts sometimes specified this in any event.

David Bornor, of Children's Mutual, speaks of the need for a good working relationship with the outsourcing company:

We have a dedicated Outsourcing Relations Manager for this contract. We have monthly meetings, but can meet more regularly if necessary. If there are matters that we can't resolve, we go to the directors of our companies.

An emphasis on good communication systems was also highlighted by Rob Wortham, of RWA Ltd, the software company. He says:

We have worked hard to build the personal relationship between us and the workers for the company we outsourced to in India. We go

143

there and they come to the UK. To avoid misunderstandings and ensure the quality of their work, we have spent a lot of time on developing language skills. The close contact also means we can monitor their work.

Most clients do not have the ability, or perhaps desire, to have such a close relationship with the outsourced workforce. Several others in our case studies said that they would never directly involve themselves with the outsourcing company's workforce, as they think this leads to confusion and can undermine the position of the company. If, say, a worker of the outsourcing company damages equipment, is frequently late for work, offends customers, clients, etc., or is often involved in disputes with workers for the client, what can the client do? The matter has to be responded to promptly, but only through the managers of the outsourcing company. There will be occasions when a particular worker will need to be taken off work, but again, only the outsourcing company can do this. However, the contract may have delegated this to the client or set up a particular form of dispute resolution procedure. The type of 'people' problems likely to be encountered should any way have been discussed when considering whether to outsource (see Chapter 3) and negotiating and devising the contract (see Chapter 7).

Performance management and agency work

As with outsourcing, the employment relationship is with the agency, and matters of performance should be handled there. Where there is a highly integrated or partnership arrangement between the client and agency, there will likely be a representative of the agency on the client's premises. Clearly, most day-to-day people issues can be dealt with on the spot. It should also be borne in mind that, as a result of either legislation or the development of good practice, agencies are increasingly both training and screening temps and providing some sort of quality assurance.

If problems arise, clients are generally able to ask for the recall of a temp, and there is provision for compensation to the client. A particular issue that has arisen regarding performance management in the UK is the concern that if the client disciplines or too closely supervises the temp, the temp might consider the client to be his or her employer. If the assignment is ended by the client because of poor performance by the temp, the temp may then respond by claiming for unfair dismissal against the client. As has been suggested elsewhere, this issue will not arise where the agency provides temps with contracts of employment.

Jean-François Denoy, of Manpower, France, is clear where the performance management of the temp should lie:

> Our job is to recruit, train and develop our temps and ensure they are equipped for assignments. We need to maintain and develop their skills. If things go wrong, it is for us to sort out.

Although most of our respondents were positive about their management systems regarding the performance of temps, others were not so sure. Where temps are numerous and routine, they can easily merge into the client workforce. This can carry over into performance matters. In one organization we surveyed, a manager told us that:

> HR staff were so confused about who was a temp and who not that they applied our standard appraisal system to a temp!

This situation arises particularly where the client's managers have wide discretion in the recruitment of temps, and HR departments are hardly involved in the process. The same manager quoted above said:

> Our business has multi-million pound risks every day. Yet we do not treat the employment of temps as a risk. There is then the risk they may bring employment claims against us. We have to educate HR as well as the line managers in this matter.

The central messages about the performance management issues regarding temps are fairly clear. An agency that itself invests in training and development and guards its reputation carefully will want to manage the performance of its temps, albeit working in association with the client.

The self-employed and performance management

Curiously, this topic was rarely touched on by respondents, unless prompted. In addition, literature sources are not numerous. Yet where there is no other source of performance management aside from the client (and the self-regulation of the self-employed person), the matter is clearly a vital one.

It is generally assumed that freelancers, contract workers and the like have the skills and experience to work successfully in the client organization. Where the freelancer comes recommended or is supported by good references, many clients may well think they can relax. If there are specific provisions in a contract that refer to performance and related matters such as conduct and access to confidential matters, there are further grounds for confidence. However, there were some problems regarding performance reported in our case studies. Sometimes, it appears, there were misconceptions about what was expected, sometimes claims and counterclaims that the self-employed worker was 'inflexible or out of touch', and sometimes clashes about compatibility of style and culture. Others reported personality clashes.

By contrast, some respondents reported very successful use of free-lance staff, consultants, etc. They wanted to get the best out of them, rather than letting the self-employed fail to perform at their highest level.

Laura Sykes, from a Regulatory Body in the UK, which employs many consultants and contract workers, says:

> It is always vital to give them [the self-employed] a foundation on which to build. They need to understand our organization. You cannot expect someone to simply slot in without any preparation. Mostly this works well, and we involve project managers and other staff in preparatory meetings. We have had a few problems, though. Once a trainer came in to develop a team. He came from a manufacturing background and had quite the wrong attitude. He kept referring to production lines and used other terminology that alienated the people he was supposed to be training.

Self-employed people also want to develop their own skills and widen their horizons. To keep up to date, many have invested considerable sums in their own training – but obtaining training is not easy.

Summary points

- The expectations and aspiration of non-employees are often markedly different from those of employees.
- Despite many non-employees occupying key roles in employing organizations, the nature of the psychological contract they have is underappreciated. The different groups of non-employees have distinctive psychological contracts.

- Many non-employees report a strong sense of marginalization and stereotyping, and some report a blame culture.
- At the same time, it is clear that positive attitudes by managers, coupled with attention to the distinctive skills and needs of non-employees, can achieve high performance.
- Attention may need to be paid to HR policies and practices as regards their relevance to non-employees, and adaptation may be required, if appropriate.
- Managers, especially line managers, require effective and sustained training in the management of non-employees.
- HR has a key role in the definition and execution of the psychological contract of non-employees.

6

Regulating the use of non-employees

Prescient tales

A Portuguese national, employed by a Portuguese outsourcing company, worked on a contract to provide concreting work in Berlin, Germany. When he was not paid, he sued the building site operator under the 1998 German Social Security Law. This requires organizations employing outsourcing companies to act as guarantors of wages due from the company up to the level of the national minimum wage. German courts considered this amount inadequate, as it would deter mobility of labour.

The matter was referred to the European Court of Justice (ECJ) under the provisions that provide for freedom of movement and the removal of barriers to that movement. The ECJ supported the German law, as it did provide a minimum level of protection and, anyway, national legislation can take measures to protect itself from unfair competition.

Cross-border outsourcing is considered unfair by many, as it often undercuts local wage levels, and there were questions raised in the case as to why a Portuguese national should be covered by the law itself. Nonetheless, there was no question regarding the basic legal principle that the employee in question was able to make the claim against his employer's client.

(Wolff and Muller v. Pereira Felix 2004 C-60-03)

In 1990, in a complex UK case, Viasystems Ltd (V) engaged Thermal Transfer (T) to install air conditioning in its factory in the UK. T subcontracted the work to SP Ltd, which in turn arranged for CM Services to supply fitters on a labour only basis. They were supervised by a man subcontracted to by SP Ltd. While undertaking the work, the fitters acted negligently and caused considerable flood damage to V's premises. Who was to be responsible for the fitters' negligence?

It was held that SP Ltd and CM Services were both *liable, 50/50, to V. This was despite the fact that SP Ltd was not their employer. It has always been thought that for an employer to be vicariously liable for the carelessness of a worker, that person had to be their employee. Not so, said the Court of Appeal: 'As the employee in question [who caused the harm] is so much a part of the work, business or organization of both employers [SP Ltd and CM] it is just to make them both answer for his negligence'.*

(Viasystems v. Thermal Transfer Ltd and others CA (2005) EWCA Civ 1151)

These two very different and recent cases illustrate a number of important issues:

- The regulatory framework that applies to the use of non-employees is drawn from international (here, the EU) and national legislation but also – especially in the UK, but also in the so-called common law jurisdictions – from rules developed by judges
- The judges themselves are very alert to the complex economic, political and employment realities
- There are concerns to see that regulation and its application reflects workplace realities
- Courts are reflecting the major changes in the ways that businesses and people are working today, and aiming to provide practical outcomes.

Aims of this chapter

- To raise awareness of the regulatory framework that applies to the use of non-employees; although it should be noted that there are major differences between different states, the main focus is on EU and UK law

- To identify regulations that apply specifically to the use of non-employees, but also key regulatory areas that may have particular relevance to their employment – anti-discrimination and data protection provisions are of special note here
- To identify the policy objectives of those regulations
- To explore the role of HRM in responding to regulation and in developing effective strategies and good practice.

Non-employees: the 'regulatory framework' in general

There are two major elements of the regulatory framework. The first is the legal rules that may apply to the process of outsourcing, agency work and employing self-employed people. Regulation may apply to, say, whether you can outsource or use temps at all, what legal protections the non-employees have, and their access to social welfare and other benefits. The term 'regulation' is used to comprise both various types of legislation and its interpretation through case-law.

The second is the contract that translates the expectations of the parties into a legally binding document. Contracts are considered in Chapter 7.

Preliminary issues

Regulation and controversy

Regulation is often resisted, with opponents referring to it as 'red tape' and 'burdens of business' while claiming that regulation adds to costs and inhibits innovation, flexibility and competitiveness.

Sally Worsley-Speck, a former manager in a further education college in eastern England, reflects on the practice in her college regarding the employment of temps. The temps left after being at the college for thirteen weeks. She said:
It was not at all clear to me why. I think it was to do with the college not wanting to get lumbered with expensive legal responsibilities.

Many opponents of regulation have specifically identified its assumed negative impact on competitiveness more generally. In fact the evidence is less clear-cut, with economies with highly regulated labour markets often performing as well as those with lower levels of regulation (OECD, 2002). This debate is very long-running, and remains inconclusive. Nonetheless, negative attitudes remain in many employing organizations and amongst policymakers.

Caroline Waters, HR Director, BT, UK expressed a very different view. BT uses several thousand agency temps on any given day. She is well aware of recent UK legislation tightening the regulation of both how agencies operate and the relationship between agency and client. Asked if this is a burden she said:

> Our business philosophy dominates our thinking. We set our own labour standards. We always go beyond the statutory requirement in any case. For example, we have to ensure that the people who go into peoples homes [to install equipment, deal with faults, etc.] meet our standards. As we prescribe these standards, the statutory requirements are unimportant. We live in peace with them!'

Some practitioners are therefore happy with the current level of regulation and work with it – but calls for less regulation are getting wider support. This is especially true in the EU, but also in other countries such as Australia.

In the EU, there were dramatic developments in the autumn of 2005. The European Commission announced that, in the interests of better regulation, many proposed ideas for regulation would be withdrawn. Of 183 proposals on the table, 68 were withdrawn immediately. Others were put on hold. A point of interest for this book is that the proposed regulation of temporary agency work was one of those put on hold.

In the future, it was declared, regulation would only be proposed if:

- it would contribute to competitiveness
- it would improve regulation (making it easier to use/comply with)
- there was a realistic chance of it being made law.

Commenting on the changes, Vice-President Gunther Verheurgen said:

> This is just the beginning. We want to tackle red tape and over-regulation on all fronts. It will only work if member states do their

bit as well. This exercise is definitely not about less Europe but about a better Europe. EU regulation makes sense when it adds value – but where it doesn't, we'll scrap it.

(EC, 2005a)

Regulation and litigation

The consequence of any regulation being broken is a critical consideration, especially where this regulation provides individual worker rights. The threat or reality of a claim can have a major impact on an employing organization, and on the HR function in particular. Claims, even where made by someone who is not an employee, can be divisive and stressful. Indeed, the fact that the claimant is not an employee and is therefore less integral to the organization and perhaps less susceptible to dialogue and mediation may make it more difficult to deal with. There are few research data on this issue, although anecdotal evidence suggests that all claims can lead to internal tensions, a blame culture and real damage to the psychological contract.

There can also be increased emphasis on 'defensive' management strategies that can appear as an exaggerated compliance with regulation. A 'bad' experience of litigation often leads to intense new training regimes, increased bureaucratization and a lessening of trust. In terms of using non-employees, defensive strategies can take the form of aiming to distance the non-employee even further from the organization. This can increase the individual's sense of isolation, which can in turn affect his or her engagement and motivation.

Features of non-employee relationships

Most of the employment regulatory framework is geared to standard full-time employees. This relationship is essentially linear, with no-one else involved. The nature of the relationship where outsourcing companies are used, agency workers relied on and freelance staff employed is not only distinctive from the standard employee model; each relationship is markedly different from the others. Figure 6.1 highlights these differences.

These relationships are intrinsically complex and often challenging for legal analysis. Many aspects are unclear. More importantly, strict legal analysis is often at variance with the perceptions, understanding and

153

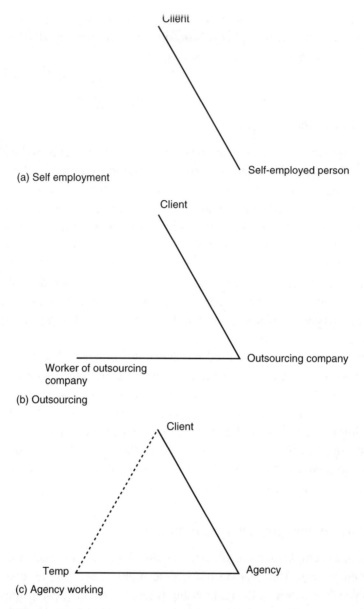

Figure 6.1 A reminder of the features of non-employee relationships

expectations of the parties. For example, many temps on long assignments consider the client rather than the agency to be their employer; while many self-employed people believe that after working for many years for a particular client they have 'mutated' into an employee.

Outsourcing staff, even those wearing the uniform and using the facilities of their employer's client, may be clearer regarding the identity of their own employer. Nonetheless, they may also consider that the day-to-day involvement in their work by employees of the client and their day-to-day involvement in the organization more generally have created some sort of employment relationship, although one that they cannot, themselves, easily define.

These are all important matters in applying the regulatory framework. Confusion and misconceptions as to who the 'employer' of various groups is clearly have considerable relevance for their effective management of these non-employees. An important practical question is the extent to which the regulatory framework clarifies the position and enables HR managers to respond effectively.

The regulatory framework itself

Let's turn now to the regulatory framework in more detail. This may cover the circumstances in which outsourcing or using agencies is permitted by law and the rules applying to the business relationship between the client and the outsourcing company or agency. For example, there are legal rules regarding health and safety (see Chapter 8), equal opportunities and minimum pay. These may also extend to tax and social security/insurance, and whether, say, the client can 'poach' a temp.

Similarly, there is a need to be sure about the legal responsibilities owed to a self-employed/freelance worker. It is not the case that self-employed workers have no employment rights. Many employers have been surprised when an individual for whom they consider they have no legal responsibility has brought a claim in employment law to a court or tribunal for, say, unfair dismissal.

The regulatory framework is often influenced by important political and industrial relations considerations. In Chapter 2, we noted the controversies and even conflict that outsourcing and agency work can generate. Trade unions often resist the process. Agencies are still unfavourably regarded, by some, as undermining state/public employment services or being used to drive down wages or employment conditions.

Today, agency work is probably less controversial, not least because there has been a growth in collective agreements between agencies and employing organizations and the public/private (agency) partnerships to support labour market restructuring. The controversy does, though, help to explain the tight regulatory framework in some countries affecting the use of both agencies and outsourcing.

What does the framework apply to?

The regulatory framework in different countries applies to a wide range of issues – for example:

- The legality or otherwise of employing non-employees to provide skills
- Limitations on the use of non-employees at the workplace – for example, to break strikes, or to employ for more than a maximum period or particular purpose
- Regulations to provide legal protections for employees affected by outsourcing
- Rights and protections for workers for temporary work agencies and workers for outsourcing companies
- The employment rights and protections of freelance/self-employed persons
- The regulations affecting fiscal matters, such as income tax and social security contributions and protections
- Regulations affecting some basic protections for most non-employees, such as for pay, health and safety, paid holidays, etc.
- Rights for non-employees under wider areas of regulation, such as for data protection and human rights
- Access to and opportunity within employment. There is now a massive regulatory agenda, especially from the EU, covering protection on grounds of sex, age, race, religion, disability, nationality, etc., and on grounds of being a part-time or fixed term worker. Given that freelancing and using an agency are typical ways in which new entrants or disadvantaged people gain access to employment, this is clearly a highly important topic.

Regulation can be complex. This is especially so regarding non-employees. An HR manager cannot usually be an expert in all the areas covered, and specialist advice may be required. Nonetheless, the role of regulation needs to be appreciated. Where the regulation has been carefully prepared and widely consulted on, and is clearly drafted, the hope is that it has a beneficial effect. Law is not drafted so as to deliberately cause chaos or problems, add to costs, etc.; sometimes the motivation is to ensure that there is so-called 'level playing field' of regulation. Within the EU, laws are explicitly designed not just to protect workers but also to ensure that competition is not bought on the back of poor working conditions, low pay, etc., in a particular member state. Regulation that is common across the EU can also ease mobility of workers and help responses to skills shortages. At the heart of many areas of EU regulation is the firm belief that better trained, better protected and better rewarded workers are more productive and effective. This thinking underpins the so-called European social model.

Nonetheless, many consider that the cost of regulation, which anyway primarily focuses on providing protection for employees, is a strong motivator for moving to the employment of non-employees (see Chapter 3). It is thought that non-employees attract few regulatory protections, with the consequent financial and administrative savings. This is not generally the case, especially within the EU and most developed economies, and it is therefore important to identify which rights are available to which groups of workers. Most rights under anti-discrimination law in most developed economies are available to most non-employees. In some respects, health and safety protections are more rigorous for non-employees than for employees. The reason for this is not hard to identify; it is because the use of non-employees may well increase hazards and risks. Non-employees are disproportionately likely to suffer accidents, etc. Chapter 8 considers the matter more fully. Other protections are more dependent on the category of non-employee and sometimes the sector/occupation.

Key areas of regulation: hard and soft law

Employing organizations and their HR managers are affected by two types of law: 'hard' law and 'soft' law. Although both types of law have long existed, it is only in recent years that this terminology has been used.

Hard law or regulation is the type of regulation most familiar to HR managers. It provides employment rights that can be enforced, usually by individuals, who take claims to employment/labour courts and the like and seek compensation. Other forms of hard law, such as health and

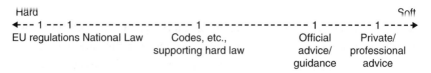

Figure 6.2 Hard and soft law

safety legislation, provide sanctions for its breach, enforced by public authorities, again through courts or tribunals.

Soft law provides codes, guidelines, recommendations and the like, usually based on good practice, which should be applied in given situations. In the UK, the Highway Code, codes of practice under health and safety legislation and the ACAS Code on Discipline and Grievance at Work are examples. The failure to comply with soft law does not of itself lead to direct legal sanction, although evidence of the failure could well be used in court or tribunal action under hard law – such as, in the UK, the Employment Rights Act, 1996.

Figure 6.2 provides a spectrum of regulation. To the left is hard law and to the right is soft law. Some soft law, however, is 'harder' than others. This is especially so where the soft law carries with it the possibility of investigation or 'naming and shaming'. This is in contrast to 'softer' forms of soft law that simply provide advice, guidelines and the like which are helpful to employing organizations but if ignored have no direct legal repercussions.

In recent years there has been a shift towards soft law. This is especially true in the area of discrimination law, in part as a recognition that providing individual rights for members of various typically disadvantaged groups does not, of itself, appear to ensure major change (Leighton, 2004). Examples of soft law in this area are national or organizational equality plans and gender or disability mainstreaming. These are well developed in many EU states, including in the UK, and in Australia and New Zealand. Pressure for change occurs through the process of target setting, monitoring and formal review of progress, and 'naming and shaming' those who are failing on their soft law duties.

Hard law and non-employees

Although regulation varies from country to country (as do the mechanisms for dealing with disputes and providing remedies for those who have suffered a detriment from the breach of regulations), within the EU there is a commonality of regulation affecting some aspects of the employment of non-employees. This is as a consequence of EU Directives and Articles of the Treaty of the European Union.

Within the EU there are specific and demanding regulations affecting outsourcing and aspects of agency work, through both national legislation and EU provisions. Such legislation has a very clear philosophy. It is to encourage labour market flexibility, but not at the expense of the working conditions of the people affected. The regulation of outsourcing has generated detailed legislation and particularly complex case law. In the UK, regulation affecting outsourcing and some forms of agency work is referred to as 'TUPE' – a term that often sends shudders down the spine of HR managers. Outside the EU there is relatively little regulation of outsourcing – a fact that has facilitated off-shoring.

Within the EU there is also growing concern about the situation of some self-employed workers. They have some, though typically few, legal rights against their employer. However, increasingly they are referred to as 'dependent workers'. This is where an apparently self-employed and independent worker in reality has only one employer, and is thus dependent on that one employer for his or her livelihood. Such workers typically exhibit no entrepreneurial characteristics. There is speculation that the position of dependent workers will be regularized within the EU, but this is unlikely to be imminent.

In Australia, recent legislative moves towards deregulation have made it easier to employ contractors (Independent Contractors Act, 2006) and have removed protections for, for example, people employed in small firms. This is as a consequence of the Work Choices legislation of 2005. These changes have caused considerable industrial strife and legal challenge. The unions are concerned that the shift in the balance of power in Australian industrial relations is taking many of the casual and self-employed in Australia, especially those in low-paid work, towards a two-tiered system of employment, more like the United States system, where little real power in the employment relationship exists for those with few or antiquated skills. It is inevitable that there will be increasing problems in motivating and managing such workers.

It is, of course, vital that HR managers keep abreast of developments in hard law affecting the use of non-employees. Not least, this is to avoid entering into contractual relations that become different or more complex due to the intervention of new hard law. This applies to general areas of regulation as well as to those specifically applying to outsourcing and agency work, etc.

Soft law and non-employees

The most important and directly relevant soft law is that of the European Employment Strategy (EES). The strategy is driven by the need for the EU employing organizations to be flexible, adaptable and productive so as to ensure its ability to compete effectively in a global economy.

The EES is an important initiative. It represents an innovative way to develop labour market policy based on the Open Method of Coordination (OMC). This encourages the sharing of best practice between EU member states regarding such matters as increasing labour market participation, responding to long-term unemployment, promoting entrepreneurialism, and increasing adaptability and flexibility at the workplace and within economies. All this is done within the context of the European Commission setting benchmarks (called Guidelines) for the EU as a whole and for individual member states.

There are particular concerns that as many as possible should be active in labour markets – especially young people, older people and members of various disadvantaged groups, such as migrant workers, people with disabilities and those disadvantaged on grounds of their religious beliefs. Targets have been set for participation rates and for other matters. These are the so-called Lisbon Targets (from an EU summit in 2000 in Lisbon).

Recent reviews of the EES in the context of increased global competition have led to an intensification of measures and the convergence of EU economic policy with employment policy. Some interest groups, especially trade unions, fear that the result of the 'new' EES from 2005 will put the European social model under threat. However, the broad consensus is that, without change, the EU will fall back in the global competitiveness race.

The key notion – a compromise between liberal economic policy and the European social model – is that of 'flexicurity'. This aims to provide a balance between the needs of employers to be more flexible and competitive with the needs of employees and workers to have appropriate levels of job protection and benefits. This intention is particularly relevant to times of 'transition' for workers – from unemployment to employment, for example, or from temporary to permanent work, or when moving towards retirement. In this context, freelance work, reputable agency work and good forms of outsourcing are seen by many as having a valuable role to play in increasing labour market participation. Agencies, for example, often work in partnership with public authorities to train and deploy long-term unemployed people. Many governments have policies targeted at young people to become self-employed. There are EU initiatives to encourage women entrepreneurs and for older workers to set up businesses.

The following statement from the 2005–2008 Employment Guidelines provides a flavour of where EU employment policy is today and how the flexible forms of working considered in this book have particular relevance.

> *Europe needs to improve its capacity to anticipate, trigger and absorb economic and social change. This requires employment-friendly labour costs, modern forms of work organization and well-functioning labour markets allowing more flexibility, combined with employment security to meet the needs of companies and workers . . .*
>
> *Enterprises must become more flexible to respond to sudden changes in demand for goods and services, adapt to new technologies and be in a position to innovate constantly in order to remain competitive.*

Guideline 21 includes the following policy objectives:

- *adaptation of employment legislation, reviewing where necessary the different contractual and working time arrangements*
- *the promotion and dissemination of innovative and adaptable forms of work organization*
- *support for transitions in occupational status, including training, self-employment, business creation and geographic mobility.*

In the light of these policy objectives, agencies, outsourcing and self-employment can be seen to have a positive role. This assumes, however, that the workers involved are effectively managed and there is an appreciation of their distinctive aspirations and expectations as derived from their psychological contracts (see Chapter 5).

The changes promoted through this type of soft law – whereby the governments of the member states have to demonstrate that they have introduced labour market measures to ensure compliance – have, in effect legitimized agencies and similar employment service providers. This, in turn, has led to an increase in the number of both collective agreements covering agencies and their workers, and the growth in public/private partnerships between state bodies and agencies. This is especially marked in France, Belgium, the Netherlands and the UK.

Nonetheless, regulating the employment of non-employees remains difficult, complex and often controversial. The technical details of regulation probably need to be left to a legal specialist. Despite this, it is vital that HR practitioners have an understanding of the general direction, scope and, most importantly, policy aims of the relevant areas of regulation.

The next sections explore the regulatory framework applying to each category of non-employees. However, there are areas of regulation that tend to apply more generally and are not dependent on the employment category or status. An obvious example is health and safety law, where risk of injury or illness is the key issue rather than the victim belonging to a particular category (see Chapter 9).

Regulation with wide application

In some legal jurisdictions, especially the EU, certain legal protections cover 'workers'. These are people who undertake to do work 'personally' for an organization, but not necessarily as an employee. This means that they are required to do the work themselves and do not have an entitlement to send a substitute or delegate the work. Temps will therefore generally be classified as 'workers', as will many freelance, self-employed and consultancy staff. Within the EU, 'workers' have access to important rights such as personal data protection, privacy, breaks from work (including paid holidays) and, for example, in the

UK, the national minimum wage (NMW). Although many HR practitioners are unaware of the extension of these important rights to non-employees, the implications are clear. There must be, for example, the same level of care regarding the obtaining, storage and use of personal data of non-employees as for employees, and the same level of care in terms of surveillance and monitoring. Even in countries where specific regulation does not exist, there is merit in considering the following practical issues:

- Personal details of temps and freelance/self-employed staff must be subject to the same secure internal processes as for employees. Particular care must be taken with the CVs of freelancers. The mere fact that they present themselves as entrepreneurs or are with the organization for only a short while does not mean that that less care can be taken with the storage of their personal details, or that they can be passed on to others without the consent of the non-employee.
- Data on freelancers or temps must not be kept for an unjustified period of time.
- The same rules apply to references for non-employees as for employees. A reference is a confidential document.
- Non-employees are also entitled to the same protection afforded to employees regarding surveillance, monitoring, interception of emails, etc.
- Non-employees are not 'outside the frame' and should not be outside thinking on matters of privacy, personal data and monitoring. If appropriate, consents should be obtained.
- Policies to deal with these matters at the workplace should refer to and apply to 'workers' and, if appropriate, be discussed with agencies and with freelance/self-employed staff.
- Within the UK there should be compliance with the NMW and no unlawful deductions made from pay. Deductions for, say, damage caused or alleged contract failures should only be made with the consent of the worker.

It should be noted that the application of anti-discrimination law to non-employees is considered at the end of this chapter (see p. 184). Health and safety is considered in Chapter 9.

Key regulations: outsourcing

This section focuses on EU and UK law. The decision to outsource has an inevitable impact on the host workforce. Where an outsourcing company is replaced by another, there will be some (although less) direct impact. Where a decision is made to revert to insourcing, there will again be changes to the workforce.

Where work is outsourced for the first time, without the intervention of regulation, those affected will likely lose their jobs. As has been seen, this can also lead to industrial unrest and increased social security costs in dealing with the displaced employees.

In 1997, the EU intervened to protect the employees affected by mergers, acquisitions and outsourcing. It adopted the Acquired Rights Directive. The 1997 Directive aimed to deal with the anxieties of those whose work was to be outsourced by providing as much job security as possible and also by securing their 'acquired' terms and conditions of employment. In effect, the legal strategy was to treat the employees affected by outsourcing (and takeovers, mergers, etc.) as 'stock-in trade'. They should normally transfer to the outsourcing company and retain their acquired employment rights. If they are dismissed 'in connection with the transfer' (through outsourcing), the dismissal is normally automatically unfair and entitles them to compensation. In addition, the transferee is responsible for any occupational or legal claims outstanding against the transferor by employees at the date of transfer.

The Directive, the national law to implement it – the Transfer of Undertakings (Protection of Employment) Regulations (TUPE) in the UK – and subsequent case-law applying the law have all been controversial, in particular regarding outsourcing. There have been uncertainties regarding the scope of law, especially concerning the definition of a 'transfer'. When outsourcing for services – say, cleaning, maintenance, security services, professional services such as architecture, occupational health and financial services – the central legal question has often been whether there is, indeed, a 'transfer' of a discrete activity. If so, EU legislation applies.

Most outsourcing contracts are covered by EU and national legislation. It explicitly includes even short-term professional services outsourcing. Regulation refers to 'service provision changes' rather than a 'transfer'. This includes legal, financial, ICT and HR and other management services. It is only in unusual circumstances that outsourcing will avoid legal demands. There is as yet no case-law on the most recent (2001) Directive, so at this stage the best advice has to be of caution.

An example from recent UK case-law (although prior to the implementation of the 2001 Directive) shows that there are circumstances where outsourcing professional services may not be covered.

> In 1997, Cheshire County Council outsourced its architectural services to a private firm of architects. The contract was then transferred to another firm. The local authority decided it wanted to operate its architectural services in-house. However, it decided to obtain the services from architects on a freelance basis and to use them as and when required. It was decided that this change was not covered by the UK's TUPE regulations, as there was no identifiable business entity being transferred. The architectural work was to be undertaken on an entirely different basis.
>
> (Cheshire CC v . Astley (2005) IRLR)

HR practitioners tend to face problems other than those revolving around technical legal definitions. Very often, employees do not want to work for an outsourcing company. They worry about their long-term prospects, and the loss or reduction of occupational pension rights. They do not want to be 'stock-in-trade'. At the same time, outsourcing companies do not always want the current staff of the client either. They often see them as insufficiently skilled, inflexible and with poor employment records.

Jeff House, Industrial Relations Specialist, Contractor Activities, BP, Coryton Refinery, UK, reflects on some of the ironies of the regulations. BP has long outsourced for many skills and services. He said, looking out of his window at staff walking by:

> Some have been here for over twenty-five years, with several different employers as a result of the outsourcing process. There is no real change in the way the work is done. Indeed, we are facing an ageing workforce, as staff simply move from one outsourcing company to the next.

Regulation also applies where there is a change from outsourcing to insourcing. The employing organization will normally have to absorb the employees of the previous outsourcing company, assuming the regulation applies to the change. This inevitably places a considerable responsibility on the HR function and, given the widening definition of service provision changes, may not be welcomed by all employing organizations. They fear that their previous employees, who had been transferred out to an outsourcing company, will now be 'recycled' back to them. Dealing with these sorts of changes can be demanding and stressful.

Provision of workforce data

Another important and relevant change introduced by the 2001 Acquired Rights Directive is the obligation on the client organization to provide key workforce data for the outsourcing company prior to the transfer. This is to enable the new employer to better prepare for the new employees. The Directive is not explicit about the data that have to be provided. UK regulations require a significant amount of information. The following information has to be supplied in writing at least two weeks before the transfer date:

- the identity of the employees that will transfer
- their age
- information on terms of work as required for a Section 1 Statement of Terms of Work under the Employment Rights Act, 1996
- relevant collective agreements
- information regarding disciplinary action taken against employees in the previous two years
- information regarding any grievances pursued by the employees
- information on legal actions in the previous two years against the transferor, or any likely to be pursued.

Interestingly, there is no requirement to provide data on health, disability, sickness absence and accidents, etc. Nonetheless, the list is a long one. Compiling such data is likely to be the responsibility of the HR department. The requirement supports the notion of outsourcing as a partnership, or one of co-sourcing.

Until this change, one of the major complaints of outsourcing companies was that until the transferor's ex-employees moved into their own employment they were unaware that so many were, say, subject to final disciplinary warnings or were bringing equal pay or negligence claims. However, one of outsourcing companies' major complaints has not been addressed. This is that health and absence records are not covered, although an outsourcing company may well ask for these. There are major penalties for the failure to provide the legally required information, so this is a legal duty that has to be taken very seriously.

The legal obligations set out above apply to all states in the EU. The UK has probably taken EU law further than other member states in that, in the interests of certainty, more types of outsourcing contracts are covered by TUPE, and the range of employee information to be provided is wide. It should be noted, though, that there are no legal limitations on outsourcing in either EU or UK law; the legal obligation is simply to ensure that the procedural and legal obligations are met. In particular, the procedural rules require:

- provision of information for employees affected by the proposed outsourcing
- consultation with such employees on the possible implications of outsourcing
- that such consultation take place before a decision to outsource is made.

Recent case-law indicates that the Directive, in conjunction with national legislation, requires consultation to be meaningful and to minimize any potentially negative consequences of change. This cannot be done if the key decisions have already been made. There is a real difference between 'consultation' and a 'rubber stamp'. This has been recently strongly reinforced by case-law.

There are no legal rules on the length of outsourcing contracts, the terms of contracts or their renewal. Contractual matters are dealt with by the client and outsourcing company, and are considered more fully in Chapter 7.

Summary of regulatory provisions applying to outsourcing in the UK and EU

The basic regulatory provisions applying to outsourcing in the UK and EU can be summarized as follows:

- There are no prohibitions or restrictions on outsourcing under EU or UK law (although there may be under other national regulation).
- Outsourcing is increasingly consistent with the 'new' EES in providing for efficiency, flexibility and competitiveness.
- Most outsourcing, unless it is for a one-off task or service, such as a promotional activity or the installation of a specific piece of equipment, will be subject to regulation (TUPE in the UK). Explicitly, professional services outsourcing is covered.
- Where there is an 'organized grouping of employees' providing specific skill needs for the client, such as cleaning, payroll, security and vehicle maintenance, they will transfer to the outsourcing company, retaining their statutory and contractual employment rights.
- The transferor must provide workforce data for the outsourcing company prior to the transfer.
- Any dismissal of employees by the client 'in connection' with the transfer amounts to an automatically unfair dismissal. Justifying such dismissal is difficult.
- Employees who refuse to transfer lose any job security rights, such as redundancy payments. They need to be aware of this, and this is an important matter for discussion between them and the HR staff.
- Any attempt to avoid the legislation by, for example, excluding regulation through the outsourcing contract, will be ineffective.

Impact on HR

Our case studies tend to show a fairly low level of HR involvement in setting up and managing outsourcing. However HR's involvement is desirable and, some argue, essential for effective people management of outsourcing. Otherwise, the process tends simply to focus on service specification and delivery and neglects the people issues.

It is likely, therefore, that the HR managers will:

- need to be aware of whether a proposed skills change has legal implications and in what way

- need to be aware of the general requirements of law, especially regarding the need for effective consultation, and be responsible for devising and disseminating relevant information that is required for consultation
- be called on to provide the workforce data on the employees affected by outsourcing prior to the transfer – data will include any outstanding obligations and liabilities of the transferor
- need to respond to questions and anxieties of staff affected; to explain the implications of refusing to transfer
- need to respond to questions and anxieties of those 'left behind'
- need to contribute to the smoothness of the transfer itself
- be required to manage the 're-entry' of previously outsourced employees when the contract has come back in-house and they with it.

There is also the role of international soft law to consider, especially where outsourcing involves off-shoring. The main sources of soft law are the International Labour Office (ILO), to whose standards most developed and developing countries subscribe. Soft law standards cannot give rise to penalties or claims in courts by individuals who consider that the standards have been broken. However, increasingly, employing organizations – especially those with a commitment to corporate social responsibility – are building into contracts with service suppliers the ILO and other standards as a contractual requirement. The prohibition of child labour or forced labour, and the requirement of a fair wage and the general prevention of exploitation are examples of the standards set down by the ILO.

In similar vein, the Organization for Economic Cooperation and Development (OECD) has Guidelines for Multinational Enterprises. Some of these are leading outsourcing companies for ICT, HRM and, increasingly facilities, management. Guidelines IV concern Employment and Industrial Relations, and include the following:

- Respect trade unions and provide facilities for collective bargaining
- Contribute to the abolition of child labour and forced labour
- Prevent discrimination
- Provide employment terms and conditions not less favourable than those provided by comparable employers in the host country, and ensure health and safety

■ Where change involves likely job losses, provide information, aim to minimize the job losses and cooperate with state bodies concerned with employment.

Many of these guidelines refer to collective labour rights, and mirror those of the ILO. Although they also represent good practice, what is their relevance to outsourcing and similar arrangements if there are no direct sanctions?

As a minimum, they provide a benchmark against which to judge an outsourcing company. As considered above, there is no reason why compliance with them cannot form part of the outsourcing contract, especially where the outsourcing company is from one of the thirty OECD countries. This might also provide some reassurance for employees who might be taken on by the outsourcing company. A company that tendered for a contract and was unaware of the Guidelines, or one that intended to ignore them, could usefully be screened out of the selection process. Often 'soft' law guidelines turn into 'hard' law, so soft law can point you in the direction of future legal change.

Regulation during the outsourcing contract

While an outsourcing contract is ongoing, a number of problems may crop up – many of which will have been anticipated by the contract and can be resolved in accordance with it. However, some legal issues go beyond the contract. As touched on earlier, within Europe, the Convention on Human Rights determines that a client's (or their employer's) invasion of privacy through intercepting mail, inappropriate use of CCTV cameras and the UK legislation on Protection from Harassment Act applies to the workers of an outsourcing company. That said, workers mostly look to their own employer for redress of breaches of regulations and for general employment support.

Ambiguities can creep in where workers of the outsourcing company work on the client's premises and alongside its staff, especially during a long contract. These workers may begin to 'lean on' the client, seek its support or, indeed, claim employment rights. For reasons of simplicity, this should be resisted and line managers advised and trained accordingly. The outsourcing company is the relevant employer, and although good management suggests effective liaison with the company over work itself, employment relations should be unambiguously left with the company itself. Where the client's supervisory staff had previous responsibility for the currently outsourced staff, there may well be particular tensions.

Sally Worsley-Speck, from Capita Learning and Development, and previously a manager in a further education college, said:

> When we outsourced cleaning work at the college, we felt the cleaning standards declined. Most of the cleaners were previous employees of the college. The caretaker, who continued to be directly employed by us, could no longer tell them off. He could see that standards could be better, but we had to ensure he did not get involved. We had problems with ending previous practices whereby cleaners gave gifts to the caretaker. We had to enforce the 'boundary' between the employers.

Health and safety presents particular issues, and EU law has devised specific duties where premises are shared by two or more employers, as is the case of on-site outsourcing (see Chapter 9).

Key regulations: agency work

Agency working is intrinsically the most challenging and complex of the employment situations considered in this book. The triangular nature of agency working presents many legal and managerial ambiguities (see Figure 6.1). There is usually clarity about the nature of the relationship between the client and the agency, and this is one of a commercial contract to supply one or more staff to the client. There is then a contractual relationship between the agency and the temp, although the precise nature of that relationship can be unclear. The relationship between the temp and the client is even less clear. Most lawyers in the UK took a view until recently that it could not be a contractual one, as there is no payment from one to the other.

As considered elsewhere, attempts have been made in the EU since 1983 to develop a directive to provide employment protective rights for temps. This is now on the back burner. In the UK, the agencies themselves have long been tightly regulated but the process of intermediation (supplying labour) is unrestricted, aside from a ban on their use in supplying labour to replace workers on official strikes.

Most other (especially European) legal jurisdictions have some sort of framework that applies to agencies and their use. This is usually through the regulations of agencies themselves, and through regulation of their activities to a greater or lesser extent. For example, in some countries there are limitations on the circumstances in which agencies can be used.

UK regulation

In the UK, there have been obligations since 1973 for agencies to provide documentation for temps and clients and to comply with fiscal demands. Most critically, they have to inform temps as to whether or not they are employees of the agency. If they are employees of the agency, the agency has to provide for the employment rights of temps – for example, dismissal, redundancy, maternity and time-off protective rights. If the agency does not provide employee status, it has relatively few obligations beyond those of providing payment and the more basic rights provided for 'workers'. This inevitably creates problems for the temps and, most importantly, can then lead to pressure on the client to provide the legal and occupational protections.

Under the Conduct of Employment Agencies and Businesses Regulations 2003, important new requirements for temping were added. The prospective hirer of the temp has to provide the agency with precise information regarding the skills, qualifications, professional memberships, etc., required for the job, and whether there are particular health and safety risks. If there are, the prospective client has to tell the agency how the risks are being minimized.

The agency, for its part, has to undertake the screening of the temp. This covers verifying professional and other required qualifications, police checks and, where the work includes dealing with vulnerable children or adults, at least two references from previous hirers of the temp. This is a very useful quality assurance process for the client. As there are major costs involved in the screening process, the agency may well want a regular, committed workforce. Hence, they may offer employee status to achieve that end.

The client is well advised to check the type of employment status provided for temps during their initial enquiries with an agency. It may be slightly more expensive to use an agency that provides employee status, but the benefits to the client are both numerous and valuable. If the temp is an employee of the agency, that fact precludes any argument that they have become, especially on long assignments, the employee of the client.

Caroline Waters of BT, from a client perspective, explained that BT had developed close working relationships with a number of agencies on their preferred supplier list. She said:

> We only use agencies that provide employee status for the temps. We require the agencies to train them and provide holidays and, in effect, meet our own labour standards. This removes the worries of low pay and poor terms of work, and enables the temps to focus on their skills. In a way, these legal rules regarding agencies are not relevant to us. We encourage our skills suppliers to be forward thinking and add more value, regardless of the minimum required by law.

A different perspective was offered by Nick Stephens from RWA, the specialist agency in pharmaceutical work:

Reflecting on the regulatory framework from the agency's perspective, Nick Stephens said:

> Regulation is not that important. Our temps are highly motivated, highly talented and can command high fees. They value having an 'exit strategy' rather than being tied down. The 2003 Regulations give us choice on employment status and they [temps] want self-employment.

RWA is a highly specialized agency providing highly skilled temps. Employment status may be less important to particularly well-rewarded temps. It is perhaps understandable in these circumstances that market worth is more important to both temps and the agency than are protective regulations. However, managers in other agencies held different views.

Darren Cox, HR Director of Kelly Services, UK said:

> Increasingly, we are giving employee status to our temps. The market is beginning to demand it. I think the role of regulation should be to stamp out poor practice, improve the status of temps and clarify the employment status of workers themselves.
>   Unfortunately, the 2003 Regulations have not helped much in any of this and there are problems with the Regulations themselves. We,

therefore, have to go beyond what regulation requires, especially in a consolidating market. We have to set our own standards.

Although employment status may be less important to especially well-rewarded temps, it is still important to reflect on the rights that are only available to employees. Along with job security rights and maternity and 'family friendly' rights, the increasingly important rights to information and consultation are only available to employees. As consultation is required before organizational and workforce changes that are especially important for non-employees generally, their exclusion leaves a big gap in the law.

Can the client become the employer of a temp?

This is a particularly 'UK type' of problem. Until recently, the answer was 'no'. The legal orthodoxy was that, in common with the position in most developed economies, the only employment contract that could arise was between temp and agency. Unless an agency decided to provide individuals with employee status (as more are doing today), a temp would generally be denied employee status by courts and tribunals. This was because the relationship lacked 'mutuality of obligation' – i.e. the agency was not contractually obliged to provide an assignment for a temp 'on their books' and the temp, if offered an assignment, was not obliged to undertake it.

In recent years, courts and tribunals have recognized that the operation of this legal rule has meant that many temps, even those who have worked for an agency for many years, have been, in effect, consigned to an 'employment rights desert'. In a growing number of cases in the UK, it has been decided that a temp may have rights against the client. This has been a shock for many client organizations, especially where the *raison d'être* of using an agency has been to avoid employment law responsibilities.

A particular case of interest is that of Bushway v. Royal National Lifeboat Institution (RNLI) (2005).

B was assigned to RNLI for three months. This was to cover a post, but one that had not initially been authorized to be filled on a permanent basis. Following authorization, B was offered the post,

*but, following a dispute, B claimed she had been constructively
dismissed. She could make a claim to an employment tribunal if she
had completed one year's service as an employee. This she could
only do if the three-month temporary period was 'counted'. The
documentation between the agency and RNLI and agency and
B apparently clarified that B was not an employee of the agency or
RNLI. Despite this, it was decided that the whole period of work at
RNLI could count, as the way she was treated before and after she
became a permanent employee of RNLI was very similar.*

This case illustrates that there can be circumstances where, despite
carefully worded documents that expressed a clear intention that
Ms Bushway was not to be an employee, employee status can arise. Clearly,
a wide range of employment protective rights can then be enforced
against the client. Using a temp on an assignment as a way of assessing
abilities before formal recruitment can therefore have its drawbacks.

Recent case-law in the UK indicates that there is an increased likelihood of the temp being able to enforce employment rights against a
client where:

■ the agency states in the contract with the client that the client should
provide employee status, and/or
■ the client makes changes to the working conditions of the temp, or
negotiates directly with the temp about their terms of work, and
■ the assignment is a long one, and
■ there is minimal contact between the temp and agency
■ there is a conversion from temp to permanent, at least where the
post/role remains constant.

Discussions during the case studies revealed this situation to be one of
the most challenging for many clients. The central dilemma is this. The
law is indicating that if clients do not want to take on employment law
responsibilities for a temp, it is important that they ensure they do not
take on the HR management role *vis-à-vis* the temp or integrate them
closely within the employing organization. This can seem counter-
intuitive for good HRM practice.

Nonetheless, in situations where employing temps is seen as a useful
type of 'probationary' arrangement for the client, there are risks that the

temp may drift into employee status. The client may want to see whether to offer the temp a permanent post, by assessing skills, providing firm-specific training and integrating the temp into a work team in order to check out team-working skills. Practices such as these may well suggest to a court or tribunal that the temp has already become the client's employee.

Our case studies included several organizations that make heavy use of temps. They are well aware of the recent UK case-law developments sketched out above. Some have developed close 'partnership models' with agencies.

Caroline Waters of BT, UK, said:

> We have representatives of agencies who work on our premises and we use temps to see whether people share our values and can work with us. Some transfer to jobs with us. However, while they are temps, their employer is the agency. We set the labour standards. However, if there are problems with a temp, we insist that disciplinary matters must be handled by the agency. It is clear cut.

A similar approach was explained by Jeff House, of BP.

Jeff House, of BP, expressed the need to have a 'divide' between client and agency even more strongly. In the light of a recent UK case that had opened up the possibility of an employment relationship developing between the client and temp, he had reissued guidelines to managers regarding the use of temps and was setting up training in the matter at the time of the case study. He was especially concerned about the implications of taking a temp onto a permanent contract. The guidelines and training emphasize:

- the need to manage carefully a transfer from temp to permanent
- the need to reinforce the idea that temps are just here for a short time – 'We want to prevent them being part of the furniture'
- the need to clarify a range of issues with the agency, such as provision of sick pay, paid holidays – 'We must make sure the agency takes ownership of this' – and, most importantly, 'they must handle disciplinary matters'
- the need to involve temps, but 'when we have team briefings we include temps where routine matters are considered but not more strategic ones'.

In other parts of the EU, many agencies provide employee status or a particular type of employment contract that provides certain, but not all, 'employee-like' rights. These are generally the larger agencies.

Nonetheless, it is important to bear in mind that temps do anyway have a number of legal rights when working for a client. These include (in the UK and other parts of the EU):

- Many rights under health and safety law. These include both statutory and (in the UK) common-law protections. For example, agency temps who are injured at the client workplace, allegedly through the negligence of the client, can usually make a claim for compensation in much the same way as can an employee of the client (see Chapter 9).
- Anti-discrimination law/equal treatment provisions that can be enforced by a temp against the client. Case-law suggests that this can include some maternity rights – for example, if a temp on a long assignment goes on maternity leave but is refused her 'old' job back on return from leave she may have a claim. This is not so much because it is a breach of maternity rights (which are only available to employees in the UK), but because it is potentially an act of sex discrimination. For this right, the worker simply has to be 'personally executing work'.
- In the UK, a right to be accompanied by a colleague or trade union representative at any grievance or disciplinary meeting at the client's premises.
- Rights under data protection and human rights law.

Although the issue of employment status for temps has become highly controversial in the UK, outside the UK the situation is generally more straightforward.

Jean-François Denoy, of Manpower, France, explained that in Germany all temps are employees. The agency needs flexibility, so they have to offer high pay to keep the temps. In France, he says:

> We have to operate with little margin for profit. We do offer an employee contract and provide many incremental benefits. The contract is not a permanent one [it's a CDI], as this would cause inflation and the essential nature of the relationship would change.

The type of employment status provided by an agency is probably today less to do with regulation and more to do with a business decision to maximize the performance of temps.

Darren Cox, of Kelly Services, UK, reflects on the influence of regulation. In the agency work sector he thought an increasing issue was the need to attract and retain the 'best' temps. These temps had 'A clear idea of the type of protection they wanted and how they wanted to be treated'. He thought that the Conduct of Employment Agencies and Business Regulations, 2003 had not helped very much:

> *There are problems with the regulations. They are too technical and do not deal with the real HR issues.*

Summary of regulatory provisions applying to agency-working

The time when agencies were unlawful or heavily limited by regulation has passed. They have been legitimized in many states. There is still some way to go, and agency work has not entirely freed itself from suspicion and controversy. The particular rules that apply to agency work in different countries need to be checked out. There may well be special rules that regulate when temps can be used, the maximum length of assignments, and specific terms of work for temps.

In these circumstances, the following must be considered:

- The provisions of the regulatory frameworks for agency work should be well understood – they often offer useful safeguards for clients and put into legal form good practice.
- The circumstances when agency temps can be used for the organization must be clearly specified, as must the issue of who is authorized to hire them.
- Approved agencies should be identified and managers provided with a checklist, especially on the issue of the employment status provided for temps.
- Clients should define and require standards for the relationship between agency and temp.
- Where the agency does not provide employee status, care must be taken to ensure an 'implied' contract of employment does not arise; assignments should not be open-ended, and there should be clarification of procedures when a temp is offered a permanent post.

- Managers must be aware of the employment rights that temps do have; it should not be assumed they are outside anti-discrimination and health and safety provisions (in particular).

John Raywood, of GlaxoSmithKline, UK, summed up the view that many expressed in our case studies. He said:

The environment is now of acceptance of temps. Managers need to introduce ways of working that recognize that fact. At present there are ad hoc *arrangements based on individual managers. Therefore, there should be guidance for managers to ensure temps are integrated and become effective, and that we avoid any legal pitfalls.*

Key regulations: self-employed workers

The temptation is to think that self-employed people are largely unregulated. It is correct that they are only covered by a few areas of employment regulation – this is broadly the case in developed economies. The area of regulation that does apply to them is in the commercial/trade area, as they are properly seen as the concern of business regulation.

The legal obligations associated with standard contracts of employment, including both the express and implied obligations, will not be automatically present in the contract with self-employed persons. In Chapter 3 we considered the advantages that a standard contract of employment can provide. These include the implied obligations concerning:

- a duty of 'faithful [loyal] and honest service'
- a duty to obey lawful orders
- a duty to comply with the warranty of competence [skills] provided when applying for work.

If there is the need to enforce obligations, for example, of confidentiality and restraint of trade/competition, these will need to be spelt out in the contract, as they will not automatically arise (see Chapter 7). Although there are major differences between the regulatory framework for self-employed people and that for employees, especially in the UK, non-employees do have certain protective rights. Most are derived from EU regulation. They include:

- Health and safety and anti-discrimination rights (see Chapter 9 for health and safety, and below for discrimination law). These rights are available to those who are not employees but who are 'personally executing work'. This means that any delegation of work or provision of a substitute person is tightly controlled or forbidden by the client/ employer.

- Protections in civil law – for example, the law of negligence where they are working on the premises of someone else.
- Protections taken from regulation that does not require a particular employment relationship to use them, such as under the Human Rights provisions, data protection and protection from harassment, bullying, etc.
- Rights concerning security of earnings – i.e. no deductions without consent and an entitlement to the fee as agreed in the contract if the non-employee is 'personally executing work'.
- Some rights under working time regulations, including the rights to breaks from work and to paid holidays – again, if they are 'personally executing work'.

However, the main and almost universal regulatory problem is, how can you decide whether a freelancer/consultant/etc., is really self-employed? There are some exceptions to this, and one such is Australia, where legislation considers virtually all at work to be employees. This simplifies matters considerably. In the UK and some other states, the problem is compounded by the fact that there are only two basic employment categories: a person is either an employee or is self-employed. In many other states there are gradations of employment status and special types of employment relationships. These are often linked to a particular occupation or sector. Such relationships generally provide access to a range of employment rights, depending on the type of employment relationship. In the UK the division between employee and self-employed is stark and has led to much highly controversial case-law, from which the basic rules are derived.

Many people, when working for an organization, want to be considered self-employed – usually for tax and other benefits. This is especially the case with highly skilled and professional workers. However, a large proportion of these workers only provide their skills to one organization on long contracts, and are sometimes highly integrated into that employing organization.

The employing organization is freed from many fiscal, insurance and employment law obligations as regards the self-employed. This can, of course, heighten the attraction of freelancers, contract staff and consultants. There are also many traditions in different employment sectors. In ICT, the media, performing arts, taxi/mini cab work, publishing, and craft and construction work, a large proportion of the workforce is employed on a freelance/contractor basis. Sometimes this is due to the fluctuations or uncertainties in work, sometimes because there is a strong sense of autonomy in certain types of work, and sometimes because there are strong traditions of self-employment.

Nonetheless, the regulatory framework is applied to them and people are not 'free' to choose what suits them best. In the UK, EU member states and many other non-EU states the following apply:

- Courts reserve to themselves the right to declare whether someone is, legally, an employee or self-employed.
- Legal tests have evolved that place emphasis on the extent to which the employer can control, direct or otherwise subordinate the worker, and whether the worker is 'dependent' on that employer.
- It is unlikely that workers will be seen as 'dependent' if they have a range of clients, employ an accountant, market their services, provide their own equipment and otherwise give indicators of being an entrepreneur.
- An issue of increasing importance is the ability to delegate work where the freelancer/contractor is unable or unwilling personally to do the work. Where delegation is possible (and takes place), the chances are that a court will see that as evidence of self-employment.
- Where the employing organization of a freelance worker is the worker's only source of income, courts are, when asked, likely to conclude that the worker in question is, in reality, an employee of the organization.

Practical points

Getting employment status correct is crucial. It can be a real shock if someone considered to be freelance makes a claim for unfair dismissal after being told that the company no longer requires their services. If a claim is made and the individual is found to have been, in legal reality, an employee, there are likely to be messy repercussions in terms of tax and national insurance/social security, as well as the employment law claim.

The responses to regulation affecting freelance staff, etc., in our case studies were very varied. Mostly, the respondents were clear regarding their policy of granting either employee or self-employed status. Some saw contractors/self-employed people as 'coming with the territory' of the type of work they did. They were also aware that the major area of regulation of such people is tax law rather than employment law.

In the UK, the Finance Act, 2000 and the so-called IR-35 provisions have, in effect, limited the right to be taxed on a self-employed basis to only those clearly self-employed. Those who have this IR-35 status do not want to jeopardize it, and will want to ensure that the client they work for does not adopt policies and practices that integrate the individual too closely with the organization.

Rob Wortham, a Director of RWA Ltd, a software company based in South Wales, said:

> *Our contractors will go to enormous lengths to protect their position. They present us with standard form contracts devised by their professional body. This is specifically designed to distance us from them and satisfy the tax authorities.*

Others in the case studies were more relaxed about employment status. Typical comments were:

> *We are not too bothered about this. If they want to be self-employed, we go along with it. They have to carry the risks then.*

> *We treat all our staff much the same, regardless of employment status. If someone wants to turn funny and claim that they are really an employee (after months of claiming they were freelance) we will defend our position.*

> *People can spend too much time worrying about this. Lawyers try to frighten you. Its just something you have to get on with in our sector [IT].*

It should be borne in mind that, even with the agreement of tax authorities, courts and tribunals can 'go behind' an apparent self-employed contract and declare the nature of the relationship. Many freelance workers are provided through agencies. There have been major concerns that changes in UK regulation that have reinforced the relationship between temps/freelancers and the agency have presented risks to the continuation of their self-employed status for tax purposes. Many professional bodies now advise freelancers to deal directly with clients rather than through an agency.

On the assumption that the employing organization wants to employ individuals on a self-employed basis, yet also to create unambiguous employment relationships, the following points might be considered:

- Changing an existing employee relationship into one of apparent self-employment where work continues much as before is rarely legally effective. This is even where documents are signed to declare self-employed status. There might also be the risk that this can be seen as a plan to defraud tax and other authorities.
- When entering a self-employed relationship, it is important to explore the business practices of the individuals concerned. Do they have other clients? Do they have an accountant, insurance cover for both liability and loss? Do they market their services? Do they belong to associations set up for self-employed people?
- Where a contract is of short duration there will normally be few legal problems. Where it is longer and even open-ended, care must be taken to ensure that the individual has an appropriate level of autonomy, and is not 'disciplined' for poor work standards or unacceptable conduct. The correct approach is to work through the contract and its remedies and procedures, and not simply merge in the freelancer with employees.
- Work practices should be carefully managed. Most freelance workers will want to adapt their work practices to those of the client. However, this should not be formalized. For example, freelancers can work more flexibly, especially from home, and use skills in their own way.
- The language of the employee should not be used. Reference should be made to 'contracting', to 'fees' not 'pay', and to the 'discharge' of the contract duties, not 'performance management', etc.
- Care should be taken with a long contract not to let it 'drift' into one of employee status. Some people want this to happen (just as others will guard their self-employed status vigilantly). Managers must be alert to this and trained in dealing with self-employed staff.

Key regulations: other relevant provisions

Other major areas of work apply to non-employees. Aside from health and safety, which is well-known, there are anti-discrimination laws and a few rights that can be claimed so long someone is a 'worker'. These rules apply across the EU, but clearly detail will vary from state to state. Some have been considered above, including the protection of personal data and entitlement to, say, paid holidays.

Anti-discrimination law

Anti-discrimination law has particular relevance for the self-employed and agency temps, so long as they are 'personally executing' work for the agency. (It will not generally have relevance for outsourced staff, as the outsourcing company will have the anti-discrimination duties imposed on them.)

In the vast majority of cases, temps and self-employed people will be covered. They will only be excluded from protections if they have a power to delegate work and do actually exercise that power. Agency temps will not have this power at all. They will also be seen in all likelihood as 'personally executing work' for both the agency and the client.

The legal protection regarding unlawful discrimination now covers a wide range of groups in the labour market. Protections are provided in the EU on grounds of:

- sex
- racial or ethnic origins
- disability
- age (from October 2006)
- sexual orientation
- religion or belief
- gender reassignment (in the UK)
- working part-time (but not generally if working on a fixed-term engagement)
- nationality if an EU national.

Outside the UK there are often other grounds for legal protections, such as political beliefs, family name, education/background and physical appearance. These provisions always need to be checked out.

Sex discrimination also has wide application in terms of discrimination regarding pregnancy. Pregnancy rights relate to treatment of an individual and to health and safety protections, but not to maternity leave and pay, as the latter are only open to employees. Specifically, an employer of an individual 'personally executing work' can contravene sex discrimination provisions by subjecting that individual to a 'detriment'. This might be by failing to undertake a risk assessment of health risks to pregnant women, by allowing them to be subjected to harassment or bullying, or by adopting a more rigorous and/or unsympathetic approach to sickness when connected with pregnancy.

Where the woman is self-employed, or a temp has been on a long assignment to a particular client, discrimination law may be infringed by providing time off to have the baby and then refusing to re-employ the worker in the same role as before. There is, to date, very little case-law on these matters, but the prudent employer/client will have the fair treatment of a woman in mind and will not assume the woman has no rights.

Similar comments can be made regarding equal pay, where there is an explicit entitlement for self-employed people to receive comparable pay to that of a self-employed person of the other sex.

In an EU context, anti-discrimination law has recently been greatly tightened. There have been other important policy changes, and these changes have direct relevance to the employment of non-employees as much as to employees. They include the following:

- The reduction or removal of most exemptions from anti-discrimination law, such as for small firms, security services and private facilities.
- An increasingly wide interpretation of what constitutes a 'detriment' to a claimant, which is vital in order to make a claim. Being refused work, paid less, etc., are obvious detriments. Abuse, damage to status and reputation, and hostility are also considered detriments.
- A narrowing of the opportunities to justify unequal treatment. A justification has to be for a 'legitimate reason', and the response must be proportionate and reasonable. Arguing that clients of the business prefer a temp to be young and female, or clients using an interior designer prefer a middle-aged, male, native English speaker, or perhaps stating that 'our firm has always done it this way', will not do. With freelance staff, the risk is that pay will be so linked to market

forces or traditions in an occupation, that unfairness creeps in. These practices are getting more and more difficult to defend. Particular attention has therefore to be paid to setting fees for consultants and freelance staff, especially where the organization employs many such staff.

From an HRM perspective, a number of practical issues derive from the application of anti-discrimination law to non-employees. HR managers should therefore ensure the following:

- That those hiring freelance staff or using an agency need to be aware of the impact of anti-discrimination law on the way in which the hiring is done and the treatment of the individual non-employees.
- That an agency recruitment/search agency that the company uses has robust equal opportunities policies, and that the specification for a temp or, say, consultant is not discriminatory by, for example, setting age bars, indicating that adjustments cannot or will not be made for people with disabilities, that certain 'types' (for example, homosexual people) would not 'fit in', etc.
- That the treatment of a temp and other non-employees while working for the organization is not discriminatory, and that line managers and others are aware that the legal duties do extend to temps, etc. Care should be taken with the allocation of duties, and when a woman is pregnant, for example, in ensuring that temps, freelancers, etc., are subject to risk assessments.
- That the fact that someone is self-employed and also, perhaps, works from home or part-time, does not exclude that person from at least some anti-discrimination protections, including equal pay for male and female self-employed.
- That there is awareness that some legal protections extend beyond the end of the assignment or contract. Hence, care should be taken in providing references, testimonials and reports that might negatively affect a career.
- That all organizational anti-discrimination/equal treatment, etc., policies and training specifically makes reference to the rights of non-employees who are personally executing work.
- That policies to deal with bullying or harassment explicitly remind readers that they also cover non-employees.

Summary points

- Regulation is today generally more supportive of outsourcing, skills supply through intermediaries and self-employment, although within the EU there is emphasis on regulation that provides for 'flexicurity' – i.e. a balance between the employer's need for flexibility and the worker's for adequate protections. The role of the EES is especially important in providing pointers for HRM as regards EU employment priorities.

- Regulation is frequently complex and fast-changing; case-law is similarly complex, and care must be taken to ensure that the organization has up-to-date knowledge and/or advice.

- It is important to note the policy objectives of regulation, as well as its wording, and the role of 'soft' law should be appreciated as establishing best practice, benchmarking and guidance.

- Although the legal rights and protections available to non-employees are limited, it should not be assumed that non-employees have no rights.

- Key areas of both 'hard' and 'soft' regulation have particular relevance for non-employees. These are health and safety, anti-discrimination, data protection and human rights.

- In the UK, particular care should be taken with the issue of employment status. There are particular risks of both temps and self-employed people 'drifting' into employee status and gaining access to employee rights. Where this is not desired, care should be taken in advising, training and monitoring line managers where they have key roles in the recruitment and management of non-employees.

7

Contracts and the use of non-employees

Prescient tales

At a time when outsourcing was becoming a feature, Virgin Atlantic outsourced its on-line flight booking to a part of BA [British Airways]. BA took the opportunity to 'divert' prospective Virgin customers to BA. The problem led to acrimonious litigation in 1994. The outsourcing contract had not anticipated the risk of 'diversion' of customers or that there might be divided loyalties on the part of staff.

(Arnold, 1995), p. 3

A cleaning contract in a London hospital was under the spotlight when a patient in the hospital slipped and broke his leg on vomit left on the ward floor by another patient. No-one had cleaned it up. The cleaning contract had carefully specified what had to be cleaned, and set down hours when it was to be done.

The contract cleaners argued that the failure to clean up the vomit was not their fault as that was 'human waste' and was the responsibility of nursing staff. The nursing staff argued that it was not their job to clean the ward as it was 'down to the contract cleaners to keep it clean'.

Both arguments had validity but the contract had not anticipated emergencies, or the need to clean out of the set cleaning hours. The issues regarding hygiene in hospitals remain highly controversial and do need to be planned for and incorporated into the contract.

(Leighton, 1995)

These two cases illustrate the vital importance of contracts that antici
pate and respond to the complex working relationships, expectations, divisions of responsibility and environments that managing non-employees entails.

The people management implications of the contracts or agreements are significant where contracts provide for:

- outsourced services (where working relationships are often deter-mined solely through service level agreements rather than direct dialogue with the workers responsible for implementing them)
- agency work (where employment status in terms of management and control is often complex in the context of a 'triangular' relationship)
- self-employed assignments (where expectations between client and worker are complex and rarely effectively reflected in letters of appoint-ment or contracts).

Yet because establishing these working arrangements is generally seen as a procurement function, often undertaken by either centralized finance functions or local line managers in immediate and pressing need, the input of HR practitioners at the point of procurement is often lacking or given insufficient weight.

Aims of this chapter

- To appreciate the role of contracts in the creation and management of non-employees
- To gain an understanding of the basic principles of contracts as legal documents
- To explore ideas for appropriate strategies for the nature and content of contracts
- To consider how the need to change or adapt contracts can be responded to
- To explore the possible content and role of the contract for the employment relationships with non-employees.

Contracts with non-employees: general considerations

At the heart of any employment relationship with a self-employed or freelance worker, the arrangement with an agency for the supply of skills and the undertaking of services by an outsourcing company is a contract. This defines the obligations of the parties and establishes their mutual expectations. However, the function of contracts varies considerably between the different groups of non-employees covered by this book.

For outsourcing, the contract deals with the delivery of particular skills and services, and it is essentially a document dealing with practical, procedural and financial concerns. The specification and service level agreement will be at the heart of the contract. Employment relationships are not essential to this process, as the people in question will typically be employees of the outsourcing company.

In agency contracts, the employment relationship is central but overwhelmingly in terms of the tasks to be undertaken by the temp for the client and the skills needed to undertake them. Matters of fees, contract length, etc., will also be important but, from a regulatory aspect, the employment relationship of the temp is with the agency.

Where the work is being undertaken on a freelance, self-employed basis, the situation is very different. Here, of course, the employment relationship is only with the client. How that relationship is negotiated and defined is therefore critical.

Contracts can be made in most legal jurisdictions simply by word of mouth. More typically, especially in the UK, they are lengthy and complex written documents. Typically also, those contracts are drafted by specialist legal advisors. Frequently, those legal skills are also outsourced. With the growth of outsourcing and agency work, firms of lawyers are emerging which have developed a reputation for negotiating and writing agency and outsourcing contracts – especially for public sector employers. By contrast, contracts of self-employment have tended to be developed in a more informal or *ad hoc* way. This can present problems, as the legal rules apply in a broadly similar way to all contracts.

So, why should HR specialists be concerned with such a technical and highly specialized matter? The answer is because they must make an input into the contracting process so as to ensure the 'people aspects' of the contracts are effectively dealt with. This is especially important where the non-employees are working on the client's premises; or they have access to confidential or market-sensitive material; or they are performing a role that has the ability to cause the client harm if it is not undertaken correctly. Examples are where temps or contract or freelance staff

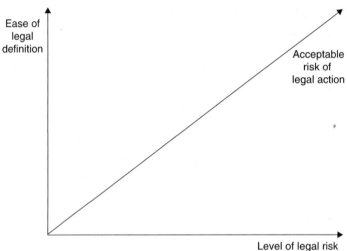

Easy to define legal risk High level of legal risk Result: *Success* with little or no value added results	Easy to define Low level of legal risk Result: *Success* with value added results
Difficult to define High level of legal risk Result: *Failure,* lots of problems, damage, decline in value added results	Difficult to define Low level of legal risk Result: *Success* with some value added results but increasingly difficult implementation

Figure 7.1 Legal risk model
© P. Leighton/M. Syrett 2006

work with vulnerable children or adults, in a research and development department, in a sales function or in health care.

Problems can arise in many ways. There is no correlation between, say, short contracts or the provision of basic skills, and a lesser likelihood of disasters or difficulties. There can be practical, direct issues, and less obvious problems such as longer-term damage to business reputation or client base. Figures 7.1 and 7.2 are illustrative of the issues.

Moderate risk	Low risk
Outsourcing of business sensitive activities (e.g. care for children where there is risk of worker having criminal record or history of abuse)	Outsourcing of transactional activities (e.g. security, catering, technical support)
High risk	Moderate risk
Agency temping where there is a strong risk of a claim by the worker for employment rights	Use of freelancers or self-employed workers in self-contained, home based activities

Figure 7.2 Legal risk model: examples

As the promotional literature for the government funded 'baby bonds' from one of our case studies, The Children's Mutual, puts it when explaining its values and priorities:

> A brand is a 'space' that a company can own in its market. All sorts of qualities can be attributed to a brand, many of them at a subconscious level, and we will be working together to make sure that our brand becomes known for the qualities we respect and value. A successful brand is something that people have learned to recognize, respect and trust. We must therefore ensure that our brand personality remains focused and consistent.

In these circumstances, the brand has to be protected through the quality of any non-employees as much as through employees.

Along with input from HR to the contract issues applying to non-employees, there is a commensurate need to have input from appropriate line managers and other staff. An important relationship is being created, and it is essential that all those potentially affected are involved.

The Principality Building Society in Wales, UK, operates within a very tight regulatory framework for the provision of financial services. The quality of any external service provider is critical. In terms of outsourcing, 'due diligence' tests have to be undertaken where the service or facility to be outsourced is core or 'material'. This is an essential aspect of pre-contractual procedures. This process involves line managers, legal services and other specialists as well as HRM.

Brian Kushlick, the HR manager, identified some key issues for the pre-contractual processes and the contract. The contracts for outsourcing need to reflect tight control, and then provide for auditing and monitoring. He was more concerned about the contracts for agency temps and self-employed people and the need to bring together all the relevant expertise within the building society.

Although outsourcing was generally closely and centrally controlled, he thought that:

> *Staff dealing with agencies may not be adequately prepared or supported in the process. We may have overestimated the screening processes at agencies and we may need to formalize matters more in contracts.*

He also referred to matters such as data protection, saying 'That will almost invariably need to be addressed in the contract.'

Relevant practical issues should be considered and responded to. The professional lawyers who will actually draft the contract will usually be unfamiliar with the particular workplace. They may want to use an 'off the peg' (standard form) contract. Such a contract may not be appropriate for the particular business priorities of the employing organization. HR practitioners need to ensure they are consulted and involved in the process of contracting.

Rehman Noormohamed, solicitor with Morgan-Cole, stated:

> *It is vital that you get together the 'right' people at this time, especially those that are familiar with the HR issues that will inevitably arise with outsourcing. You will have to manage the fears of those affected by outsourcing and contribute to the process of change management. But also, importantly, they must assess potential service providers when they say they can manage the work. The skills they provide must at least equate to or improve on existing standards.*

Contracts in practice

This chapter does not aim to turn every HR professional into a contracts lawyer. It seeks to provide information on the nature of contracts and the role of other documents. The legal rules relating to contracts across different countries fortunately do tend to work with some common understandings. There are, though, some differences between the so-called 'common law' or Anglo-Saxon legal world that comprises the UK, Ireland, USA, Canada, Australia and many African and Asian countries, and the so-called 'civil law' legal world that comprises most of continental Europe and South America. Some countries combine the concepts of common and civil law. The former countries tend to a tradition of detailed and prescriptive (if not exhaustive) contracts, whereas the latter countries tend to place greater reliance on broader principles and concepts. These differences have major practical implications for the role that the contract plays in the management of the employment relationships created by the contract.

In all countries, a contract is a legally binding document that should express the expectations of the parties. Contracts have particular features. In the UK these are as follows:

- Contracts are based on deep-seated notions of agreement and consent. This means they can only be changed with consent and neither party can simply decide they want to make changes on their own.
- Where the legal expectations of one side of the contract are not met there is a breach. A breach usually entitles the other party to claim compensation.
- Where the breach is very serious, this entitles the 'wronged' party to end the contract.

Contracts can be made by word of mouth. However, in some jurisdictions, such as the UK, overwhelming importance is attached to the written and signed contract. Such documents dominate any other sources of information, such as emails, letters, memos and, of course, the spoken word. Contracts can be used defensively and protectively, as well as creatively. The temptation for many is to try to think of and put in the document everyday detail and everything that could happen or could conceivably go wrong. In the UK we therefore tend to have lengthy complex documents, especially for outsourcing.

However, by contrast, it appears that many contracts for self-employment/freelance work and small-scale outsourcing – such as for office cleaning, gardening, and equipment maintenance – are made on one A4 sheet of paper headed 'Purchase order' or 'An agreement'. This is despite the fact that there will often be major risks in buying in such skills. Conversely, the freelancer or outsourcing company may provide their own documentation and simply ask the client to 'sign on the dotted line'. Given that research consistently shows that few people, when confronted with documents to sign, actually read them or raise questions, this practice carries with it major risks.

Lawyers often advise that with cross-border contracts the client should state that in the case of dispute, English law applies. Although widely recommended, some in our case studies rejected this very legalistic and technical approach to contracting.

RWA outsources its software writing to a firm in India. The contract is governed by Indian law. When asked whether this was a bit risky, Robert Wortham, a Director of the company said:

> We had a mindset that we would make this relationship with the Indian company work. We didn't go into this to catch them out. We wanted them to be successful and we appreciated that their success would be ours. If things did not work out, what would be the point of suing for breach of contract?'

Chris Sharp, of Capita Learning and Development, UK, took a slightly different view of the role of contracts.

Capita provides many consultants and is outsourced to by many UK organizations. Chris Sharp stressed that the important issue is that of 'creating partnerships'. He thought that some clients had developed 'contracts that work well' and are 'consistent with effective partnering'. Others were 'very incompetent', especially in defining expectations and preparing for the contract. 'Some are reluctant to take the time and pay for what they really want and this can impact on the contract.'

The contract must also reflect the essentially different levels of control available to the employer, bearing in mind the different types of non-employees. Once again, it is important to note the different issues and different potential for control.

Figure 7.3 demonstrates the continuum of control and quality assurance depending on employees and types of non-employees. The more the type of employment relationship is towards the right end of the spectrum, the more care has to be taken with contracts and their management. The potential may be greater for problems and for practices to develop that challenge quality assurance, etc.

Figure 7.3 Control and quality assurance

Contracts: the link with effective management

A positive view is that contracts are important for defining the expectations of the parties. They set standards and encourage good practice, along with being helpful in avoiding disputes. The last issue could arise where the contract sets up an internal dispute resolution process. A less positive view is that contracts 'keep people in line', protect the company's interests and are a very useful 'weapon' where the company is not happy with the work of non-employees.

The latter approach is very symptomatic of the common law/ Anglo-Saxon world. An HR manager in parts of continental Europe, especially the Nordic countries, would reject the notion that contracts are important in that they define employment relationships. These managers argue that trust is at the heart of all employment relationships, and that formal legally binding documents can undermine trust. Written contracts tend to be defensive documents and are unhelpful, they argue, for good HRM. The incidence of the employment of non-employees at work in these countries is, though, very low.

Whatever the view on contracts and how they should be used, it is clear that there can be many problems in using non-employees at the workplace. These are often cause by assumptions, neglect, confusion, ambiguity, etc. A well-crafted contract may help in anticipating and responding to some of these issues.

Typical problems might include the following.

- A freelance worker, who you have employed for the past three months on a six-month contract, wants to move on before the end of the contract to work for a business rival. The rival is offering a higher fee, and you consider that market-sensitive material might be lost to the rival. The development is surprising, as the freelancer appeared very grateful for the contract and happy in her work. The arrangement had been arrived at following a series of letters and telephone calls. Nothing was said or written down about working for 'rivals' or about confidential or market-sensitive material. You negotiate a higher fee during lengthy and sometimes acrimonious meetings so as to try to 'stop' the defection.

- A consultant, engaged to develop and deliver a staff training programme, has decided to work mainly from home. He takes on work for another employer nearby and fails to attend team meetings where training is on the agenda. The consultant, when challenged, reminds you that he is self-employed and can work in his chosen manner. He also says that he is 'in business', so if work is offered by another employer he needs to accept it. Further, that there was no mention of attending team meetings when the work was discussed. You decide that the relationship is not working and terminate the contract, although providing significant compensation for the consultant. The consultant, nevertheless, claims for breach of contract.

- You recruit an agency temp to work in your community-based mental health charity for a six-month assignment to cover maternity leave. Most of the clients are from minority ethnic groups. The particular temp has expressed himself uncomfortable working with members of certain ethnic minority groups because cultural and religious factors often make it difficult for him to respond to their mental health problems. You ask the agency to withdraw the temp. The agency refuses, pointing out that the worker in question is particularly well qualified in mental health interventions and the sensitivities regarding ethnic minority groups were never explicitly referred to by you when seeking a temp. The temp is withdrawn eventually, though the agency demands, and you pay, the fee for the remaining part of the contract.

These are but some hypothetical examples of the myriad problems that can arise through a lethal combination of oversight, assumptions, ambiguities and lack of attention to detail. Where the contract is one for a complex and long-running outsourcing contract, the consequences can be very expensive indeed. (Today, as has been noted, contracts of twenty years' length are not unusual. Recently, in the UK, concerns about the nutritional value of school meals – which are typically provided through outsourcing contracts – have caused difficulties because the contract price for school meals was originally negotiated on the basis of 'less nutritious' meals. The contract was made many years earlier.) Renegotiation of contracts is generally highly problematic, so it is essential to 'walk the contract' through and anticipate developments and problems before signing it.

This is particularly important for the people issues. There is a need to have a clear strategy for the development and management of the employment relationships created by the contract, not least because some of the matters that can be taken for granted in an ordinary contract of employment (loyalty, obeying orders, confidentiality, etc.) will not be automatically present unless specified. Courts tend not to be sympathetic to arguments that the client forgot to mention a key obligation to a freelance worker (as it was obvious, wasn't it?) and now seeks enforcement of the alleged obligation through litigation.

Contracts: the link with effective HRM input

The first reason for effective HR input is to ensure that there is attention to the people issues. These include: skills and professional requirements, security, health, safety and welfare, data protection, and information and communication.

Close HR involvement in the negotiation and then management of these contracts is also important to ensure that the employees directly employed by the employing organization are taken into account during the recruitment, negotiation and introduction of non-employees into the organization.

Freelance people may work in or alongside teams of employees. Other non-employees may work as security staff employed by an outsourcing company, with directly employed reception staff. People employed by another outsourcing company or temporary work agency, and non-employees covering maternity or sickness leave, will inevitably be an integral part of a work project or activity. It may be that the security, reception and, say, maintenance staff are all wearing the company uniform – but that might be the only thing they share with the organization.

The interests and well-being of third parties might be affected by the employment of non-employees. Where the third parties are children, patients and clients/patients in care homes or community support projects, it will be important to ensure appropriate standards, in terms of not just the skills and qualities of the non-employee staff but also their attitudes and behaviour towards the people they are caring for. There are too many instances of violence, abuse and paedophile behaviour across the world for this not to be considered a critical issue.

Where the third parties are customers and commercial clients, it will be equally important to ensure that non-employees are professional and present well. They may also have to be fully aware of the organizational values, culture and priorities of the employing organization. This enables them to represent it better.

It is particularly important to determine the basis on which such staff can be 'disciplined' or removed from the work. This may entail terminating a freelance contract, or requiring an agency to withdraw a temp or outsourcing company to redeploy a particular individual. Many of these decisions are difficult or even painful to execute. The expectations of the parties to a contract need to be clear and unambiguous, including performance standards and matters of conduct. This, in turn, will depend on developing an appropriate relationship with the intermediary provider of those skills or the self-employed/freelance workers themselves. These are exactly the type of matters that need to be considered during the negotiating and contracting process.

As Rehman Noormohamed, a legal expert in outsourcing and agency contracts, says:

It is always important in these contracts to retain strategic management control. Always consider exit strategies before signing the contract. You must always have the option to remove the incompetent person.

The knack in this process is the ability to identify and assess the areas and issues of risk and to use the legal process to minimize or eliminate those risks. For this process to be successful, it is essential:

- that HR specialists are aware of the regulatory framework as outlined in Chapter 6, and the extent of its 'intrusion' into employment relationships with non-employees
- to involve HR specialists who will have the knowledge and experience of anticipating and dealing with likely problems and risk areas regarding 'ordinary' employees, and to seek their views on likely problem areas in using non-employees
- that there is input from people with 'front line' experience of the work – the clients, customers, etc.
- that the process is formal and its outcomes are fed back to those responsible for devising contracts and ensuring legal compliance by the organization.

Contracts for outsourcing

Devising and managing outsourcing contracts has now become the subject of many publications, and there are numerous written sources of advice. There are also many specialist advisors, from professional bodies and trade associations to firms of lawyers. Some produce 'standard form' contracts (i.e. ones that can be taken 'off the peg' and possibly amended by the parties). On the other hand, to the question 'are there many sources of advice and support that deal with the topic of this book, i.e. the people issues of outsourcing?', the answer is 'no'.

Before turning to consider these issues, including input from our case studies, some general points need to be made.

There are some global trends regarding outsourcing contracts. First, they are becoming more formalized and detailed as the outsourcing market matures. Second, the contract periods are tending to be longer. Mistakes made at the time of contracting can therefore be even more problematic. As contracts are legal documents, the failure to comply with them or to deal with omissions or day-to-day problems can have major management and cost implications. Third, and critically, research and information from the case studies developed for this book indicate that people issues often have a low priority in these contracts.

Traditionally, outsourcing contracts (for example, for cleaning and catering) have mirrored contracts for the purchase of goods. The procurement or purchasing function at the employing organization has dominated the negotiation and contracting process – even where the outsourcing in question has concerned aspects of HR itself. This might include payroll, recruitment or training.

Chris Sharp, from Capita Learning and Development, saw possible tensions between the need to 'get the contract right' and the people issues. He said:

> We attach considerable importance to building and evolving the working relationship between ourselves and the staff at the client organization. In fact, in the contract I have in mind the relationship evolved very quickly. A too formal rigid contract might have inhibited this and have given out all the wrong signals. The client staff might not have become, in effect, the extended members of our team.

Most of the advice on effective contracting for outsourcing has concerned IT outsourcing, but thankfully this can be used to extract broader issues. There is much useful advice on developing a specification for the work to be done, the tendering process, selecting the provider, devising contracts and setting standards through service level agreements. Some offer advice on responding to problems relating to the service level agreement and dealing with termination.

However, there is much less advice to draw on for other types of outsourcing, including the traditional lower-skilled areas of cleaning, catering, security and maintenance. Pursuing the issue through our case studies, it is confirmed that the 'people issues' are generally poorly reflected. Sometimes they are entirely absent.

In terms of the supply of skills, attention should be paid in the contract to the following:

- The style of the contract documentation itself. Is it clear, accessible and readable, and is there recognition that the contract is for the supply of people, not widgets? Is it attractively presented? Is it likely to be used as a working document? Does it have guiding principles that are helpful to achieve clarity or resolve ambiguities or problems? Does it state what it is aiming to achieve? How are the parties referred to? Is the language of collaboration, partnership, etc., used, or just client, supplier and the like?
- Careful construction of the service level agreement – particularly so as to ensure sums are paid to the client if the service standards are not met.
- Contract price and changes, which should be pegged to some certain indicator, such as the retail price index or similar.
- Building in change and ensuring that problems have a mechanism to deal with them and there is a clear exit strategy for the client.
- Providing for flexibility and potential for development.

The last point is well illustrated in comments by Rob Wortham, from the software company RWA, which had outsourced a significant part of its work to India:

Rob Wortham was sure that he wanted flexibility from his contract. He clearly saw a need not only to build an effective working relationship with the staff in India; he also wanted it to evolve. In fact, the relationship did evolve very rapidly with a higher level of integration with colleagues in the South Wales headquarters. He said:

A highly formalized and rigid contract might have inhibited this; might have given out all the wrong signals, and they might not have become what they now are – extended members of our Wales work teams.

Most of those offering advice for successful outsourcing do recommend that a project management group should be set up, meet regularly and have the authority to deal with some, at least, of the day-to-day problems. However, very few recommend that HR (from the client or the outsourcing company) should be represented on the group. This is extremely unsatisfactory.

Even where the outsourcing is for HR services, there seems often to be a battleground between the procurement professionals and HR. The former stress the cost and measurement issues of outsourcing, while the latter strain to ensure that outsourcing does not simply become 'too commodified'.

Andrew Lewcock, Manager of HR Procurement at BT, UK recently commented that 'There is a big difference between buying widgets and buying intellectual capital'. He went on to comment that in HR outsourcing you 'need to think of value – not just cost'.

There is a slowly emerging view that current contract practices on outsourcing have major problems. One leading observer of the situation said recently that: 'Procurement professionals are good for cost-cutting, but perform poorly on contract management and customer services'. Similarly, there is an awareness that many of the problems associated with outsourcing and the contracts that create it fail because of the lack of attention to the people issues.

The rhetoric of partnering, co-partnering or rejecting the notion of outsourcing in favour of co-sourcing or some other label, is popular. Indeed, there is every reason to see that the provision of skills by an intermediary requires input from the client as well as the service provide on a regular basis. Insofar as there is a reality of co-partnering and collaboration, it has still typically tended to focus exclusively on the service level agreement that specifies what has to be done, when and by whom. But what of the people involved?

The people issues in outsourcing contracts

First of all, there has to be consideration of what precisely are the people issues that need to be a part of the contracting process and its management. Clearly, this depends on the type of outsourcing and the culture and practices of the employing organization – although general issues can be addressed.

It might be useful to pose the following key 'people' questions where a decision has been made to outsource but the contract process has not been completed:

1. Is the work of the contractor being performed on your premises?
2. If so, does it raise issues of health and safety, evacuation procedures, health and safety training, including perhaps that representation on health and safety committees be dealt with?
3. Will the workers of the outsourcing company have access to confidential or sensitive material or equipment, either on or off your premises?
4. Will the workers of the outsourcing company have access to or be working with your own employees?
5. Will the workers of the outsourcing company have access to or work with vulnerable people?
6. Will the workers be sharing or have access to common facilities, such as canteens, car-parking or other social facilities?
7. Is there likely to be a need for emergency health care, counselling or other support services and, if so, how will it be provided?
8. Is there a need for firm-specific training, especially where the contract is a long one and/or involves working alongside your employees? If so, by whom and on what basis will it be provided?
9. Is there a likelihood of interpersonal conflicts between your employees and the workers of the outsourcing company? Are some of the outsourcing company's employees former employees of yours?

There are also broader issues that need to be considered from an HR perspective:

■ Are there organizational, cultural or ethical issues that must be considered before a contract is signed? Where the client organization is a charity/not-for-profit/third sector employer, or operates in sensitive areas of work, what safeguards need to be built in? Can unsuitable staff be removed? Is there the requirement for induction of outsourcing company staff? Are there any particular skills or personal characteristics that are required (or, indeed, not required).

- Are HR practices at the organization likely to be jeopardized by the presence of non-employees? Are HR accreditations, such as 'Investors in People' in the UK, going to be at risk?
- Are conflicts likely to arise over people management issues between your employees and the workers of an outsourcing company? Are pay differentials and other employment benefits so wide that resentment and tension might arise? How might such issues be dealt with?

Laura Sykes, of a Regulatory Body in the UK reflected on the possible difficulties of having highly paid outsourcing staff working alongside less well-paid employees. It worked because, although there were major pay gaps, the higher-paid group were very 'hands-on' and experienced, and they were treated as though they were employees. However, she did comment that: 'They did not want to be seen as employees, and this was quite complex to manage'.

If there is a positive answer to any of the above, it is vital that HR and probably other people-related specialists (such as occupational health and health and safety) are involved at the pre-contract stage. This might cover situations where the specification or service level agreements for the contract are being drawn up. It is no good if the people issues and problems surface after the contract has been agreed. Contracts will likely be hard to change, especially where responding to 'forgotten' people issues will add to costs.

A checklist for outsourcing contracts

- Do HR specialists within the organization know when outsourcing for a service is being contemplated? Are they automatically informed, or do they only learn about it when the issues of terminating the contracts of employment of existing staff or, perhaps, dealing with the fall-out of transferring work to a third party, come on stream? How can the HR function become directly involved in the process if it is currently excluded?
- When a specific service is being outsourced, has HR identified the specific 'people' issues that need to be considered? Are they matters

of skill level, quality assurance, attitude, safety, security, confidential-ity, induction, training, etc.? How are they best addressed – formally through the contract, or less formally through management systems? If the latter, what is appropriate and how might they be set up?

David Bornor, of Children's Mutual, which had outsourced its customer relations services under a long contract, had devoted considerable time and energy to the contract – specifically, to ensuring that the core issues for them were recognized and correctly responded to in the contract. Children's Mutual specializes in the provision of so-called baby bonds for newborn children. Sometimes, such children died or became ser-iously ill soon after the company was notified of their birth. It was essen-tial, therefore, that the outsourcing contract required the outsourcing company to provide bereavement training for its customer relations staff at its premises.

- Is HR represented in the selection of the outsourcing contractor?
- When a service has been outsourced, is HR represented on project management/monitoring groups, or the like? If not; why not? If there are specific 'people' problems associated with the delivery of the service by an outsourcing company, how are these issues highlighted and responded to? Where the outsourcing is for HR functions such as recruitment and training, do the HR specialists have the key decision-making role? Can they require change or even termination of the contract?
- What are the specific contractual and other provisions for dealing with disputes or amendments of the manner in which the service is delivered?
- Is HR familiar with the HR procedures and practices of the outsourcing company? Has a 'partnership' model evolved between the HR function in the outsourcing company and the HR function in the client organiza-tion? There is clearly a need to avoid a situation whereby the people issues are simply referred to by a hospital HR manager as, 'day-on-day crisis management' (Leighton, 1995).

Contracts with agencies

Outsourcing contracts have become specialized and formalized. Contracts between clients and agencies for the supply of temporary workers can also be formal and complex, but they can also be more 'hit and miss'. The major agencies have sophisticated procedures and documentation, but smaller agencies use simpler and, typically, standard form contracts.

From our case studies, it is clear that contracts for agencies have become high agenda items for many organizations, and the nature, content and management of these contracts is currently subject to much concern and debate. Sometimes this is because of specific regulatory issues (see Chapter 6), sometimes, more day-to-day practical concerns.

An important difference between agency contracts and outsourcing contracts is that HR is more likely to be involved in the contracting process itself. This may be in a 'hands-on' role but, more typically, through the development of guidelines, policies and monitoring. Contracting with an agency is now rarely seen as a procurement issue, and so HR managers can directly influence the process. The people issues can therefore be provided for in a well-designed contract that clarifies the important issues, whoever drafts it. This can be no easy task.

One of our case study organizations in the UK uses several agencies that provide considerable numbers of temps to supply their skill needs. So important is this activity that the organization employs specialist resource consultants that act as 'the pivotal link between law, HR and the businesses'. One such consultant described herself as 'a problem solver, an internal consultant, though one that does not have complete control'. Interestingly, she is not part of the HR function. She noted the dilemma that arose because both HR and line managers were insufficiently aware of the risks of employing temps that could then try to assert employee-like protective rights. She reflected that 'We need to do something about this or live with those risks'.

Although she provides support and advice to others regarding the contracts and the terms of work of temps, she felt that there are considerable tensions and unresolved issues regarding the control of such contracts.

The agency contracts themselves are distinctive from outsourcing. Their duration tends to be short, and the contract usually applies to the assignment of one person. Nonetheless, the type of people supplied by agencies can range widely. An agency may supply an interim manager for a high fee. They may do so for a specific purpose. They may do so for a research scientist at one end of the spectrum, to a security guard or receptionist for one day at the other.

The people issues can vary enormously. They will, though, need to be reflected in the formal negotiations and in the contract itself. As seen in Chapter 2, the reasons for using an agency can vary enormously – to deal with an emergency or a short-term skill need, or as part of a wider strategy of bringing in different skills, a strategy for partnering, bringing in new ideas or, as might be the situation with interim managers, to drive through change. These reasons may also need to be reflected in the contract.

What is the contract for? In the words of Nick Stephens, CEO of RSA, a UK agency in the pharmaceutical industry:

It's quite simple, really; the contract defines what the client is paying for.

At the same time, there are several matters that need to be spelt out in relation to the people issue of agency contracts. Where, as is normally the case, the agency provides the draft contract, it is important to carefully consider it and ensure the following matters are included to your satisfaction:

- The qualifications, skills and experience needed for the post in question – the evidence of these have to be provided by the agency
- The circumstances in which a temp will have to be withdrawn by the agency from the assignment by the agency, such as poor performance, but also attitudinal matters and the failure to adapt to the culture and ethics of the organization
- The circumstances in which the temp can leave the assignment if he or she finds the assignment difficult, and the legal consequences, if any, for so doing
- Matters of compensation if the temp causes damage or loss or is injured or harmed
- Matters specific to particular occupations and professions, such as accreditation, confidentiality and ethical concerns.

The client needs to be satisfied on these points, especially where there are special occupational or professional concerns. The question of references for temps to work in health, child and elder care should be carefully explored, and a bland statement in a document that states, for example,

'We satisfy ourselves that all our temps are honest and reliable', is inadequate. This applies to qualifications required for the post as well.

In addition, other people issues might also be addressed, such as whether the temp will have access to training at the organization, social facilities, parking or benefits such as travel expenses, preferential shopping facilities and health-care facilities. It is especially important to consider whether use is to be made of counselling services and employee assistance programmes.

It is also important to find out what facilities are provided by the agency. These might well include training, and some of the benefits referred to above. Temps do not usually expect the client/employer to provide many facilities, but it is wise to clarify the position with the agency and later with the temps themselves when they arrive.

Standard form contracts

Agencies provide standard forms for clients. This is clearly a convenient measure. Contracts are sometimes required for legal reasons other than simply to clarify the rights and duties of the parties. Nonetheless, there is no obligation to accept the terms if they do not suit your needs or properly address the people issues you are concerned with. However, once contracts are signed, even if they are not read or checked, they will usually become legally binding documents and the terms set out will be hard to escape from.

An example from UK case law

An agency provided a man to Reuters News Agency. He worked for them for nine years and undertook different jobs at the company. Reuters decided they did not want him any more and ended the contract with the agency He made a claim for unfair dismissal against Reuters, despite the fact that the agency had paid him throughout the assignment at Reuters. It was decided that he could make claim for unfair dismissal, even though there was no contractual relationship with Reuters. A key factual point was that in the contract between Reuters and the agency there was a clause that required Reuters to treat him as their employee during the assignment. Reuters were under no legal obligation to do so but the fact that they did not challenge the term in the contract when it was negotiated and backed that up by treating him as if he were their employee was the major reason for them losing the case.

(Franks v. Reuters (2002) CA UK)

Where a standard form contract is used, there is sometimes a temptation to negotiate other terms of work with an individual temp after he or she has arrived – for example, hours of work may be arranged to provide the client with more flexibility. The agency may be unaware of this. This negotiation with a temp can be a key element in leading UK courts to conclude that the client has, in effect, taken over the employment relationship. This then enables the temp to assert employment protective rights against the client, and possibly the agency as well.

If clients in the UK wish to avoid this risk, it is important to ensure the contract reinforces the employment relationship of the temp with the agency. All variations to the work undertaken by the temp, or other changes, should only be done via the agency. This includes where the temp is an interim manager.

The key issue to clarify through the contract is the employment status of the temp. It is wise to ensure that the agency treats the temp as its employee – not as a self-employed person. This avoids the possibility of employment law claims being made against the client (although liability under anti-discrimination and health and safety law cannot be avoided by contract).

A checklist for agency contracts

- What is the role of HR in contracting with agencies? Is the matter left to the complete discretion of line managers, or is it controlled by HR?
- If HR is playing a major role in the contracting, what is their strategy?
- What is HR's policy agenda for contracting for temps? Does HR provide a framework, guidelines and advice? Does the advice have to be complied with? Does HR provide training in the recruitment of agency temps, and provide a preferred list of agencies?
- Are there key people issues that must be in a contract with an agency? This might cover health and other screening, the compensation package provided for temps by the agency (any anomalies?), provision of training, access to support facilities, maximum length of contract, etc.

- Are the quality control issues sufficiently reflected in the contract? For example, is there an emphasis on the disciplinary role only being directly undertaken by the agency and, similarly, that grievances should be taken to the agency not the client?
- If the contract provided by the agency is not appropriate, especially regarding the HR management aspects, what is the client's policy – is it to renegotiate the contract, find another agency, or anticipate that any problems can be resolved informally?

Contracts with self-employed persons

These contracts are different from any others considered in this chapter. There is no intermediary involved; the self-employed person deals directly with the employing organization. Typically, work is obtained through networking rather than a formal recruitment process.

Although there are many accounts of the lives of self-employed persons and how they obtain work, there is:

> little attention to the concerns and practices of the client/employer. Rarely do we hear the voices of managers who commission and supervise the work. This includes the process whereby employment is negotiated.

> (Platman, 2004)

There is generally more variety and flexibility in the content and form of the contracts. Partly, this is because self-employed people are, typically, better informed about what they want from the employer. They also tend to know what they want from the basics of the contract. There can often, therefore, be real and sometimes, tough, negotiation.

The nature and terms of a contract with an individual (remembering that terms can be created orally as well as in writing) are an important part of the process of managing expectations. Many of the problems that arise with self-employed persons are over a mismatch between what they want or expect and what they will get out of the deal. It is vital, therefore, that the mutual expectations are talked through and not left to chance. If there are likely to be any ambiguities or 'gaps', there should be mechanisms to resolve them.

The category 'self-employed' encompasses many different types of people. They can range from contractors, freelancers and consultants through to 'cash in hand' craftsmen. They generally work on the client's premises, and therefore the issues to address by the contract are not only varied but also very important.

HR specialists need to be involved, especially where the self-employed person works alongside employees. They will need to ensure, for example, that the appropriate qualifications, experience, induction and familiarity with workplace procedures are all in place. There is also a whole range of matters, such as team-working and quality assurance, to take on board when employing a self-employed person. These can be complex. A strategic decision needs to be made as to whether they need to be set out in a contract or dealt with more informally.

In devising the content of a contract, an important preliminary issue affecting virtually all legal jurisdictions is the question of employment status. This has been previously considered in Chapter 6. It is vital that the contract avoids uncertainties, especially where the employer does not want employment law and social security responsibilities. Where this is the case, the following is suggested:

- Use language in the document indicative of self-employment and entrepreneurialism. Use 'fee' rather than 'pay', 'project/assignment' rather than 'work', 'termination' rather than 'dismissal', etc. The title of the document should avoid a phrase such as 'Employment contract' or 'Terms of work for contractors'.
- Ensure the document is signed, so as to signify agreement to the terms set out.
- Confirm formally in the document that it is one of self-employment and is not a contract of employment; confirm that it cannot develop into one.
- Confirm that: the organization is contracting with an independent business; the individual is free to work for other employers providing there is no conflict of interest or issues of confidentiality, etc.; the individual can generally provide a substitute if he or she is unable to attend.
- Avoid the language of control and discipline; encourage the language of partnership and dialogue. If problems arise over, for example, work performance, these will be resolved through discussion or arbitration rather than 'disciplinary hearings', etc.

■ If some control is required, for example over confidential or market-sensitive information, use language that stresses the business reasons rather than an obligation that ariscs through the subordinate relationship of employer/employee.

On the question of drafting contracts, Sue Nickson from UK employment law specialists, Hammonds, says:

Employers need to narrow restrictive covenants down and make sure restrictions are regularly reviewed so they have specific restrictions relating to the individual concerned. The worst thing is to have a blanket, 'don't-do-anything-naughty-and-go-off-to-work-for-someone-else clause'. The courts consistently say they will not enforce such clauses – the important thing is to look at what people do, what information they have access to, what they should not do, making sure the clauses are tailor made.

(*Employers Law*, March 2005)

What do the self-employed want from contracts?

Contracts are two-way documents. However, there has been relatively little analysis of what self-employed people typically want in the contract and expect from the relationship. Anecdotally, they want to avoid high taxation and enjoy considerable flexibility. It is, though, reported that in terms of contracts, many self-employed people consider that they are in a weak bargaining position. This is especially the case when they are older (younger consultants, etc., appear more confident and demanding in negotiations). According to recent research on freelance staff, the major 'negatives' facing them are:

employers who tend to cut corners, rather than issuing fair and open contract terms; a reluctance to offer feedback on work; a failure to offer appreciation and a reluctance to provide any training.

(Platman, 2005)

Platman's research highlights the frequently difficult negotiation of contracts and mismatch of expectation and perceptions. For example, employers attach considerable importance to the following, on the part

213

of the self-employed person. flexibility (the ability to start work when wanted and to work around the employer's needs); affordability (they do not want to feel 'ripped off'); and instant knowledge and orientation (familiarity with state-of-the-art systems and an ability to 'fit in').

Employers were also suspicious that self-employed people would bring 'baggage' with them in terms of experiences and attitudes and, especially if older, might tend to be out-of-date and complacent. These attitudes can lead to very hard bargaining and the inclusion of 'defensive terms' in the contract itself.

For their part, the self-employed people in the research considered they had to be 'amoeba-like' – i.e. opportunistic and adaptable. Directly relevant to obtaining work and the contract, they stated that they were well aware of the demands of project work and deadlines, etc. They should not be seen as difficult or demanding, and they should be very cautious about fee-setting with the employer. Most expressed themselves as feeling in a weak bargaining position and not able to get the best out of the deal. Some stated they felt discriminated against on grounds of sex, racial group and age.

The self-employed people in our case studies reflected carefully on the process of contracting. They were aware of 'banana skins' and the need to be sensitive and cautious.

Dominic Brender, consultant and freelance writer over a period of twenty-five years, said:

> I am lucky in that after many years of experience I am generally able to get into the contract what I want. I can, to an extent, shape the content. I get a sense of what the budget is and rationalize my role to fit in with it. However, sometimes you have to second guess what they want. If it goes wrong, you are the one who takes the blame.

Our respondents were also acutely aware of their weak position if there was a dispute over the contract. Dominic Brender said:

> When things go wrong you have no recourse – contracts are impossible to enforce and you have no grievance procedure.

His conclusions are shared by Pattie Pierce, who combines agency secretarial work with office work offered directly to clients under self-employed contracts. When asked which form of contract suits her best, she commented:

I could pick and choose assignments more effectively as an independent but had no come-back if anything went wrong. Many of the problems I encountered were due to procurement mistakes by the HR department. But it was far simpler to sweep me under the table than confront this. Even if I had been aware of my legal rights, I would not have protested because I might have wanted work elsewhere in the organization and did not want to get a bad reputation.

This, clearly, makes it doubly important that contracts with self-employed persons are carefully negotiated and drafted. It is essential that potential disputes are identified and misunderstandings or misconceptions addressed. Dominic Brender also suggested that a topic for contract terms should be a procedure to deal with disputes and problems. This would be preferable to the current situation of rancour and often premature ending of the contract.

Dominic Brender further commented on one of the core issues, as he sees it. He said:

It is often difficult to get precise terms that are of importance to you, such as IP rights, rights to vary some contract terms, onto the contract agenda. It sometimes seems a one-way rather than a bargaining process. Most of the things I suggest are really quite helpful generally, as well as being important to me.

Questions of fixing the fee for the work featured strongly in case studies. As the basis for payment can vary greatly, it is important to get the right payment basis for the type of work being done. So-called 'ticking clock', usually daily fee rates, are popular, providing there has been careful analysis of the time the work should take. Where the work is not dissimilar to that undertaken by employees, this can be the simplest way to pay. Where work is project-based, the realistic estimate of time to do the work is critical. It is also important that both parties to the contract feel comfortable with the time allocation per day, etc.

A 'lump sum' payment is most appropriate for genuine project work, but again there has to be a realistic assessment of the time to complete the work. Closely allied to fixing pay by day or by project are issues of agreeing quality standards – who determines them, and whether the work can only be performed by the contracting party. There are many problems associated with the substitution of a (frequently less experienced) person to do the work. If delegation is to be allowed, questions regarding the qualifications and experience of the substitute should be agreed at the outset; they should not be allowed to evolve informally during the contract. This may risk quality and also perhaps, if freely agreed to raise the possibility of the self-employed person having 'worker status', or even being seen as an employee (see Chapter 6).

The other key matters to be considered for inclusion in the contract are:

- Hours of work or attendance at the workplace
- Attendance at meetings, briefings, etc.
- Timescales for the completion of all or parts of the work
- The situation if the self-employed person is ill, injured or otherwise unable to work
- Access to accommodation, facilities and technical and other support
- Availability or otherwise of expenses
- Identification of key personnel/groups/teams, etc., to report to
- Tax issues
- Clauses to deal with exclusivity, confidentiality, competition, intellectual property rights and restraint of trade following termination
- Procedures to deal with alleged breaches – e.g. failure to reach performance standards or behave appropriately or, alternatively, alleged failures on the part of the client to provide equipment or back-up
- Provision for dealing with unanticipated problems such as natural disasters, economic crises, business takeovers or liquidation
- Provision for notice to terminate.

Well-informed self-employed people are concerned that the contract should not only deal with the basics of pay, role, length of contract, termination, etc., but want it also to address matters such as the support they need from the employing organization, training needs and access to workplace facilities. An example of how this can work is provided by Laura Sykes.

Laura Sykes, a senior manager at a Regulatory Body in the UK, who has wide experience of dealing with non-employees, stated that:

We use lots of contractors. They are treated as well as employees. They earn good money and we want the best out of them. They are a lot more reliable than temporary staff, and are clear about their work intentions. They all sign a personal contract. Some can be very demanding.

For example we took on a consultant to undertake training. He wanted a lot of support from us over and above the contract terms – more than we were expecting. Indeed, we felt he could have been a lot more understanding of our position. We thought he did this because he was under a lot of pressure to ensure quick success. For our part, we thought the best way to provide the support was to give him the foundations, i.e. the basics he could build on.

He became 'one of us'. He also knew 'not to overstep the mark', as he was aware of our culture and we had put a lot of effort into that. We did not think we needed to write all this down. We had involved managers in the project development, and so what could have been risky was a great success. Leaving it all to chance can be problematic, though. We had another trainer from a manufacturing background who treated staff as if they were on a production line. It was useful that we had an exit strategy in the contract.

This relationship appeared to work well due to attention to detail in the contract, combined with the provision of a clear organizational framework within which the trainer could work. Setting the parameters of the relationship is vital. Where the role undertaken is highly professional and is subject to the demands of a professional body or guidelines, the matter is generally clear. Employers should incorporate those guidelines or practices within the contract. Where the role is not subject to those provisions, it is important to consider expectations and, if appropriate, spell them out.

Managing contracts

Negotiating and devising contracts is usually undertaken in a practical yet optimistic way. What about if problems arise, changes need to be made or there are major disputes?

Regardless of the type of contract – outsourcing, agency or self-employment – there are some common issues. In the words of Rehman Noormohamed, legal expert on contracts in the UK:

Always consider the exit strategy before contract signing. A contract is a bit like a marriage: first the honeymoon, then things tend to go wrong. Expectations are not met and there are other disappointments. It is vital that time is invested to keep the contract going. It is too easy to turn to divorce! You don't always want to end it and may want guidance. This might be Alternative Dispute Resolution [ADR]. This should help you to sort out the problems. You need always to 'nurture the contract'. If you do not have an exit strategy, assuming it is not possible to resolve problems, it costs twice as much to deal with.

It is always important to bear in mind that a written, signed document is a powerful document – at least in the common-law world. It is virtually impossible to argue that what was written down is not what was meant, or that either client/employer or self-employed person changed the contract through the manner of the work being done.

Even where the specific matter under dispute is not dealt with by the contract, it is difficult to get a court to agree that the matter should be implicit in the contract. Courts, not unreasonably, consider that the parties are able themselves to agree the basis of employment, and should not ask courts for help when things are unclear or contested. All this places emphasis on the need to have dispute resolution provisions within the contract itself.

Evidence from many of our case studies suggests that where an organization employs a significant number of non-employees at the workplace, especially through outsourcing, it is useful to consider:

- a central post/role for managing and monitoring the contracts and their operation
- establishing project management techniques for the management of non-employees – this might include management boards, risk management teams and steering groups
- the provision of information specifically designed for those on non-employee contracts
- procedures and practices to explain the situation of those on non-employee contracts
- discrete training for managers concerned with the recruitment and management of non-employees
- a procedure to deal with day-to-day problems or issues regarding the contracts for non-employees
- formal procedures for monitoring and review of contracts and their management.

If there are complex management procedures for the contract, this will need to be reflected in contract prices. From our case studies, it appears that many employers have detailed structures and processes.

Laura Sykes, from a Regulatory Body in the UK, reported that the Authority simply applies project management techniques to contracts for non-employees. It has adapted general project management techniques to the management of agency contracts, outsourcing and the self-employed. There are Project Boards, Risk Management Teams and Steering Groups, all focused on the contracts and their management.

David Bornor, of the Children's Mutual, emphasized how important it was to spell out in the contract the 'direct links' between the regulatory and quality issues and the management functions at Children's Mutual itself. A manager has the job title 'X' [name of outsourcing company] Relations Manager. Monthly meetings are held with the outsourcing company. Although the meetings are held in a very 'positive atmosphere', the contract also deals with the exit strategy if things go wrong. Most importantly:

> *A separate document exists on the situation if the contract is ended. It identifies who would be affected, who has responsibility for what and what the outsourcing company's responsibilities are regarding the exit. Our contract also allows us to specifically monitor the performance of the customer relations staff provided by the outsourcing company.*

Summary points

- There should be a clear understanding of what role contracts play, what they can achieve and how best they can be used.
- The people issues must be reflected in the commercial contracts for the supply of skills. This applies to all the groups of non-employees.
- There is a key role for HR in identifying, defining and ensuring that the people issues are dealt with in the contracting process. This should be done from the outset.
- HR needs to provide key data, information about HR processes and generally play a key supportive role in the contracting process and the contract terms.
- Business and other risks need to be responded to in the contract; the same (or even more) care has to be taken with short-term as with long-term assignments or contracts.

- Contracts need to reflect the mutual expectations of the parties as well as the work realities. They need to include discussion with self-employed freelance people and ideally should be explained to other groups of non-employees. Contracts should always be living and positive documents, as opposed to negative or defensive ones.
- If documents are drawn up by legal specialists, it is important that HR staff are involved in the process and can influence their content.

8

Employment relations and related issues

Prescient tales

This was previously outlined in Chapter 1. In 1997, British Airways (BA) outsourced its in-flight catering provision to a US-owned company called Gate Gourmet. This company employed several hundred staff, largely living near London's Heathrow Airport. The workforce was drawn from various ethnic groups, especially Asian groups. Many were former BA employees. Gate Gourmet recognized trade unions, in particular the Transport and General Workers Union (TGWU). The contract was a long one and, importantly, BA sourced all its in-flight meals from Gate Gourmet. The contract was due to be renegotiated during the spring of 2005. Profit margins were always low, and by 2005 Gate Gourmet's Heathrow operations were running at a significant loss. Its parent company, Texas Pacific remained highly profitable.

In an effort to deal with the losses, Gate Gourmet proposed changes to working practices, including the increased use of agency temporary workers. In June 2005, the TGWU and other unions agreed a restructuring deal. This was rejected by members. The workers affected took unofficial strike action – i.e. they did not follow the required legal procedures prior to taking strike action. The TGWU provided advice and support.

Those who went on strike were sacked by Gate Gourmet, as they can be under UK law. Baggage handlers and other staff employed directly by BA also went on 'sympathetic' strike, leading to the cancellation of large numbers of BA flights, and those flights that went ahead were often delayed and did not have meals provided for passengers. There was wide publicity regarding the situation at Heathrow Airport. The disruption continued for several weeks.

The TGWU called for the sacked Gate Gourmet employees to be reinstated (BA did not take action against their own staff except for two shop stewards who were disciplined but who, in September 2006 following lengthy negotiations received significant compensation). Gate Gourmet refused to reinstate people they referred to as 'troublemakers', although they did offer reinstatement or voluntary redundancy to other staff. Agency staff, predominantly from Poland, made the meals during the continuation of the dispute. The industrial dispute was settled in October 2005, with some staff being reinstated but others accepting redundancy. Later in October 2005, BA and Gate Gourmet agreed a new contract with considerably higher payments to Gate Gourmet.

Rory Murphy, a Director of Morgan Chambers, commented on the dispute in *Personnel Today* (23 August 2005), under a headline 'BA Case Highlights the Need for Early HR Input'. He said:

When you have no control over how a business is run or its people management strategy – when it views its workforce differently from how you view yours – disaster is inevitable.

He went on to state that although outsourcing contracts can be complex and problems can arise:

What seems to have been missing in this case – right from the beginning of the process – was the active involvement of HR.

The case achieved international publicity. The industrial dispute lasted several months, and the damage to BA's business and business reputation has been incalculable. The case confirms one of the key messages in this book: the need to redress the absence or low key role of HR in the management of non-employees. The need is heightened to ensure that the people issues are dealt with in contracts for the supply of non-employees and their management. It also shows that there are often collective dimensions to the use of non-employees, especially those that are employees of another organization, and that when disputes do arise it can be especially difficult to deal with them or to limit their damage.

This chapter is concerned with a number of issues that go beyond the management of the individual employment relationship of non-employees. If not dealt with effectively, they have the potential to have a major (and often negative) impact on the employing organization itself. The issues can give rise to considerable controversy, as well as presenting dilemmas and choices for employers.

Aims of this chapter

■ To explore some of the management and legal issues that go beyond the individual employment relationship – these are primarily issues of employment/industrial relations and social integration at the workplace
■ To identify the specific issues posed by the use of non-employees at the workplace in the context of employment relations
■ To touch on other matters, such as the access of non-employees to social facilities such as canteens and health care, sports facilities and car-parking, as well as involvement in social activities, such as parties/celebratory events
■ To consider some useful strategies and practices that can be developed.

Employment relations/industrial relations (ER/IR) and the non-employee

This agenda includes such matters as might be termed 'collective':

■ Formal matters of union recognition, collective bargaining/social dialogue and collective agreements/social agreements, dispute resolution processes, etc.
■ Information and consultation procedures and practices
■ Team briefings and the like
■ In-house committees, such as for equal opportunities, work–life balance, customer relations and health and safety.

It might also include matters that involve an organizational activity but where the individual non-employee participates. Such activities might include:

■ financial participation, such as profit-sharing, share options and bonuses based on team or whole workforce performance
■ suggestion schemes
■ attitude surveys.

Typical questions concerning non-employees and ER/IR

- Are there any regulations affecting industrial/employment relations in the context of using non-employees? (Can you outsource or use agency staff to 'break' strikes, etc.?)
- Should non-employees be covered by organizational information and consultation procedures (even though, for example, in the EU there is no legal obligation to include non-employees)? When might this make good sense? Are there risks?
- Should the employing organization relate to or liaise with an agency or outsourcing company that supplies the staff, regarding ER/IR, and if so, how?
- Should special ER/IR procedures be set up to deal with the participation of non-employees? This might be an especially important question where the numbers of non-employees at the workplace are high.
- Should there be special dispute resolution procedures where more than one employer is involved, or can existing procedures be adapted?

There were few responses in the case studies to these types of questions. ER/IR issues were not, according to one of our respondents, 'on the radar'. This was not the only feeling (especially from respondents outside the UK), but it appears that ER/IR is not regarded as a key aspect of the employment relationships with non-employees. That said, collective agreements have been made in several EU states specifically for some groups of non-employees – in particular, agency temps.

Employment/industrial relations: background information

Despite the fact that few of our respondents spoke of ER/IR issues unless prompted, this is an important topic for employing organizations – not least because the substitution of in-house skills with skills supplied by an intermediary has historically given rise to many industrial disputes.

One of the most contentious aspects of the BA/Gate Gourmet dispute in the summer of 2005 was the replacement of some directly employed staff with (lower paid) staff provided by an agency. As many non-wage labour costs (such a sick pay, pensions and other occupational benefits) are affected by length of service (continuity), there are obvious attractions in using casual or agency staff. Driving down costs in this way will tend to have a negative impact on existing staff, especially in labour-intensive industries or sectors. Workers may fear transfer to a new employer, or redundancy.

In many countries, policies of privatization (in, for example, Japan), outsourcing and, more recently, off-shoring have been resisted by unions and workers. In the UK, most resistance occurred in the 1980s; however, more recently outsourcing as a consequence of other developments – such as the Public Finance Initiative (PFI) – has led to unrest and disputes.

Outsourcing that involves off-shoring has been especially controversial. However, there are examples of arrangements that aim to respond to worker concerns:

> *In 2005, UNIFI, the financial services union in the UK (now part of AMICUS) reached an agreement with HSBC bank. The agreement was to minimize the number of jobs lost and to find innovative solutions for the redeployment of workers within the company. The ILO reported 'This agreement now serves as a benchmark for other companies in the industry'. Despite this, the ILO also reported continuing disputes across the developed world.*
>
> (Global Employment Trends Brief, February 2005)

Increasing use of private agencies in the provision of the public employment service (PES) across the EU has been resisted in several states, although much of the direct hostility has declined in the last decade. The talk is now of public/private partnerships in the provision of services. Many of these partnerships have been forged in France, Belgium, the Netherlands and the UK. However, the underlying resentment in some countries and in some sectors should not be underestimated. The workers affected by change or the fear of it tend to become disaffected unless steps are taken to respond to their concerns.

Controversy can also arise through friction between directly employed staff and non-employees. This may be because the non-employees are not members of trade unions or are hostile to them. Where the workplace provides a union recognition agreement and formal employment relations structures *vis-à-vis* directly employed staff, tensions can increase. Indeed, employees may be suspicious that the non-employees are being used to weaken the formal employment relations structures and/or to undermine employment conditions more generally.

Given the relative rarity of major industrial disputes, it is almost inevitable that there will be considerable media coverage should such a dispute arise. This, in turn, may lead to adverse publicity for the employer. The BA/Gate Gourmet case is a prime example. The fact that the workers involved were not employed directly by the company does not necessarily protect its reputation. Disputes tend to be complex. They cannot always be contained – especially outside the UK, where regulation is less harsh on 'sympathetic' industrial action. Furthermore, the reporting of them is not always accurate. Mud sticks, whatever the truth.

Trade unions and non-employees

Recent data continue to show a decline in both trade union membership and collective bargaining within the EU (WERS, 2004; European Foundation, 2005). The trend is marked in most developed economies, though there is considerable variation in the incidence of trade union membership by age (the young are far less likely to be members), sex (women are slightly less likely to be members) and employment sector.

Employees in the public sector are, globally, more likely to be in a union. Certain sectors, such as transport, health care and education, have very high membership levels. By contrast, financial services and IT have very low levels of membership.

There are also some important contrasts in terms of how representation is organized. In the UK, Ireland and much of the common-law world, unions draw members from specific employment sectors or professional occupations. In most parts of continental Europe, unions have political, religious or other affiliations. In the UK, there have been moves towards mergers between unions to create more 'continental' super-unions.

There are other variations across countries. Fewer than 10 per cent of employees in France are union members. In some other EU member states – Malta, Cyprus, Belgium, Sweden, Finland and Denmark – the rate is over 50 per cent. Membership rates in ex-communist EU states are generally low. The rate for the USA is 12.5 per cent and falling. In Japan, it is 19 per cent and falling slightly. In Australia, it is 23 per cent. These dramatic declines, following government policies in the UK in the 1980s and political and economic changes in ex-communist EU members from 1990, have generally tailed off. Nonetheless, most commentators consider trade unions are facing major challenges to their role and power.

Union mergers are not confined to the UK. These are happening across the EU, creating 'super-unions' aiming to improve their position. It is unclear what the implications of this will be for flexible working, non-employees and collective relations. Will it lead to non-employees being pushed even further to the margins of IR/ER, or will these new bodies adopt a more inclusive and flexible membership policy? Alternatively, will new types of associations emerge? Will they be more representative of new types of employee and non-employee?

Within the EU, new forms of consultation and bargaining have emerged – in particular, European Works Councils. These must be set up where companies operate in at least two member states, and must contain employee and employer representatives, as well as meeting at least once a year.

John Raywood, from GlaxoSmithKline (GSK), is Secretary to GSK's European Consultation Forum (Works Council). GSK has operations in many EU states. As well as annual meetings, the Forum has a Sub-Committee to consider current issues. He comments that matters under discussion often include plans to outsource or otherwise change the nature of employment relationships or where work is carried out. Although an enthusiast regarding the system, he confirms that non-employees have no representation and the trade unions involved are not pushing for their inclusion. He describes the discussion process in some detail. One situation concerned the closure of a distribution centre in Belgium. He says:

> As some of the Belgian jobs were agency/temporary workers they didn't 'count'. The decision went through smoothly. In any case, getting jobs back in-house is always popular, as jobs are then on an employee basis.

Despite EU measures to encourage collective labour relations through 'social dialogue', collective ER/IR often struggles to gain influence and impact. This is not helped by trade union membership decline. This decline in trade union membership is attributable, to a significant extent, to the rise of the atypical/ flexible workforce and the increasing numbers of non-employees (such as agency temps and freelancers/consultants) at workplaces.

More recently, migrant workers are forming a large proportion of the labour markets and are often also employed in atypical work. Historically, trade unions have generally not targeted such workers for union membership, considering their main role to be maintaining working conditions for employees/standard workers. Agency work, in particular, has presented many unions with major dilemmas. Should they aim to recruit such workers and to formalize employment relations with agencies, thus providing them with legitimacy? Or should agency working be rejected as undermining labour standards and stability?

The comments of Stefan Clauwaert from the European Trade Union Institute (ETUI) illustrates the continuation of the dilemmas trade unionists face in relation to non-employees at the workplace. He expressed the concern that agency temps are sometimes used to break strikes, though he accepts that 'it can make sense, especially for SMEs, to, for example, outsource for recruitment'. In terms of increasing membership, he says: 'The first priority is to get ex-members back but also to consider flexible workers, such as part-timers, homeworkers and job-sharers'. He thinks that 'gold-collar workers' and 'strategic individualists' are 'not a top [recruitment] priority', asking himself 'do they want to be in unions anyway?'

A recently published study (Heery, 2005) has traced the evolving attitude of unions to agency work in the UK. Responses have moved on from 'exclusion' (banning them) to 'replacement' (by state bodies) to 'regulation' (to limit use) to 'engagement' with them (aiming to improve temps' working conditions). The last response has proved problematic in that union membership amongst temps at even the major agencies is low, and formal relationships have tended to focus on procedural rather than substantive issues.

However, at the multinational level, CIETT's (the employers' confederation of leading global agencies) European branch has participated in social dialogue and social agreements, for example within the ICT sector. There are also major changes in formalizing industrial/employment relations with agencies in several EU states, such as Belgium, France and the Netherlands.

Adecco and Manpower, for example – the largest and second largest agencies, respectively, in Europe – have collective agreements with trade unions. This, in part, reflects their policies of developing close and developing relationships with their temps.

Jean-François Denoy, Director of Human Resources Development at Manpower, France, reported that Manpower has eleven Works Councils in France. They cover around 130 000 temps. There are ten trade unions involved. The Works Councils meet every month. M. Denoy comments: 'It's very complicated but we do try to address the very particular concerns of our temps'.

Such comments and practices are probably not widespread. The overall position appears to be that trade unions have struggled both to retain members and also to develop a coherent response to non-employees. Disputes continue to arise over proposals to outsource or use employment agencies, and the topic remains controversial in an IR/ER context in many countries and sectors. Given the constant reassessment of the notions of core roles and non-core roles by employing organizations, it seems likely that controversy will continue.

New forms of ER/IR

The challenge for employing organizations using non-employees is not just to respond in terms of traditional industrial/employment relations, but also to note the different types of 'collectivization' that exist – especially for self-employed people. This issue was touched on in Chapter 2.

Given that the major growth in self-employment and the more sophisticated areas of agency work has been in high skills areas, the workers concerned have tended to belong to professional bodies that operate in their occupation. Some of the bodies are long-established and powerful.

Many self-employed people have access to support structures. They also rely to a greater or lesser extent on networks. There is evidence that younger workers are also using or developing networks to support their careers (Lammiman and Syrett, 2004). Nonetheless, they often lack or have problems with access to training and development facilities, financial support, pensions, etc. Specialist organizations are emerging to fill these gaps, although not as either trade unions or professional bodies.

Nic de Potter is the co-founder of CAST (Cooperative Active Age Services Trust), based in Brussels but with branches developing in many EU states. CAST provides coaching for members who are typically older

229

workers working with younger people. These 'twins' have training, advice and support from 'alternative' finance sources, and from newsletters and other facilities. He says:

> Young professionals and entrepreneurs often have to operate outside traditional support structures. They are often isolated and lack both confidence and support. We have put together an innovative yet very practical structure for them, recognizing that trade unions do not encourage them, professional bodies do not always provide the practical support they need, and chambers of commerce, etc., are not always seen as relevant to them. Whether we represent a new form of employment relations is unclear, but CAST does demonstrate the need for change.

Both CAST and the traditional professional bodies are markedly different from traditional trade unions, but they do bring a form of collectivism to the workplace. Some of the norms of these bodies and their practices do have relevance for employers, especially in terms of professional standards and ethics. They can be very useful to employment relations involving non-employees, and are growing in range and importance.

Darren Cox, Director of Human Resources at Kelly Services, UK, reports that he has had discussions with two major unions. He felt, though, that simply formalizing the discussions or recognizing the unions was not the right way forward. He says, 'Trade unions need to change their mindset'. He is unsure what the ideal form of collective relations would be in the temporary agency world, given its particular features. He is sure, though, that 'any new system must match the strategic goals of creating partnerships with clients and other initiatives'.

Issues and choices

In Chapter 1, a model is used to explore levels of control that employers either have or would wish to have over non-employees (see Figure 1.1). The model is been used to explore developing notions of the new psychological contract as applying to non-employees. This chapter now introduces a new model, based this time on degrees of participation and involvement. High involvement includes the involvement of non-employees in formal information, consultation, and possibly even negotiation procedures. It sees their involvement in other collective structures, such as consultative committees, health and safety/diversity/ work–life balance committees and similar, and in team briefing and feedback procedures. Low involvement (which could include no group/ collective involvement at all) tends to mirror the hands-off approach to employing non-employees more generally. On the other hand, employers who have adopted an 'integration' or partnership approach to the employment of non-employees tend towards medium or higher levels of involvement.

Figure 8.1 presents the model of types of involvement. It deals with collective issues (i.e. where the interests/needs of the non-employee are represented through a group, which may or may not be a trade union). It also deals with issues that might involve the non-employee, but on an individual basis.

The relevance of Figure 8.1 clearly depends on what facilities or practices the 'employer' of the non-employee has. It will also be affected by whether the non-employees work on the employer's premises. It may be worth considering whether some forms of involvement might be

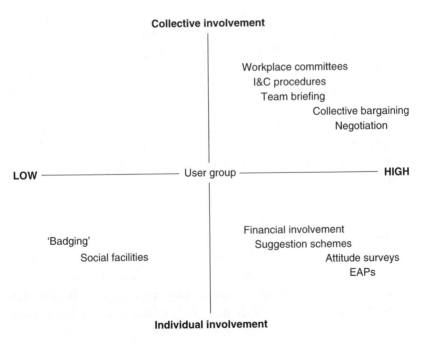

Figure 8.1 Involvement at the workplace

specifically developed for non-employees. This might be a User Committee or something similar, which would explain the employer's situation to non-employees or their representatives and enable the non-employees to express views or experiences to the employer. It focuses on the people issues. This would be different from a liaison or monitoring group that oversees the working of the outsourcing or agency contract itself.

It was noteworthy that, during the discussions for the case studies that were specially developed for this book, no respondent referred to such committees or groups unless they had a specific IR/ER role.

Developing a strategy: some preliminary questions

1. Is the direct employment relationship of the non-employee(s) with the organization, or is another employer involved? Where skills have been outsourced, another employer(s) will, of course, be involved. Clearly, self-employed people have a direct relationship with the employer. Once again, the ambiguities that often attend agency work will make that decision more complex. Chapter 6 dealt with the employment status of temps in the UK and further afield, and it was recommended that only agencies that provide employee status should be used. The temp will then look to the agency for IR/ER processes. The question of 'who is the employer?' is especially important where the non-employees are working alongside directly employed staff or are otherwise integrated with them.
2. What structures and procedures at the workplace, such as consultative procedures, might have relevance for non-employees or their employer?
3. Are there structures and procedures at an agency or outsourcing company that you need to be aware of?
4. Are there any legal obligations for involvement that need to be complied with? For example, within the EU there are several pieces of legislation that require consultation over workforce changes, restructuring, redundancy, etc. However, they only apply to employees, despite the fact that plans to restructure, off-shore, etc., tend to have a disproportionate impact on non-employees, who are often affected or dismissed first. Note that many of the obligations to inform and consult in health and safety laws do apply to non-employees (see Chapter 6).

5. What are the key drivers and policies of the organization, including cultural and ethical considerations and matters of quality assurance, that need to inform the questions concerning the involvement of non-employees? Despite the lack of legal imperatives, does it make sense to omit them from workplace procedures? Can, for example, Investors in People accreditation from the UK Government be maintained without some involvement by non-employees and/or their employer? This will be especially important where the non-employees constitute a major part of the total workforce.

6. Are there explicit gains to be made through the effective involvement of non-employees and/or the agency or outsourcing company? Where the organization has seen merit in an integration or partnership model for the supply of skills by of non-employees, adopting inclusive IR/ER practices and providing appropriate levels of involvement for individual non-employees might well make sense.

7. Are there legal or other risks in involving non-employees? Where employment status is unclear, might close involvement with ER/IR practices or access to facilities and activities at the workplace suggest employee status? Care might need to be taken and there may need to be an effective balance between the HR objective of a harmonious and well-integrated workforce, and the risk of taking on employment responsibilities that were not wanted.

In most countries, there are few rules or IR/ER procedures that must apply to non-employees. As a minimum, non-employees do have so-called 'association rights' – i.e. the right to be a union member. Many self-employed people belong to professional and trade bodies, although such membership does not usually attract collective rights at the workplace.

An overview

The implications of the above are that employers of non-employees are faced with the following situation:

1. Where the non-employees are employed by an agency or outsourcing company, they may have employee-based IR/ER rights applying to them in their own employment. They have the right to be consulted, and may even have representational rights in European Works Councils.

233

Works Councils apply formal information and consultation rights and structures for certain EU multinationals. The individuals have these rights to representation, despite the fact that they may work a long way away from their employers' premises and have very little contact with them.

2. In the overwhelming number of cases, the freelance workers, agency temps and staff supplied under an outsourcing contract have few, if any, IR/ER rights *vis-à-vis* the client/employer. They can therefore be excluded from current or planned procedures and practices for employee involvement.

3. It will therefore be a matter of choice or policy whether non-employees are included in workplace IR/ER practices and whether they are involved in matters such as suggestion schemes, questionnaires, staff meetings and social events. Where the workers involved are free-lance staff or consultants, care needs to be taken with these choices. As with agency temps, there are risks in the UK and in other juris-dictions if the apparently self-employed person is very closely inte-grated into the organization, benefits from IR/ER procedures and becomes almost indistinguishable from an employee. The individ-ual's self-employed status may then be challenged by tax authorities. This is a matter that needs to be carefully explored with those con-cerned and, if appropriate, legal advice should be sought.

4. Most importantly, traditional IR/ER practices, law and writings have not come to terms with the forms of flexible workforce considered in this book. Despite statistical evidence that more people, for a variety of reasons, are not part of traditional employment structures or reject them, no alternatives appear to be emerging yet.

The case studies tended to confirm this situation:

John Raywood is a specialist HR manager at GlaxoSmithKline (GSK), being Secretary of GSK's European Employers' Consultation Forum in the company. This acts as a works council under EU law. The discus-sions at the works council only involve permanent employees, and this has caused him to reflect on the role of non-employees. He believes such workers are not interested in involvement. Existing representa-tives on the works council would informally recognize them, but he doubts whether they would want their own representatives. John Raywood concludes that the fact that non-employees are not part of the structures does not always make sense, given that it is often their jobs that are 'on the line' in proposals for employment change within GSK.

Some possible approaches

The groups of non-employees considered in this book are each in very different situations when it comes to IR/ER. They have relatively little in common for these purposes, beyond the fact that they are not employees. Where the non-employees are self-employed, it is only the individual that becomes a part of organizational practices. Where a temp is used, there is the individual to consider but also the agency. With outsourcing, another separate employer is involved, though the outsourcing workers may work alongside the employer/client's own staff.

Any policy on these matters cannot, therefore, be a simple 'one size fits all'. There will be many factors to consider. Not least will be the distinctive circumstances and needs of self-employed people, temps and employees of outsourcing companies. Collective arrangements may exist for pay bargaining, but will likely not be relevant to individual self-employed people. However, such workers may well be interested in social facilities and support services, and may have much to offer in terms of attitude surveys and, say, suggestion schemes.

Where an organization has outsourced a core service to a large outsourcing organization on, for example, a twenty-year contract, there may well be a need to ensure that there will not be industrial/employment relations problems. If the outsourcing company is unionized and is subject to collective agreements but the client has few union members and no formal agreements, what issues are there to address? What if the outsourcing company's staff, who may well work on the client's premises, want to hold union meetings there, or ask to be involved in consultation procedures or meetings, or have a policy to recruit the client employer's staff?

If the outsourcing company's service is provided on site, what other aspects of involvement might be explored? Should key outsourcing staff join team briefings? Should they be members of a health and safety group, or a bullying or an equal opportunities policy group? Should the aim be – through closer involvement – a more seamless web of involvement that might well add value to the contract? What might the advantages be?

Where the non-employees are agency temps, the issues can be more complex. Much will depend on the length of an assignment/mission. If a temp is with the client organization for a few days, it is likely that most of the existing collective or individual methods of involvement will not be relevant. With a longer assignment or the provision of a group of people for project work, or where there is a preferred or sole supplier agreement in place, questions might be usefully posed about the temps' degree of involvement and integration. If a bonus is paid to employees for good performance, should temps who also contributed to the success receive some form of financial recognition? This might well need to be agreed with the agency.

Where matters of Employee Assistance Programmes (EAPs) and other support facilities are concerned, it might be asked whether it makes sense to exclude temps on long assignments, or freelance and contract staff (subject to the legal issues considered in Chapter 7).

Laura Sykes, of a Regulatory Body in the UK, an organization that at any given moment has around 40 per cent of its staff as non-employees, when asked about the involvement of non-employees, says:

> When we use temps or consultants, we treat them the same as employees. They need to be just as involved in the organization. Why treat them differently? The fact they do not want to be employees is not the point. When they are here, they are one of us!

Industrial disputes

Although industrial disputes are less a feature of workplaces than in previous decades, the BA/Gate Gourmet dispute considered at the beginning of this chapter reminds us that one of the key messages is that industrial disputes cannot easily be 'ring-fenced'. Involving workers who have other employers does not necessarily protect you from the consequences of industrial disputes at their employment. Strike action is typically carefully regulated in developed economies, and reacting to workers who have not complied with regulation by sacking them is also tightly controlled – generally more so than in the UK. Within the EU, the regulation of outsourcing generally requires transfer of previous in-house staff to the outsourcing company. They tend, therefore, to be familiar with both their previous employer and the employer's remaining staff.

Action short of a strike might be involved – for example, withdrawing goodwill, working to rule or refusing to cooperate with the workers of an outsourcing company or agency. Disputes may reach a point where premises are closed. This will clearly impact on the ability of self-employed persons or agency temps to carry out 'their' work, which will in turn affect both their earnings and the agency. If there is a withdrawal of goodwill or other less dramatic action, there may well be implications for the ability of, say, freelancers or contract workers to work efficiently. Their contract may well be jeopardized, especially if it is a 'ticking clock' type of contract based on completing work within a set time.

These eventualities need to be part of the HR dimension and part of contracts. Who is to bear the losses? Can adjustments be made to enable completion of contracts? Our case studies showed that many self-employed people felt aggrieved by the fact that not only were their services sometimes dispensed with abruptly, but also, in situations beyond their control, they were completely disregarded. It is self-evident that this can have a major impact on trust and the psychological contract with the organization.

Summary points

Industrial/employment relations regarding non-employees are subject to little regulatory control. Employers broadly have choice as to how they approach the matter. It is suggested, therefore, that the following points be considered:

- Before outsourcing, using an agency or recruiting self-employed people, have a clear inventory of your current practices for the involvement of staff.
- Find out whether the agency, outsourcing company, etc., has practices to involve staff.
- Find out whether these practices are compatible with your organization – are problems likely?
- Find out the typical length of relationship with temps and consultants, as opposed to the theoretical contract length. Our case studies showed that many 'short-term' contracts tend to drift, and people become embedded in the organization and its practices.
- Review information and communications systems, not only with, say, agencies and outsourcing companies, but also with the staff

they provide. This process should also apply to self-employed people. It is the latter group that is the most likely to be 'at the margin' and unsure as to where members 'fit in'.

- Set up and invest in formal communications systems with agencies and outsourcing companies specifically to deal with people issues. Consider whether workplace committees, such as on health and safety, equal opportunities, etc., might have as *ex officio* members non-employees and/or their employers.
- The outcomes of research (Leighton, 2002) that indicates that non-employees especially value involvement in social and corporate activities at 'their' workplace should be drawn on. Access to parking and leisure facilities is often referred to, but meetings about business plans, feedback on the state of the employing organization and meetings where the views of staff are sought can usefully include non-employees. They do often make helpful contributions, and their identification and engagement with the organization might be enhanced.
- Question whether there are other benefits to be gained through involving non-employees at the organization. Might misunderstandings or omissions be avoided? Might useful intelligence on the organization be obtained through the 'eyes' of non-employees?
- Consider the types of involvement that might be the most appropriate for the different groups of non-employees. Some will clearly be inappropriate, such as those related to long-term matters like financial participation, although bonuses related to projects ought perhaps to include freelance staff who have contributed to the work. Similarly, team briefings, TQM processes and the like can usefully involve freelance and consultancy staff.
- Consider the possibility of disruptive industrial actions, sometimes as a consequence of the employment of non-employees. Ensure that there is awareness of the regulatory framework and of the fact that 'containing' disputes is not always possible. Especially where outsourcing is concerned, bear in mind the 'sympathy' between the client's and the outsourcing company's employees. Ex-employees in particular often have strong emotional bonds with their ex-employer, and this has to be carefully managed so as to avoid problems.

9

Health and safety

In 2000, a rail disaster occurred near Hatfield in the UK that killed several people. The cause of the disaster was poor rail track maintenance. Track maintenance had been outsourced to Balfour Beatty, a major UK engineering company. Prosecutions under health and safety legislation were brought against both Railtrack (at the time the privatized company responsible for track, stations and other facilities) and Balfour Beatty. Several senior managers from both companies were charged with manslaughter, despite the fact that only the outsourcing company had direct contractual responsibility for the track's maintenance. The manslaughter prosecutions were unsuccessful, causing Bob Crow, the Rail Union General Secretary, to state:

> *Justice will not been done until Britain has a corporate manslaughter law that holds individual executives to account for negligence that kills innocent people.*

Railtrack was, nonetheless, fined over £3 million and Balfour Beatty over £10 million. These are exceptionally high fines, and reflected the court's view that the outsourcing contract had been poorly undertaken by Balfour Beatty, and Railtrack's overall management in terms of health and safety had many deficiencies.

(*Personnel Today*, 10 October 2005)

The outcomes of the Hatfield tragedy and other major disasters in the UK and elsewhere, along with the 'changes in the organization of work', have highlighted the particular issues for health and safety presented by the use of non-employees. In particular, it has been the role of outsourcing and its management, although pressure has been mounting to ensure higher levels of accountability for health and safety. Analysis has led to conclusions that there are particular risks that also arise from using non-employees through intermediation or employment of self-employed people, as well as through outsourcing.

Aims of this chapter

- To outline the principles of health and safety regulation of relevance to non-employees
- To analyse the application and implications of the regulations
- To consider management strategies to respond to the legal and other issues, and reflect on examples of good practice.

The issues relating to health and safety are in marked contrast to most of those considered in this book. Whereas there is little regulation applying to non-employees in general, health and safety matters are tightly regulated in all developed economies.

Within the EU, there is, in effect, a pan-European comprehensive and coherent body of regulation. The EU's approach has been hugely influential way beyond the borders of the EU. Many non-EU states have adopted the EU's approach and structures, and its central concept of risk management is therefore familiar in most parts of the developed world. Part of this core concept is the managing of the particular risks faced by non-employees.

In addition, there is considerable research and numerous statistical data to draw on (Gospel, 2004). Most of this shows that, typically, non-employees are at especial risk from accidents and ill health when compared with standard employees. The reasons are not hard to find:

- Non-employees tend to be less familiar with work premises, work practices and the particular risks that exist
- Non-employees tend to have less training in health and safety matters
- Non-employees tend to have little access to the important structures for health and safety, such as health and safety committees, or roles

as safety representatives, and are unlikely to be consulted on health and safety matters

■ There are often ambiguities in the management of non-employees that present particular issues for health and safety.

The last point has been emphasized by the National Institute for Occupational Safety and Health in the USA, which reports that:

Concern also exists that organizations may shift hazardous jobs and tasks to members of the alternative [flexible] workforce, that these workers may be less likely to recognize and report hazards and injuries and they may be at increased risk of stress owing to their precarious employment.

(NIOSH, 2002)

Research also shows that health and safety risks are increased for non-employees, especially agency temps and the self-employed, through their exclusion from, or only limited access to, occupational health schemes, health screening at the workplace and policies for fitness support.

The health and safety agenda

Health and safety used to be dominated by accidents and incidents in the heavy industrial sectors of employment and construction. Construction remains a sector that has high accident rates, but the shift to service economies and the decline in manual labour has meant that a new agenda has emerged. The accident statistics are still dominated by trips, falls and various sorts of accidents and occupational diseases, but matters of general health, especially musculoskeletal problems and stress, are causing major loss of working days and other economic consequences. There is also the pain and suffering for the individuals concerned. Where those individuals are non-employees, they are less likely to be insured or to have access to state benefits.

The agenda for employing organizations is a wide one. It includes:

■ The safety of work premises – there are specific issues where premises are shared
■ The safety of work materials and equipment

- Safety management, including the undertaking of risk assessments and the implementation of preventive measures
- Health and safety training and retraining
- Monitoring, including through the use of surveillance, feedback and committees, and communication systems, leading to review of procedures
- Health surveillance and support facilities, including for stress
- Special provisions where premises or work activities are shared (this clearly has particular relevance to outsourcing and agency partnering arrangements).

The topics covered by health and safety management are not confined to accidents and ill health, but also include matters such as bullying at work, violence, and ensuring that working time is managed properly. Policies on health and safety are, across economies, driven by notions of risk management and the need not only to identify risks and measure them but also to respond to them in a systematic and comprehensive way. The key legal duties in most countries are to:

- assess workplace risks for all at work and for others who may be affected by work
- minimize those risks through putting in place preventive measures, such as through training, supervision, equipment quality and good work practices
- monitor safety standards at the workplace and ensure adjustment when work practices change (for example, through the employment or increased employment of non-employees).

Why is it important?

Health and safety is a matter that cannot be neglected, not just because the consequences can be so serious in terms of cost and publicity but also because, unlike most matters affecting the employment of non-employees, they cannot be resolved through a contract. The law in virtually all countries will not allow for delegation (or outsourcing) of these legal duties. Two or more organizations or individuals can be liable in law for the consequences of one incident. The duties are also shared with the non-employees themselves, although often their degree of responsibility is lower. The situation is that all at work have strict legal duties, they cannot be ignored or passed on, and criminal penalties cannot be insured against.

There are also major implications in terms of insurance. An employer with a bad health and safety record will find this is reflected in premiums, and insurance companies are well aware of the extra risks that the employment of non-employees can bring. With more and more employers moving to self-insurance the costs may be more hidden, along with the costs of dealing with an accident or legal action. Hidden they may be – but they are very real.

The problems in terms of accidents and ill health are so serious that, within the EU, there are several pieces of legislation that are specifically designed to deal with non-employees and agency temps. This legislation has three main strategies:

1. Recognition that, where more than one employer is engaged in working on the same premises, the work must be subject to 'cooperation and coordination' between the various employers. This law was developed with the construction industry particularly in mind, but the principle has wider impact. Clearly, where more than one employer shares premises the idea has particular relevance. This covers not only obvious matters (such as access to and use of electricity and gas, and building and maintenance work) but also policies on smoking, violence and shared social facilities. It is also important to bear in mind that where a worker for one employing organization is subjected to violence or, say, harassment by a worker for another organization, the situation is likely to be extremely complex. The complexity will not, though, provide an 'alibi' for an employer.
2. To ensure the sharing of information on health and safety between, in particular, the client and the temporary work agency. In the UK, for example, when contacting an agency for a temp, the law requires the client to explain the nature of any relevant health and safety hazards, such as dangerous chemicals or biological agents, noise and electromagnetic fields. There must also be information on other activities, such as the manual handling of goods that present particular risks. The client must also tell the agency what procedures and structures there are in place at the workplace to minimize those risks. The agency must inform the temp about health and safety issues affecting assignments. There must also be appropriate training, just as there should be for

self-employed staff (Conduct of Employment Agencies and Businesses Regulations, 2003).

3. The legislation applies regardless of employment status, though there are some distinctive duties on an employer regarding employees. The fact that people are not employees and/or do not have long periods of employment does not take them outside legal protections. If people are at work, including in their own home, the law will apply.

4. Areas of law that provide compensation for people who have been injured or suffer illness similarly do not require them to be in a particular employment category. They again simply need to have been 'at risk' of harm. Legislation also recognizes that some people are at greater risk of harm, including young people, older people, women and people with disabilities. This category of higher risk includes most groups of non-employees. All these matters need to be taken into account by the employing organization, because the fact that someone is at the company for a limited time or brings his or her own equipment or works at home, for example, rather than restricting legal responsibilities can actually increase them. The risks to non-employees must, therefore, be addressed. Risk assessment processes need to refer explicitly to non-employees, and staff with occupational safety and health responsibilities must be made clearly aware that non-employees are within the 'risk assessment frame'.

These specific pieces of EU-wide legislation are set in the context of the essential topic of risk management. Employers, as referred to above, must undertake risk assessments, including for when an activity is undertaken (or might be undertaken) by, say, a temp or freelancer; have preventive measures in place to minimize those risks; and must monitor risks. Figure 9.1 sets out a health and safety risk triangle with particular application to using non-employees. It aims to illustrate the typical types of injuries suffered by non-employees, and their typical causes.

The substantive causes of these problems are a lethal combination of lack of familiarity with hazards at the premises or in the use of equipment, lack of training, and failures in communication systems.

Change at work typically presents particular problems. If work procedures are changed, a business is relocated or new machinery is introduced, the level of risk may change. Change in personnel is a critical risk factor. It is self-evident that when work is outsourced, it is almost inevitable

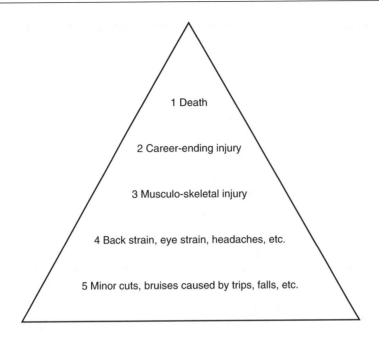

Pathology:

5 = Caused by unfamiliarity with building, and for example, its uneven stairs, wet floors when being cleaned, difficulty in summoning help

4 = Injuries caused by, for example, using other people's pcs, chairs and different lighting and ventilation

3 = Back injury caused by lack of training in lifting heavy loads, unfamiliarity with lifting equipment, reluctance to seek help

2 = Major injury caused by being struck by a vehicle at the work premises while standing on a walk way. The driver said, 'I did not expect anyone to be there. No-one told me we had a temp working in the despatch office'

1 = Death caused by falling through lift shaft. As employees knew, but temps and other workers did not, the door to the lift shaft was never locked and there was no warning of the danger.

Figure 9.1 Risk triangle and non-employees

that there will be a knock-on effect on the level of risk. It may be reduced by, for example, work being done off-premises or off-shore, or it may increase through, perhaps, incompatibility of work practices between the outsourcing company and directly employed staff.

Responses to health and safety risks

In all developed economies, health and safety law is part of criminal law/criminal code. Breaches of law can, and often do, especially in other parts of the EU, lead to imprisonment. Many of the leading cases that have led to major fines or imprisonment have involved the use of outsourcing companies or employment of consultants, etc. The need is therefore for awareness of law, and caution and care in complying with it.

Most of the respondents in the case studies expressed awareness that this was an issue for the use of non-employees. They realized that non-employees present particular challenges for health and safety management. The problems are identified in terms of classic health and safety (i.e. accidents and diseases) rather than the newer health and safety agenda of, say ill health, violence, stress, etc. No-one in our case studies referred to stress as a particular issue for non-employees, despite the fact that many are used in traditionally highly stressful areas of work, compounded by a lack of training and support structures.

Some, though, felt that a carefully drafted contract and well-selected insurance policies could reduce problems. Only rarely was health and safety discussed unprompted.

Sadly, problems cannot be avoided, and it is axiomatic that greater care has to be taken with regard to non-employees than employees. Some respondents, especially where work was outsourced, aimed to address these health and safety issues through some form of liaison or monitoring committee or the work undertaken on an explicit partnership model. This was not a feature of using an agency or employing self-employed people. They appear to remain generally outside health and safety management structures, although there are examples of good practice.

Clearly, there are major issues where the use of non-employees has been explicitly set up on a hands-off model. This aims to distance the two organizations, or the organization from self-employed people. The temptation or intention will be to 'push' the idea of personal responsibility to the non-employee. This is one of the areas where such a policy cannot work, and some sort of management structure has to be established to ensure that the client/employer is not responsible for poor health and safety standards for the non-employees. Contracts, notices, disclaimers – for example, stating in a contract document that 'You are entirely responsible for your own safety when working here. We do not accept responsibility should you suffer an accident or ill-health' or 'You accept that when you enter these premises you do so entirely at your own risk' – will be ineffective.

The simplest way is to require the non-employees to comply formally with the client/employer's health and safety policies and practices, and to see failure to do so as a clear breach of the service contract. For the client/employer to be free of liability, it will have to show that the standards were enforced, breaches or poor standards were dealt with and overall management was effective. This is especially important in terms of information about health and safety issues, and the provision of a procedure whereby problems can be communicated and responded to.

To take a very simple example: a leading UK organization in the media sector had had a number of problems with its outsourcing and agency contracts – all of which were done through the raising of a purchase order, mostly by line managers. One such was for the maintenance of office equipment. The engineer from the outsourcing company had been making sexually explicit comments to a secretary and had molested her. This had happened on a number of occasions. She reported this to her manager, who said 'That's nothing to do with us. They are a separate company'. She took it up with the company and was told, 'If you have problems with any of our staff, take it up with your own manager. If there was an incident, it was on your premises.'

She left her job, feeling that her legitimate health and safety concerns had been ignored. Had she not done and, say, she had suffered from a stress-related problem as a consequence of the engineer's conduct, she may well have had a claim for unfair dismissal, a claim in negligence against her employer who was aware of the problem and the matter could have led to the intervention by the enforcement authorities. Both organizations washed their hands of the problem and left her feeling helpless. And then there would probably have been media coverage!

(Leighton, 1990)

Another important health and safety issue is whether the employer can be responsible for harm inflicted by non-employees on others while working for the organization. Traditionally, employing organizations have only been accountable for their employees. In many jurisdictions, liability extends to harm caused by non-employees. This approach, as is seen from the case-law at the head of this chapter, is gaining support in the UK. All this emphasizes the need to be alert to the need to apply proper training and supervision standards to all who create or are exposed to risks.

The UK is generally seen as having good health and safety standards and as complying well with the huge EU legislative agenda. We found also, through our case studies, that outside the UK, many said that rules had been 'tightened up' recently.

Jean-François Denoy, of Manpower, France, which has 80 000 customers/clients in France at any given moment, has developed relationships that he describes as *proximité* with those customers/clients. He does not say they were on a *partenaire*/partnership model. He explains that his company takes health and safety very seriously, not least because many of the temps work in manufacturing industry and construction where accidents are more common. He appreciates that, as in the UK, where there is an accident to a temp, Manpower might be liable. Insurance costs in France are high, and so there is every incentive to avoid problems. The strategy at Manpower is to provide temps with relevant health and safety information and require that they pass a health and safety test before an assignment/mission – 'We do a little training in the branch – it is very systematic'. The temp, according to the contract with a client, has to be treated as though he or she is the client's employee for the purposes of health and safety. M. Denoy also said, 'If an accident occurs to a temp, I say "You are my customer and I cannot accept that my staff are working in dangerous conditions".'

This discussion illustrates both the importance that is attached to health and safety and that in the case of agencies (and outsourcing) it is a shared responsibility. Effective health and safety management is not an optional extra. It is essential.

Discussions in case studies mainly focused on accidents in an industrial context. However, it must be remembered that non-employees are often used in work activities that may subject them to stress or other health problems. Workers in customer relations, health care and various sorts of manual work are prone to illness and well-being problems.

It must be reiterated that how health and safety issues generally are dealt with depends on a number of variables. These include:

- *The nature of the work and the workplace risks*. It should not be assumed that the areas of work where agency temps and self-employed people work are 'safe'. Indeed, many work in construction, where there are notoriously high risk levels. Alternatively, there are risks from less serious accidents, stress, fatigue, headaches, etc., in the standard office environment. Good practice, backed up by law, suggests the need to assess for any particular risks to non-employees as well as to employees. The greater the risks, the more management systems need to ensure risks are minimized. Clearly, one of the major risks for non-employees is often being unfamiliar with buildings and work procedures, including emergency procedures. Several of our respondents have said:

We simply do not know at any given moment how many temps and consultants are on the premises.

One comments:

If there was a fire or a bomb scare, I am not sure we could count them or that they would know what to do.

Another says:

We are thinking of developing a special Health and Safety Handbook for temps and contract workers.

- *The location of work and extent of involvement by non-employees with employees of the employer/client.* Where individual self-employed persons or employees of different employers work together, the risk of confusion increases.
- *The nature of the employment relationship and which model of control applies.* Is it 'hands-off', integrated or partnership? For health and safety purposes, the hands-off model presents real problems. Clearly, the lack of day-to-day contact between managers and a policy that says 'Out of sight out of mind' is dangerous and unworkable. The integration and partnership models, with higher levels of day-to-day involvement by the various parties and the development of explicit management structures, will fairly easily incorporate the issues of health and safety.

The MEDEF (France) Esprit de Service's Guide du Partinariate de Services (Guide to Shared Services), which is the equivalent of outsourcing or co-sourcing, stresses *proximité* (integration) between the client and outsourcing company and *partage d'experiences* (working together). The French notion of co-sourcing appears particularly appropriate for dealing with health and safety concerns.

- *The nature, structures and culture regarding health and safety organization at the client/employer*. These may need attention.

Discussions in our case studies produced the following statements, most of which could give cause for concern:

> *Oh! Health and safety. It's done by our premises people. They deal with contractors for maintenance and cleaning.*

> *Occupational health is, of course very important for all staff.*
> *We have a friendly relationship with our OH people.*

> *We try to do health and safety training when temps arrive but, you know, there isn't always time. Anyway, most only stay a week.*

> *We tend to assume consultants are intelligent enough to know the basic rules and can look after themselves.*

- *The role or function that drives health and safety policies and practices*. Is this HR, premises and maintenance, occupational health? This was reportedly often unclear in our case studies, and it by no means always included HR staff.

The hands-off model, whereby control and management is the overwhelming responsibility of self-employed persons themselves, the agency or the outsourcing company, will not work for health and safety. Integrated and partnership models are clearly better suited, but should still clearly incorporate health and safety in their management systems.

There are aspects of HR management that have relevance to health and safety, in the context of risks to non-employees. As a minimum, these include the following:

- *Recruitment/procurement* (the process whereby the service provider is selected). At the least, the tendering and selection process affecting outsourcing companies and agencies must check health and safety standards and other management functions, such as training and internal communication systems that have relevance. Are there specialist health and safety personnel at, say, the outsourcing company or agency? What is the company's accident and illness record? Is there a discernable health and safety culture? Are policy documents and manuals, etc., shared during the recruitment process?
- *The contracting process*. Have provisions for accidents and shortfalls in safety standards been incorporated in the contract? For example, what

are the insurance arrangements? If there are safety concerns, how will they be dealt with? Will compensation be payable if injury and losses are caused to the client/employer? What are the arrangements for ensuring legal duties for health and safety are met? What if it emerges during the contract that standards are not acceptable? What if a temp fails to comply with the client/employer's standards – does the contract deal with the issue? What if the temp causes harm or injury? What reference is made in the contract with self-employed persons? Do they have to adhere to the client/employer's standards, and what happens if they do not?

- *Information and consultation systems.* How is health and safety information communicated? Are the manuals, guides, etc., of relevance? Are key personnel formally linked to both the service provider and the client/employer? Will they meet formally? Is there a safety committee and, if so, who serves on it? Is health and safety to be the subject of attitude surveys or feedback systems?
- *Training.* How will health safety training of non-employees be undertaken and updated? Who will do it? Who will pay for it? Might training be conducted through elearning/open learning, CDs or other innovative methods suited to the needs of non-employees? Might training be compulsorily completed before people gain access to work?
- *Performance management.* What are the arrangements for ensuring proper health and safety provision for non-employees – for example, in terms of the use of PPE and work procedures such as manual handling, but also in ensuring compliance with anti-bullying, violence and smoking policies, and any requirements affecting working time? How do health and safety standards feature in the evaluation processes regarding the performance of non-employees generally? Where individuals fail to comply with health and safety rules or present the potential of harm to others, how and by whom is the matter dealt with?

There are particular issues of monitoring and evaluation in terms of health and safety procedures regarding non-employees. Are accidents to them recorded, and how does the rate compare with employees? If there are problems, what steps should be taken to remedy them? Do non-employees cause more accidents and near misses than employees? Again, what should the response be? Is there representation for non-employees on the health and safety committee or other formal monitoring procedures at the workplace?

A particular issue, especially for the self-employed and agency temps, is the application of disciplinary rules regarding breaches of health and safety standards. The best advice here appears to be:

- The contract or arrangements with self-employed persons should specifically address health and safety. It should confirm the rules and procedures to be complied with, and explain the consequences of failing to comply with them. In some high-risk areas of employment, a consequence may well be termination of the contract.
- For agency temps, the best advice is to clarify the position of health and safety in the contract with the agency, confirming this by instructions to the temps themselves. Where there are problems, the matter should be raised informally with the temp but formally only with the agency. It is important that the employer has complied with its responsibilities regarding health and safety, but the disciplinary role should be undertaken by the agency.

Summary points

- Health and safety is a distinctive area of law and management. Duties are less dependent on the employment category of staff, so duties towards non-employees are significant. Responsibilities cannot be delegated or opted out of.
- Health and safety law recognizes the particular risks that are posed through the use of non-employees. This implies that extra care must be taken for those unfamiliar with the workplace, for those used to different policies and practices regarding health and safety, and for the coordination of work where two or more employers are involved in activities.
- There will likely have to be discrete procedures and practices for induction, training and supervision and, where other employers are involved, for liaison and effective coordinated management.
- There should be a clear role for HRM in these matters, and a clear assessment of the health, safety and welfare aspects of using non-employees. Such matters as access to health-care facilities, sports facilities, etc., should be considered.

10

Reflections and futures

Some reflections

In our exploration of some of the HRM issues that arise from the supply of skill needs by people who are not employees of the organization, we have made considerable use of the experience, insights and observations of those with hands-on involvement in this increasingly important topic. Research data, especially from employing organizations themselves, is limited – not least because non-employees are not yet an integral and accepted part of the HRM agenda.

Research that has been undertaken has often been from a macroeconomic perspective, with less emphasis on the motivations, aspirations and expectations of non-employees themselves. Our own case studies and interviews can in no way be considered a representative sample; the people who provided many valuable comments did so in a personal capacity and made no claims for having developed any uniquely effective systems for the successful management of non-employees. They nonetheless reported on what had worked for them and what they had learned from using or being non-employees. They were very conscious of the anomalies and paradoxes inherent in the supply or employment of the different types of non-employees. They also generally appreciated that this is a topic that, for many managers and for most academics and textbook writers, is 'off the radar'.

A number of clear impressions have emerged from the case studies, sometimes corroborating research that has been undertaken by others into the topic.

First, there is the low-key role played by HRM practitioners in the strategic decisions to, say, outsource or use agencies, but often also in the day-to-day management of non-employees once they are at the employing organization. There is often ambivalence as to how performance management of non-employees is undertaken, and an apparent unwillingness of HRM to be proactive in this matter in many employing organizations. Many we spoke to who are not from HRM regretted this low-key role and would welcome more active participation in, say, contract negotiations, monitoring contracts, and assessment of whether using non-employees is proving effective or not. We found few examples of coherent policy development regarding the use of non-employees (although there were many examples of good practice), and little evidence of a willingness to apply to non-employees best practice from the employment of employees. Often, decisions are made *ad hoc*, dependent on the preferences of individual managers. Although there are many good examples of effectively using freelancers, contract workers and temps, and of outsourcing, practices are often fragmented and variable.

We found little evidence of HRM policies and practices specifically designed to respond to the distinctive characteristics and expectations of non-employees. In particular, there is little evidence of training for line managers in dealing with the issues generated by the employment of temps, freelancers, etc. Line managers have a critical role and many are clearly, in a practical sense, very effective in dealing with the recruitment, induction and performance management of temps and freelancers, etc. Nonetheless, there are many opportunities to systemize good practice and integrate the training of non-employees into mainstream work.

Second, we have a clear sense, not just from the UK but from many other countries, that there are significant changes occurring in terms of what people want from work and how they can achieve it. Many spoke of employment relationships being on a spectrum rather than in separate boxes. The gold-collar workers are clear examples of change within standard employment, but there are also temps who now have careers with agencies and others who work serially for outsourcing companies. The growing complexity of employment relationships is a matter that emerged very strongly from the case studies and other research.

It may well be that the 'portfolio career' is not a reality for more than a handful of people, but there is continuing evidence of the rejection of standard employment by (especially but not only) young and highly

254

skilled people. For them, the traditional bureaucratic organization holds little thrall. They have an interest in greater mobility and in increased variety of work experience. Interestingly, agencies and organizations that support freelance and similar work recognize these changes and are aiming to provide different but effective work opportunities. The increasing coherence among intermediaries, especially the larger agencies, is also reflected in their involvement in partnerships and similar relationships with employing organizations. This brings greater structure and reliability to supply of interim skills. Such developments mean that the often assumed precariousness of temping and freelance work is considerably reduced, and notions of a 'career' are dramatically changed. We are unsure from our discussions regarding the extent to which these changes are informing HRM thinking.

Third, we note the different approaches and attitudes towards non-employees in employing organizations. In some, they remain marginal or within the shadows. Managers are still suspicious of people who do not appear to have or want a 'proper job'. They are apparently unwilling to invest time and energy in them, and see employee status as the only or primary basis for effective employment.

In others, there is a strong sense that although non-employees are different, they make a valuable contribution to an organization. Some in our case studies spoke in glowing terms of the high levels of skills and experience they bring. Sometimes these are reported as higher than those of their employees. When analysing what factors would tend to the latter approach to non-employees (which is also likely to maximize the performance of non-employees), we have reached a number of tentative conclusions. The types of organizations where non-employees are accepted and valued tend to combine some, if not all, particular features. These organizations generally:

- are newly established rather than traditional
- are in highly specialized/highly skilled work
- have senior staff committed to maximizing skills, regardless of the basis they are employed on
- have open and flexible management styles
- have an emphasis on measuring performance through output
- are open to new ideas, especially in a context of increased competition or work pressure

■ have an HRM function committed to reviewing options for skills delivery, skills maximizing and a strategic view of human resource management, combined with a policy to integrate HRM in all aspects of workforce development.

Interestingly, these are the self-same features that appear likely to ensure equal opportunities at work. Research shows that organizations that have diverse workforces and do not present barriers to traditionally disadvantaged groups in the labour market also tend to be new, fast-moving, open and flexible, and to recruit, reward and promote purely on the basis of talent (Leighton. 2004). There is considerable food for thought here.

Futures

This section is concerned with a possible agenda for the effective management of non-employees. The agenda has been devised in the light of the experience from case studies and other research data.

Effective management of non-employees depends on transformation of a number of key organizational assumptions and procedures. HRM is critical to these changes. It is suggested that attention be given to the following issues.

1. *Attitude/culture/behaviour*:
   ■ Recognition that non-employees now make up an important part of the labour market and, at individual employing organizations, comprise anything up to half of the total workforce. They are, though, distinctive from employees in many ways, not least in terms of their aspirations and expectations of the workplace and individual employers.
   ■ Recognition that these workers are not 'marginal', 'atypical' or 'peripheral', but now perform core services that underpin and maintain the organization's competitiveness, brand image and reputation.
   ■ Recognition that while some outsourced, agency or self-employed workers see their pattern of work as a second-best option, the majority choose to work this way for distinct social and economic reasons – and consequently they have needs and expectations that are distinct from those of employees but that require equal and specific attention.

- Recognition that attention needs to be paid as to the extent to which existing HR practices are relevant to non-employees and/or whether distinctive practices need to evolve.
- Recognition that the attitudes and role of line managers is crucial to effective management of non-employees.
- Recognition that if there are moves to increase or change the composition of the non-employee workforce, there needs to be a direct link with organizational policies regarding change management.

2. *Processes.* The central issue is whether HR processes reflect the attitudinal requirements referred to above. If the attitudinal and cultural issues are taken on board, they need to be mainstreamed in all aspects of HR decision-making. The processes by which these workers are selected, supervised, appraised and motivated need to reflect this change in attitude and culture. Whether undertaken directly by the parent organization or by an intermediary, processes that need specific attention include:

- Identification of the appropriate model for use of non-employees (hands-off, integration or partnership).
- Contracts and work agreements that reflect the realities and distinct requirements of these ways of working.
- Induction and training that supports non-employees' work.
- Supervision and management control, firmly grounded in project- and team-based principles, that properly integrates the non-employee into the mainstream operations and culture of the organization and that ensures they are as motivated and engaged in their work as are their full-time colleagues.
- Performance management and appraisal that recognize the distinct and varying needs and aspirations of outsourced, agency and self-employed workers while at the same time reflecting the core goals and aims of the organization.
- Data management and protection procedures that reflect the temporary or off-site nature of many of these relationships but protect the integrity of sensitive, organization-specific information.

3. *Role of HR practitioners*:

- HR practitioners need to be actively involved in the contract specifications, service level agreements, manpower planning, skills assessments and change management strategies that precede and underpin outsourcing, agency and consultancy agreements. This should be left to procurement managers as, inevitably, the people management imperatives and requirements of these agreements, which our own and other research suggests are so important to the success of the contract, may be overlooked or downplayed.

- As part of their emerging role as 'partners to the business', HR practitioners should be able to advise and support line managers in their effective use of outsourced, agency and self-employed workers – based on the portfolio of HR services and processes outlined above.
- Even when the recruitment, training and supervision of these workers is undertaken by an intermediary organization, the relationship of these workers to the client or parent organization should be a key HR concern – especially in those circumstances where these workers are undertaking services that directly impact on the organization's core activities, brand image or reputation. The psychological contract between these workers and the parent/client organization, although determined by different imperatives on both sides, is as important as that which shapes the relationship with its own employees.

It has to be recognized that fulfilling these roles is dependent on the position that HR occupies within the employing organization. Where HR has moved to a strategic function allied to the business objectives, its role as an advocate for people issues, especially individual ones, will likely have declined. However, much of the research for this book indicates that temps and freelance staff in particular feel an acute need for support and advocates within employing organizations. Given that many non-employees are 'semi-detached' from the organization, their need for effective communication, feedback and a sense of engagement requires a response.

This poses major challenges for HRM, especially where the HR function has been delegated to line managers to a lesser or greater extent. Establishing consistent and supportive policies with, perhaps, a clear framework requires drive and direction from HR.

How can this be achieved within a devolved and facilitating system for line managers? How can you ensure that temps are recruited from 'good' agencies? That the qualifications and experience of freelancers have been fully vetted and they will respond to the culture of the organization? How can you ensure that a cleaning contract or a contract for the provision or watering of plants for the reception area is carried out by people who do not have a criminal record or other problematic factors in their background? Are there useful models that can be drawn on that would, for example, attach a central member of the HR team to a local function?

These are challenging and important issues. Nothing is simple with the employment of non-employees. However, what *is* clear is that with effective management and management that recognizes their distinctive qualities and motivation, using non-employees can enhance the quality of work and service delivery of an organization.

Annex A: Case studies and contact details

Clients

BP

BP is a major global energy company, and employs over 96 000 people. Its headquarters are in the UK. The case study was based on BP's Coryton Refinery in Essex, UK. There 550 staff are employed as employees, but a further 250 as non-employees – mainly agency temps.

Website: www.bp.com

Contact: Jeff House, formerly in the HR department, has recently taken early retirement (jeffhouse@talktalk.net).

BT (British Telecom)

One of the world's leading providers of communication services, BT operates in Europe, the Americas and the Asia-Pacific region. Within the UK, there are around 130 000 employees and a further 30 00 non-employees. Many of these are agency temps or freelance staff.

Website: www.bt.com

Contact: Caroline Waters, of the HR department (caroline.waters@ bt.com).

The Children's Mutual

This is a long-established mutual organization (i.e. belongs to its members) that is the only UK organization in the UK financial services sector specializing exclusively in savings for children. It is based in south-east England, UK and works in partnership with leading Banks, Building Societies and High Street retailers of children's goods and services. In 2004 it outsourced back office, support and delivery, though it keeps core leadership, marketing and customer champion activities at its headquarters.

Website: www.thechildrensmutual.co.uk

Contact: David Bornor, Head of Human Resources (David.bornor@ thechildrensmutual.co.uk).

'Further education college'

This is a medium-sized further education college in eastern England. It has outsourced for a variety of services, including cleaning and catering.

Contact: Sally Worsley-Speck, a former senior lecturer (Sally.worsley-speck@capita.co.uk).

GlaxoSmithKline (GSK)

GSK is one of the largest global pharmaceutical companies, and has grown predominantly through mergers and acquisitions. Its headquarters are in west London. Although most of the staff are employees, there are significant numbers of temps and contract workers.

Website: www.gsk.com

Contact: John Raywood, member of the HR department but also Secretary to the European Employee Consultation Forum (Works Council) (John.r. raywood@ gsk.com).

Henry Jones Art Hotel

A former 1820s jam factory and warehouse, the Henry Jones Art Hotel is situated in Hobart, Tasmania – Australia's southernmost state. In less than two years the hotel has become a national and international award winner in terms of tourism, architecture and training. The hotel's focus is on service excellence in an industry traditionally known for its use of contingent or peripheral labour.

Website: http://www.thehenryjones.com

Contact: Richard Crawford, Director and co-owner (richard.crawford@ thehenryjones.com).

Principality Building Society, Wales

The Principality is a steadily expanding mutual society in financial services with strong community links. All fifty-one of its branches are in Wales or on its borders, and its headquarters are in Cardiff. Most staff are employees, although there is a slightly growing number of temps and contract workers.

Website: www.principality.co.uk

Contact: Brian Kultschar, Head of Human Resources (Brian.kultschar@ principality.co.uk).

Regulatory Body, UK

This Body operates within a legislative framework, undertakes investigations and, as appropriate, enforces the legislation. Laura Sykes is the fictitious name of an experienced and senior manager.

RWA

RWA is a medium-sized software company specializing in products for the travel and tourism industry. It is based in south Wales, north of Cardiff. Some staff are employees, but others are freelance/contract staff. In 2004, it outsourced some of its software writing to India.

Website: www.rwa-net.co.uk

Contact: Robert Wortham, Director (r.wortham@rwa-net.co.uk).

Service providers

Dominic Brender (an alias)

Dominic Brender is a well-established researcher and management writer, based in London, UK. He has worked for leading research bodies, and is the author of several books. He has been self-employed for over twenty years, and has wide and varied experience of clients and work relationships.

Contact: michelsyrett@aol.com

Pattie Pierce (an alias)

Pattie Pierce has worked as a temp for many years and currently is on the books of a leading global agency. She suffers from an intermittent health problem that makes it difficult to sustain a permanent job. She has undertaken a wide variety of roles within employing organizations as a temp.

Contact: michelsyrett@aol.com

Capita Learning and Development, UK

Capita Learning and Development is part of the major service provider, Capita plc, which specializes in technical services, IT, business process and HR outsourcing. Capita Learning and Development provides training on an in-house as well as a public basis, and supplies consultants to clients for training and other specialisms.

Website: www.capita-Ld.co.uk

Contact: Chris Sharp, Director, UK Learning and Development (Chris. sharp@capita.co.uk).

Kelly Services Ltd

Kelly, UK and Ireland, is part of the global employment agency, Kelly Services, which was founded in the USA in 1946. Kelly operates in twenty-seven countries and is expanding, especially in Eastern Europe and the Asia-Pacific region. It offers a wide range of skills, but is moving to more specialized provision. It operates on a partnership basis with many leading UK employers.

Website: www.kellyservices.co.uk

Contact: Darren Cox, Director, Human Resources, UK and Ireland (dcox@kellyservices.co.uk).

Manpower, France

Manpower has operations in 72 countries worldwide. In France it has 1130 agencies for temporary work (intérimaires). The Institute Manpower researches labour market and HRM issues. Manpower, France emphasizes its role for people with disabilities and provides structured and supportive work opportunities.

Website: www.manpower.fr

Contact: Jean-François Denoy, Director of Human Resources (Jean-francois.denoy@manpower.fr).

RSA Pharmarecruit

RSA is a fast-growing specialist agency in the pharmaceuticals industry, and is now diversifying into other skills areas. It operates in the UK and Germany, with its headquarters in Hatfield, southern England. Although its core business is providing staff for permanent posts, it has significant numbers of specialist temps.

Website: www.theRSA-group.com

Contact: Nick Stevens, CEO (Nick.stevens@theRSA-group.com).

Searson Buck

Searson Buck is Tasmania's largest locally-owned recruitment, retention and people management firm. It offers temporary, permanent and executive recruitment services, and specializes in human resource services. A national award-winner for small to medium enterprises, it employs several hundred temps every week.

Website: www.searsonbuck.com.au

Contact: Stephen Porter, Director (SPorter@searsonbuck.com.au).

SKILLED Group Ltd

SKILLED Group Ltd was the first Australian skilled labour company to take on full-time employees to provide supplementary trades and labour hire. The company employs people in every major sector of industry and in most geographic areas of Australia and New Zealand. Rated by *Forbes* magazine as one of the best performing non-US companies with a turnover of less than US$1 billion for the years 2002 and 2003, it is effectively one of the largest employers in Australia.

Website: www.skilled.com.au

Contact: Jessica Schauble, Manager, Corporate Strategy (jschauble@skilled.com.au).

Support/advice systems, etc., regarding non-employees

CAST

CAST is an organization that provides innovative forms of support for self-employed persons and entrepreneurs. It has partners in the alternative finance sector, and aims to enhance skills and confidence through 'twinning' people with older, experienced mentors, and provision of coaching support and networking opportunities.

Website: www.cast-org.eu

Contact: Nic de Potter, Director (n.depotter@cast.org-net.eu).

ETUC-ETUI-REHS

ETUI (the European Trade Union Institute) is part of ETUC (the European Trades Union Confederation) and is primarily concerned with research and policy development in employment relations/social dialogue and related topics. This includes research and policy on atypical workers, and their regulation. It is based in Brussels.

Website: www.etuc.org

Contact: Stefan Clauwaert, Senior Researcher (s.clauwaert@etui-rehs.org).

MEDEF, France

MEDEF is the leading employers' organization in France, based in Paris. It includes the Institute Esprit Service, which is committed to developing best practice in outsourcing. It hosts a Europe-wide committee to consider best practice in outsourcing contracts, and has produced a number of key publications on outsourcing.

Website: www.medef.fr

Contact: Alain Tedaldi, Institute Esprit Service (atedaldi@medef.fr)

Morgan-Cole, Solicitors

Morgan-Cole is a well established firm of solicitors (notaries) with branches in southern England and south Wales. One of its specialisms is providing advice on outsourcing, especially IT outsourcing contracts. Its clients include many public bodies and large private-sector employers.

Website: www.morgan-cole.com

Annex B: The management models explained

The model on page 91 (Figure 4.1) is based on research by Ravi Aron, Assistant Professor of Operations and Information Management and Jitendra V. Sing, Professor of Management, at the University of Pennsylvania's Wharton School at Philadelphia (Aron and Sing 2005). This suggests that the level of risk involved in outsourcing or off sharing work to an external agency is determined by two factors:

■ The extent to which the work can be effectively 'codified', so that external workers can understand and be trained to undertake it.
■ The extent to which the output of the work can be effectively monitored and measured and thus form the basis for contractual service performance indicators (SPIs).

Thus in the model the work that is both easy to codify and to measure – often based around simple transactions – affords the least risk, while the work that is most nebulous affords the most. The latter should therefore be kept within the parent company while the former can be easily outsourced.

These decisions are fairly clear cut. More careful consideration is needed where the two measures are in conflict. This is illustrated by Figure 4.2 on page 98, which demonstrates how the model could be used to assess the risk of outsourcing or off-shoring in the case of an insurance company like Alpha Corp (see page 87).

Thus easy to codify and measure transactions like claim processing and technical support can be easily outsourced, while strategic processes such as pricing policies and product design are best kept in-house. Sophisticated SPIs are required when considering outsourcing tasks like insurance underwriting or cash flow forecasting (easy to codify, difficult to measure) or supply chain coordination and data processing (difficult to codify, easy to measure).

A similar approach is used in the model on pages 192–3. Here the risk model is applied to the possibility of complex legal actions that might arise from the use of non-employees. Once again, transactional work like catering or security afford the least risk of legal action while agency work affords the most, with a mixed level of risk in the case of business sensitive activities like childcare and the use of freelancers and self-employed people.

References and sources

Adams, D. (2005). Boot now on worker's foot. *The Age*, 17 September.

Ahlstrand, B., Lampel, J. and Mintzberg, H. (1999). Strategy, blind men and the elephant. *Financial Times*, 27 September.

Andrews, K. (2005). Media release: 'Action to protect independent contractors'. Department of Employment and Workplace Relations, 30 March.

Anonymous (2004). Nurses bid for shifts on the Internet. *Physicians Financial News*, **22(2)**, 12.

Anonymous (2005). Boots signs £400 m outsourcing deal. *Personnel Today*, 7 June, 4.

Arnold, C. (1995). *Outsourcing Contracts*. FT Law and Tax.

Arnold, J. (1996). The psychological contract: a concept in need of closer scrutiny? *European Journal of Work and Organizational Psychology*, **5(4)**, 511–520.

Aron, R. and Singh, J. V. (2005). Getting offshoring right. *Harvard Business Review*, December.

Aselage, J. and Eisenberger, R. (2003). Perceived organizational support and psychological contracts: a theoretical integration. *Journal of Organizational Behavior*, **24**, 491–509.

Atkinson, J. (1984a). Manpower strategies for flexible organisations. *Personnel Management*, 28–31 August.

Atkinson, J. (1984b). *Flexibility, Uncertainty and Manpower Management*. IMS Report No. 89, Institute of Manpower Studies.

Atkinson, J. and Rick, J. (1996). *Temporary Work and the Labour Market*, Report 311. Institute of Employment Studies.

Australia Council of Trade Unions (ACTU) (2005). *Factory Workers Forced Into Sham 'Independent Contractor' Scheme* (available at http:// www.actu.asn.au/public/news/ 1115869115_30952.html).

Australian Associated Press (2005). Government looks abroad to fill 20 000 skills gap. *Australian National News Wire*, 16 August.

Australian Bureau of Statistics (2000). *Survey of Employment Arrangements and Superannuation*. ABS Cat. No. 6361.0.

Australian Bureau of Statistics (2003). *ABS Labour Market Statistics*. ABS Cat. No. 6106.0.55.001.

Australian Bureau of Statistics (2005a). *Australian Labour Market Statistics*. Cat. No. 6105.0l.

Australian Bureau of Statistics (2005b). *Australian Social Trends: Nursing workers*. Cat. No. 4102.0.

Australian Centre for Industrial Relations Research and Training (ACIRRT) (1999). *Australia at Work: Just Managing*. Prentice-Hall.

Australian Senate Inquiry into Nursing (2002). *The Patient Profession: A time for action*. June.

Baden, S. and Peters, D. (2006). Cleaners want fair pay. *Geelong Advertiser*, 21 April.

Bahrami, H. and Evans, S. (1997). Human resource leadership in knowledge-based entities: shaping the context of work. *Human Resource Management*, **36(1)**, 23–28.

Baker, K., Olsen, J. and Morisseau, D. (1994). Work practices, fatigue and nuclear power plant safety performance. *Human Factors*, **36(2)**, 244–257.

Bamber, G. (1990). Flexible work organisation: inferences from Britain and Australia. *Asia Pacific Human Resource Management*, **28(3)**, 28–44.

Barnes, D. (1999). *Perspectives on Total Rewards: Recruitment and Retention*. Towers Perrin.

Barney, J. B. (1991). Firm resources and sustained competitive advantage. *Journal of Management*, **17**, 99–120.

Barney, J. B. and Wright, P. M. (1998). On becoming a strategic partner: the role of human resources in gaining competitive advantage. *Human Resource Management*, **37(1)**, 31–46.

Bell, S. (1993). *Australian Manufacturing and the State: the politics of industry policy in the post-war era*. Cambridge University Press.

Bernstein, B. (2003). *Economic Perspective for the Agency Work Industry*. CIETT Congress.

Berry, M. (2005). My baptism of fire: by new Gate Gourmet HR director. *Personnel Today*, 30 August, 1.

Blackler, F. (1995). Knowledge, knowledge work and organizations: an overview and interpretation. *Organization Studies*, **16(6)**, 1021–1046.

Blau, P. M. (1964). *Exchange and Power in Social Life*. Wiley.

Bridges, W. (1994). *Job-shift*. Nicholas Brealey.

Bright, J. (1994). Teleworking: the strategic benefits. *Telecommunications*, **28(11)**, 81–82.

Brown, M. and Ainsworth, S. (2000). A review and integration of research on employee participation in Australia 1983–1999. Centre For Employment And Labour Relations Law, Working Paper No. 18.

Campbell, I. and Burgess, J. (2001). A new estimate of casual employment? *Australian Bulletin of Labour*, **27(2)**, 85–108.

Cannon, D. (1995). *Generation X and the New Work Ethic*. Demos.

Cappelli, P. (2001). Why is it so hard to find information technology workers? *Organisational Dynamics*, **30(2)**, 87–99.

Capelli, P. and Rogovsky, N. (1994). New work systems and skill requirements. *International Labour Review*, **133**, 205–220.

Casey, C. and Alach, P. (2004). Just a temp? Women, temporary employment and lifestyle. *Work, Employment and Society*, **18**, 459–460.

Cetron, M. J. and Davies, O. (2005). Trends now shaping the future. *The Futurist*, **39(3)**.

China Staff (2004/2005). 'Gold collar' class on the rise. *China* Staff, **11(1)**, 33.

CIPD (2006). *Off-shoring and the Role of HR*. CIPD.

Connell, J. and Burgess, J. (2002). In search of flexibility: implications for temporary agency workers and human resource management. *Australian Bulletin of Labour*, **28(4)**, 272–283.

Conway, N. and Briner, R. B. (2002). Full-time versus part-time employees: understanding the links between work status, the psychological contract, and attitudes. *Journal of Vocational Behavior*, **61**, 279–301.

Cooper, G. and Vermey, K. (2005). *Independent Contractors and Labour Hire Workers – Proposed Legislative Reform*. Freehills (available at http://www.freehills.com.au/publications/publications_4998.asp).

Coyle-Shapiro, J. and Kessler, I. (2000). Consequences of the psychological contract for the employment relationship: a large scale survey. *Journal of Management Studies*, **37(7)**, 903–930.

Crainer, S. and Dearlove, D. (2000). *Generation Entrepreneur*. Pearson Education.

Crutchfield-George, B. and Gaut, D. (2006). Preparing university students for the globalised economy: an interdisciplinary, cross-cultural approach to discussing legal issues associated with the offshore business process outsourcing – the case of India Paper for the Association of Law Teacher's Annual Conference, Norwich, UK, April 2006.

CSIRO (1995/1996). *Annual Report*. CSIRO.

CSIRO (1996). Corporate Focus Group, Strategic Action Plan. CSIRO Australia.

CSIRO (2001). *Australian Science, Australia's Future*. ACT CSIRO.

Cummings, K. (1986). *Outworkers and Subcontractors: non-standard employment and industrial democracy*. Working Environment Branch, Department of Employment and Industrial Relations, Canberra. AGPS.

Davenport, T., Jarenpaa, S. and Beers, M. (1996). Improving knowledge work processes. *Slaon Management Review*, **Summer**, 53–65.

Deery, M. and Jago, L. K. (2002). The core and the periphery: an examination of the flexible workforce model in the hotel industry. *Hospitality Management*, **21**, 339–351.

De Vos, A., Buyens, D. and Schalk, R. (2003). Psychological contract development during organizational socialization: adaptation to reality and the role of reciprocity. *Journal of Organizational Behavior*, **24**, 537–559.

DiPaolo, A. (2004). Outsource, but train those who remain. *Chief Executive*, **November**, 20.

Dodd, J. (2003). Humane Management: Hu-Management KK: getting personal with a JASDAQ-listed outplacement performer. *Japan, Inc. Communications*, **May**.

Doeringer, P. and Priore, M. (1971). *Internal Labour Markets*. D. C. Heath.

Drucker, P. (1993). *Post-Capitalist Society*. Butterworth-Heinemann.

Drucker, P. (1999). Knowledge-worker productivity: the biggest challenge. *California Management Review*, **41(2)**, 79–94.

Drucker, J. and Stanworth, C. (2005). Mutual expectations: a study of the three-way relationship between employment agencies, their client organisations and white collar agency 'temps'. *Industrial Relations Journal*, **36**, 58–75.

DTI (2002). Discussion Document on Employment Status in Relation to Statutory Employment Rights. URN/02. Department of Trade and Industry.

DTI (2004). *Guidance on the Conduct of Employment Agencies and Employment Businesses Regulations, 2003*. Department of Trade and Industry.

EC (2005a). *Employment in Europe*. European Commission.

EC (2005b). Press release, 20 November. European Commission.

Economist Intelligence Unit (2005a). *Business 2010 in Asia-Pacific: embracing the challenge of change*. EIU.

Economist Intelligence Unit (2005b). *Business 2010 in Europe: embracing the challenge of change*. EIU.

Economist Intelligence Unit (2005c). *Business 2010: embracing the challenge of change*. EIU.

EL (2005). *Employers Law*, March. London rbi.

Emmott, M. and Hutchinson, S. (1998). Employment flexibility: threat or promise? In: P. Sparrow and M. Marchington (eds), *Human Resource Management: The New Agenda*. Financial Times/Pitmans, pp. 229–244.

Employers Law (2005). Reed Business Information.

European Foundation (2005). Industrial Relations in the EU, Japan and the USA 2003–4. European Foundation for the Improvement of Living and Working Conditions.

Evening Standard (2006). 9 February.

Finegold, D., Levenson, A. and Van Buren, M. (2005). Access to training and its impact on temporary workers. *Human Resource Management Journal*, **15**, 66–82.

Fojt, M. (1995). Leading the knowledge workers of the 1990s. *Journal of Services Marketing*, **9(3)**, 5–6.

Forbes (2002). Best under a billion. (Available at http://www.forbes.com/ global/2002/ 1028/048tab.html.)

Forbes (2003). Best under a billion. (Available at http://www.forbes.com/ global/2002/ 1028/048tab.html.)

Garrahan, P. and Stewart, P. (1992). *The Nissan Enigma: Flexibility at Work in a Local Economy*. Mansell.

Geary, J. (1992). Employment flexibility and human resource management. *Work, Employment and Society*, **6(2)**, 251–270.

Ghoshal, S. and Bartlett, C. (1998). *The Individualised Corporation*. William Heinemann, Random House.

Goldman Sachs (2003). *Economic Perspectives for the Agency Work Industry*. Goldman Sachs/CIETT.

Goman, C. K. (2004). Forces of change. *Information Outlook*, **8(5)**, 34–36.

Gospel, H. (2004). *Quality of Working Life: a review of changes in work organisation, conditions of employment and work–life arrangements*. ILO.

Grant, D. (1999). HRM, rhetoric and the psychological contract: a case of 'easier said than done'. *International Journal of Human Resource Management*, **10(2)**, 327–350.

Green and Cohen (1995).

Guest, D. E. (1998a). Is the psychological contract worth taking seriously? *Journal of Organizational Behaviour*, **19(S1)**, 649–664.

Guest, D. E. (1998b). On meaning, metaphor and the psychological contract: a response to Rousseau. *Journal of Organizational Behaviour*, **19(S1)**, 673–677.

Guest, D. E. and Clinton, M. (2006). Temporary Employment Contracts, Workers' Well-being and Behaviour: evidence from the UK Department of Management Working Paper No. 38, King's College, London.

Guest, D. E. and Conway, N. (2004). *Employee Well-being and the Psychological Contract*. CIPD.

Gruerrier, Y. and Lockwood, A. (1989). Core and periphery employees in hotel operations. *Personnel Review*, **18(1)**, 9–15.

Guerre, L. (2000). *European Guide to Outsourcing*. MEDEF/European Commission, pp. 24–25.

Guzzo, R. A. and Noonan, K. A. (1994). Human resource practices as communications and the psychological contract. *Human Resource Management*, **33(3)**, 447–462.

Hamilton, C. and Mail, E. (2003). Downshifting in Australia: a sea-change in the pursuit of happiness. The Australia Institute, Discussion Paper No. 50.

Harari, O. (1995). The brain-based organisation. *Management Review*, **83(6)**, 57–65.

Harding, M. (2005). *Independent Contractors Act: employees to contractors – why is it an issue?* Association of Professional Engineers, Scientists and Managers, Australia (APESMA) (available at www. apesma.asn.au/connect/newsletters/independent_contractors_act.pdf).

Harwood, R. (2003). The psychological contract and remote working. An interview with Denise Rousseau. *Ahoy Magazine*, **January** (available at www.odysseyzone.com/news/hot/rousseau.htm).

Hecker, R. and Grimmer, M. (2005). The evolving psychological contract. In: P. Holland and H. De Cieri (eds), *Contemporary Issues in Human Resource Development*. Pearson Education, pp. 220–259.

Heery, E. (2005). The trade union response to agency labour in Britain. *Industrial Relations Journal*, **35**, 435–450.

Helman, S. W. (2002). Training program helps hospital fill nursing void. *Boston Globe*, 1 January, B2.

Hendry, C., Bradley, P. and Perkins, S. (1997). Missed a motivator? *People Management*, **3(10)**, 21–25.

Herriot, P. and Pemberton, C. (1997). Facilitating new deals. *Human Resource Management Journal*, **7(1)**, 45–56.

Hetherington, L. (2002). Training the contingent workforce. *Canadian HR Reporter*, **15(20)**, G5.

Hill, R. and Stewart, J. (2000). Human resource development in small organizations. *Journal of European Industrial Training*, **24(2/3/4)**, 105–117.

Hiltrop, J.-M. (1995a). Managing the changing psychological contract. *Employee Relations*, **18(1)**, 36–49.

Hiltrop, J.-M. (1995b). The changing psychological contract: the human resource challenge of the 1990s. *European Management Journal*, **13(3)**, 286–294.

Holland, P. J., Hecker, R. and Steen, J. (2002). Human resource strategies and organisational structures for managing gold collar workers. *Journal of European Industrial Training*, **26(2)**, 72–80.

Holland, P. J., Hecker, R. and Steen, J. (2002). Human resource strategies and organisational structures for managing gold-collar workers. *Journal of European Industrial Training*, **26(2/3/4)**, 72–80.

Hottop, U. (2002). *Recruitment Agencies in the UK*. Department of Trade and Industry.

Housing Industry Association (HIA) (2005). *HIA Welcomes Move to Protect Independent Contractors* (available at www.buildingonline.com.au).

HR Focus (2005). Contingent workforce brings more questions than answers. *HR Focus*, **82(70)**, 6–7.

HR Monthly (1997). Succession still being left to chance, survey reveals. *HR Monthly*, **September**, 7.

Huselid, M. A. (1995). The impact of human resource management on turnover, productivity, and corporate financial performance. *Academy of Management Journal*, **38**, 635–672.

Huselid, M. A., Jackson, S. E. and Schuler, R. S. (1997). Technical and strategic human resource management effectiveness as determinates of firm performance. *Academy of Management Journal*, **40**, 171–188.

Institute for Employment Studies (2004). *Skills Pay: the contribution of skills to business success*. Institute for Employment Studies.

International Labour Review, **133(2)**, 205–220.

International Labour Office World Employment Report (2001). ILO.

International Labour Office World Employment Report (2005). ILO.

ITNTO/AISS (1999). Skills 99 – IT Skills Summary. Report to DTI and DfEE, IT National Training Organisation and the Alliance for Information Systems Skills (AISS).

Kabanoff, B., Jimmieson, N. L. and Lewis, M. J. (2000). Psychological contracts in Australia: a 'fair go' or a 'not-so-happy transition'? In: D. M. Rousseau and R. Schalk (eds), *Psychological Contracts in Employment: Cross Cultural Perspectives*. Sage Publications, pp. 29–47.

Kelley, R. (1990). *The Gold Collar Worker: Harnessing the Brainpower of the New Workforce*. Addison-Wesley.

Kennedy, C. (2001). *Managing with the Gurus*, 5th edn. Random House.

Key Note (2003). *Market Report – Recruitment Agencies (Temporary and Contract)*. Mintel.

Key Note (2004). *Market Report – Contract Cleaning*. Mintel.

Key Note (2006). *Market Report– Recruitment Agencies (Temporary and Contract)*. Mintel.

Kidder, D. L. (1995). On Call or Answering a Calling? Temporary nurses and extra-role behaviors. Paper presented at the Annual Meeting of the Academy of Management, Vancouver.

King, J. E. (2000). White-collar reactions to job insecurity and the role of the psychological contract: implications for human resource management. *Human Resource Management*, **39(1)**, 79–91.

Labour Force Survey (2000) (available online at www.dfes.gov.uk/statistics).

Lammiman, J. and Syrett, M. (2004). *CoolSearch: keeping your organisation in touch and on the edge*. Capstone/Wiley.

Legge, K. (1995). *Human Resource Management: Rhetorics and Realities*. Macmillan.

Legge, K. (1998). Flexibility: the gift wrapping of employment degradation? In: P. Sparrow and M. Marchington (eds), *Human Resource Management: The New Agenda*. Financial Times/Pitmans, pp. 286–295.

Leighton, P. (1985). *UK Report to the International Labour Office: Sub-contracting for Services*. ILO.

Leighton, P. (1990). Confidential report based on research and consultancy.

Leighton, P. (1995). *UK Report to the International Labour Office: Outsourcing for Services*. ILO.

Leighton, P. (1998). *Self-employment in the UK: Law and practice in obstacles to the creation of micro-businesses in Europe*. European Commission.

Leighton, P. (2002). *UK National Report for the European Guide to Outsourcing*. MEDEF.

Leighton, P. (2004). *Discrimination and the Law: does the system suit the purpose?* CIPD.

Leighton, P. and Proctor, G. (2006). *Recruiting within the Law.* Thorogood Publishing.

Leighton, P. and Syrett, M. (1989). *New Work Patterns: putting policy into practice.* Pitman.

Leopold, J., Harris, L. and Watson, T. (2004). *The Strategic Management of Human Resources.* FT Prentice-Hall.

Lester, S.W., Turnley, W. H., Bloodgood, J. M. and Bolino, M. C. (2002). Not seeing eye to eye: differences in supervisor and subordinate perceptions of and attributions for psychological contract breach. *Journal of Organizational Behavior,* **23**, 39–56.

Lewis-McClear, K. and Taylor, M. S. (1997). Not seeing eye-to-eye: implications of discrepant psychological contracts and contract violation for the employment relationship. *Academy of Management Proceedings,* 335–339.

Macdonald, S. (1998). *Information for Innovation.* Oxford University Press.

MacNeil, I. R. (1985). Relational contract: what we do and do not know. *Wisconsin Law Review,* **3**, 483–525.

MacNeil, I. R. (2000). Relational contract theory: challenges and queries. *Northwestern University Law Review,* **94**, 877–907.

Mallon, M. and Duberley, J. (2000). Managers and professionals in the contingent workforce. *Human Resource Management Journal,* **10(1)**, 33–47.

Mangan, J. (2000). *Working Without Traditional Employment: an international study of non-standard employment.* Edward Elgar.

Manpower Argus (2001). *Employee Turnover Costs in the US.* Manpower, 5 January.

Marchington, M., Grimshaw, D., Rubery, J. and Willmott, H. (2004). *Fragmenting Work: blurring organisational boundaries and disordering hierarchies.* Oxford University Press.

Marks, A. (2001). Developing a multiple foci conceptualisation of the psychological contract. *Employee Relations,* **23(5)**, 454–467.

Masanauskas, J. (2006). Cleaners seek better deal. *Herald Sun (Melbourne),* 21 April.

McDonald, D. J. and Makin, P. J. (2000). The psychological contract, organisational commitment and job satisfaction of temporary staff. *Leadership and Organization Development Journal,* **21(1/2)**, 84–91.

McKeown, T. (2005). Non-standard employment: when even the elite are precarious. *Journal of Industrial Relations,* **47(3)**, 276–293.

McLagan, P. (1989). Models for HRD practice. *Training and Development Journal,* **43(9)**, 49–59.

MEDEF (2002). *The European Guide to Outsourcing.* Institute Esprit Service, Comite de Liaison des Services du MEDEF.

MEDEF (2004). *Guide du Partenariat de Service.* Institute Esprit Service, MEDEF.

Mercer Human Resource Consulting (2005). *Measuring the Return on Total Rewards: 2005 Update,* August (available at www.mercerHR.com).

Meyer, J. P. and Smith, C. A. (2000). HRM practices and organizational commitment: test of a mediation model. *Canadian Journal of Administrative Science,* **17(4)**, 319–331.

Millward, L. J. and Brewerton, P. M. (1999a). Validation of the psychological contract scale in organizational settings. Unpublished Paper, Department of Psychology, School of Human Sciences, University of Surrey.

Millward, L. J. and Brewerton, P. M. (1999b). Contractors and their psychological contracts. *British Journal of Management,* **10(3)**, 253–274.

Millward, L. J. and Brewerton, P. M. (2000). Psychological contracts: employee relations for the 21st century. In: C. L. Cooper and I. Robertson (eds), *International Review of Industrial and Organizational Psychology*, Vol. 15. John Wiley & Sons, pp. 1–63.

Millward, L. J. and Herriot, P. (2000). Psychological contracts in the United Kingdom. In: D. M. Rousseau and R. Schalk (eds), *Psychological Contracts in Employment: cross-national perspectives*. Sage Publications, pp. 231–249.

Millward, L. J. and Hopkins, L. J. (1998). Psychological contracts, organizational and job commitment. *Journal of Applied Social Psychology*, **28(16)**, 1530–1556.

Mintzberg, H. (1994). *The Rise and Fall of Strategic Planning*. Free Press.

Morris, I. (2005). *Total Rewards: an old idea becomes the new approach* (available at MercerHR.com).

Morrison, E. W. and Robinson, S. L. (1997). When employees feel betrayed: a model of how psychological contract violation develops. *Academy of Management Review*, **22(1)**, 226–256.

Myer, J. P. and Allen, N. J. (1991). A three component conceptualization of organizational commitment. *Human Resource Management Review*, **1(1)**, 61–89.

Myer, J. P. and Allen, N. J. (1997). *Commitment in the Workplace: theory, research and application*. Sage Publications.

National Skills Shortage List (2004). (Available at www.workplace.gov.au.)

Neinhuser, W. and Matiaske, W. (2006). Effects of the principle of non-discrimination on temporary agency work. *Industrial Relations Journal*, **37**, 164–177.

Neuman, W. (2000). *Social Research Methods: qualitative and quantitative approaches*. Allyn and Bacon.

New Zealand Herald (2006). Cleaners battle to close wage gap. *New Zealand Herald*, 21 April.

Niehaus, R. J. and Price, K. F. (1991). *Bottom Line Results from Strategic Human Resource Planning*. Plenum.

NIOSH (2002). *The Changing Organisation of Work and the Safety and Health of Working People*. National Institute for Occupational Safety and Health.

O'Donohue, W., Sheehan, C., Hecker, R. and Holland, P. (2004). A hidden dimension? Work ideology and psychological contracts. Paper presented at ANZAM Conference, Dunedin, New Zealand, December.

OECD (2002). *Employment Outlook*. Organisation for Economic Co-operation and Development.

OECD (2003). *Guidelines for Multi-national Enterprises*. Organisation for Economic Co-operation and Development.

OECD (2005). *Employment Outlook*. Organisation for Economic Co-operation and Development.

Origin Healthcare (2005). http://www.originhealthcare.com.au/, accessed 10 August 2005.

Parker, M. (2002). *Against Management*. Polity Press.

Peck, J., Theodore, N. and Ward, K. (2005). Constructing markets for temporary labour: employment liberalisation and internationalisation of the staffing industry. *Global Networks*, **5**, 3–26.

People Management (2000). 11 July.

Personnel Review (2006). Special issue: Temporary Work and HRM. *Personnel Review*, **35(2)**.

Personnel Today (2005). 31 May.

Personnel Today (2005). 31 August.

Personnel Today (2005). 10 October.

Perulli, A. (2003). Economically dependent/para-subordinate work in the EU. Paper for Public Hearing at European Parliament, 20 June 2003. European Commission.

Pettinger, R. (1998). *Managing the Flexible Workforce*. Cassell.

Platman, K. (2004). Portfolio careers and the search for flexibility in later life. *Work, Employment and Society*, **18**, 573–599.

Porter, G. (1995). Attitude differences between regular and contract employees of nursing departments. Paper presented at the Annual Meeting of the Academy of Management, Vancouver.

Purcell, K. and Purcell, J. (1999). Insourcing, outsourcing and the growth of contingent labour as evidence of flexible employment strategies. In: R. Blanpain (ed.), *Non-Standard Work and Industrial Relations*. Kluwer Law International.

Quinlan, M. (2003). *Flexible Work and Organisational Arrangements – Regulatory Problems and Responses*. Paper presented at the Australian OHS Regulation for the 21st Century Conference, Gold Coast, Queensland, July, 20–22.

Quinlan, M., Mayhew, C. and Bohle, P. (2001a). The global expansion of precarious employment, work disorganisation, and consequences for occupational health: a review of recent research. *International Journal of Health Services*, **31(2)**, 335–414.

Quinlan, M., Mayhew, C. and Bohle, P. (2001b). The global expansion of precarious employment, work disorganisation and occupational health: placing the debate in a comparative historical context. *International Journal of Health Services*, **31(3)**, 507–536.

Redman, T. and Wilkinson, A. (eds) (2001). *Contemporary Human Resource Management: Text and Cases*. FT Prentice-Hall.

Rintoul, S. (2005). When two sides collide. *The Australian*, 16 November, 13.

Roberts, C. (2005). Me Inc's challenge. *Business Review Weekly*, 20 October.

Robinson, S. L. and Morrison, E. W. (1995). Psychological contracts and OCB: the effect of unfulfilled obligations on civic virtue behaviour. *Journal of Organizational Behavior*, **16**, 289–298.

Robinson, S. L. and Rousseau, D. M. (1994). Violating the psychological contract: not the exception but the norm. *Journal of Organizational Behavior*, **15**, 245–259.

Roe, M. A. (2001). Cultivating the gold-collar worker. *Harvard Business Review*, **79(5)**, 32.

Rothwell, W. and Kazanas, H. C. (1989). *Strategic Human Resource Development*. Prentice-Hall.

Rousseau, D. M. (1990). New hire perceptions of their own and their employer's obligations: a study of psychological contracts. *Journal of Organizational Behaviour*, **11**, 389–400.

Rousseau, D. M. (1995). *Psychological Contracts in Organizations: understanding written and unwritten agreements*. Sage Publications.

Rousseau, D. M. (1998a). The 'problem' of the psychological contract considered. *Journal of Organizational Behaviour*, **19(S1)**, 665–671.

Rousseau, D. M. (1998b). Why workers still identify with organizations. *Journal of Organizational Behaviour*, **19**, 217–233.

Rousseau, D. M. (2001). Schema, promise and mutuality: the building blocks of the psychological contract. *Journal of Occupational and Organizational Psychology*, **74**, 511–541.

Rousseau, D. M. and Greller, M. M. (1994). Human resource practices: administrative contract makers. *Human Resource Management*, **33(3)**, 385–401.

Rousseau, D. M. and Parks, J. M. The contracts of individuals and organizations. In: L. L. Cummings and B. M. Staw (eds), *Research in Organizational Behavior*, 1993, Volume 15, pp. 1–43.

Rousseau, D. M. and McLean Parks, J. M. (1993). The contracts of individuals and organisations. In: L. L. Cummings and B. M. Staw (eds), *Research in Organisational Behavior*, **15**, 1–43.

Rousseau, D. M. and Schalk, R. (eds) (2000). *Psychological Contracts in Employment: cross-national perspectives*. Sage Publications.

Rousseau, D. M. and Tijoriwala, S. A. (1998). Assessing psychological contracts: issues, alternatives and measures. *Journal of Organizational Behaviour*, **19(S1)**, 679–695.

Rousseau, D. M. and Wade-Benzoni, K. A. (1994). Linking strategies and human resource strategies: how employee and customer contracts are created. *Human Resource Management*, **33**, 463–489.

Schafer, M. (2005). Specialized HR for IT Organizations. *HR Magazine*, **50(3)**, 103–106.

Schauble, S. (2005). *Trades Shortages: the SKILLED approach*. Survey by the SKILLED Group.

Shore, L. M. and Barksdale, K. (1998). Examining degree of balance and level of obligation in the employment relationship: a social exchange approach. *Journal of Organisational Behavior*, **19**, 731–744.

Sims, R. R. (1992). Developing the learning climate in public sector training. *Public Personnel Management*, **21(3)**, 335–346.

Sims, R. R. (1994). Human resources management's role in clarifying the new psychological contract. *Human Resource Management*, **33(3)**, 373–382.

SKILLED Engineering Ltd (2004). Annual Report. SKILLED.

SKILLED Engineering Ltd (2005). *Employee Handbook*. SKILLED.

Skotnicki, T. (2005). The old team. *Business Review Weekly*, 6 October.

Smeaton, D. (2003). Self-employed workers: calling the shots or hesitant independents? *Work, Employment and Society*, **17**, 379–391.

Smith, S. (2002). Agencies, employers share duty for temporary worker safety. *Plant*, **61(17)**.

Smithson, J. and Lewis, S. (2000). Is job security changing the psychological contract? *Personnel Review*, **29(6)**, 680–702.

Sparrow, P. (2000). International reward management. In: G. White and J. Drucker (eds), *Reward Management – A Critical Text*. Routledge Studies in Employment Relations. Routledge, pp. 196–214.

Sparrow, P. and Cooper, C. (2003). *The New Employment Relationship*. Butterworth-Heinemann.

Sparrow, P. and Marchington, M. (1998). Introduction: Is HRM in crisis? In: P. Sparrow and M. Marchington (eds), *Human Resource Management: The New Agenda London*, pp. 3–20. Financial Times/ Pitmans.

Stiles, P., Gratton, L., Truss, C., Hope-Hailey, V. and McGovern, P. (1997). Performance management and the psychological contract. *Human Resource Management Journal*, **7(1)**, 57–66.

Stone, R. J. (2005). *Human Resource Management*, 5th edn. John Wiley & Sons.

Storrie, D. (2002). *Temporary Agency Work in the European Union*. European Foundation.

Stredwick, J. and Ellis, S. (1998). *Flexible Working Practices: Techniques and Innovations.* IPD.

Syrett, M. (2003). Contribution to *HR Shared Services: achieving the business benefits.* Business Intelligence.

Syrett, M. (2004). Interview in *Redefining Strategic HR.* Business Intelligence, p. 80.

Tansky, J. W., Gallagher, D. G. and Wetzel, K. W. (1995). The changing nature of the employment contract: the impact of part-time workers on the health care industry. Paper presented at the Annual Meeting of the Academy of Management, Vancouver.

Taylor, P. (1997). When pay for performance fails to perform. *Human Resources*, **2(4)**, 17–19.

Taylor, S. (2004). Synchronise your strategies. *Human Resources*, 25 November.

The Economist (2004). Working harder; employment agencies in Japan. **370(8360)**, 64.

The Economist (2005). The Bangalore Paradox. *Economist*, 23 April.

Thomas, D. C., Au, K. and Ravlin, E. C. (2003). Cultural variation and psychological contract. *Journal of Organizational Behavior*, **24**, 451–471.

Thomas, H. D. C. and Anderson, N. (1998). Changes in newcomers' psychological contracts during organizational socialization: a study of recruits entering the British Army. *Journal of Organizational Behavior*, **19**, 745–767.

Thompson, J. A. and Bunderson, J. S. (2003). Violations of principle: ideological currency in the psychological contract. *Academy of Management Review*, **28(4)**, 571–586.

Thurow, L. (1999). *Building Wealth: The New Rules For Individuals, Companies and Nations in the Knowledge-Based Economy.* Harper.

Timmins, P. (2005). Personal communication.

Toomey, S. (2005). Solo life has ups, downs. *Weekend Australian*, 17–18 September.

Tovstiga, G. (1999). Profiling the knowledge worker in the knowledge intensive organization: emerging roles. *International Journal of Technology Management*, **18**, 14–28.

Tsui, A. S., Pearce, J. L., Porter, L. W. and Tripoli, A. M. (1997). Alternative approaches to the employee–organizational relationship: does investment in employees pay off? *Academy of Management Journal*, **40(5)**, 1089–1121.

Tucker, D. M. (2005). *Knight Ridder Tribune Business News*, 4 April, 1.

Turnley, W. H. and Feldman, D. C. (2000). Re-examining the effect of psychological contract violations: unmet expectations and job dissatisfaction as mediators. *Journal of Organizational Behavior*, **21**, 25–42.

VandenHeuvel, A. and Wooden, M. (1999). Casualisation and out-sourcing: trends and implications for work-related training. Commissioned Report, Australia: National Centre for Vocational Education Research.

Van Dyne, L. and Ang, S. (1998). Organizational citizenship behaviour of contingent workers in Singapore. *Academy of Management Journal*, **41(6)**, 692–703.

Vitez, M. (2005). 50 years at one firm. It's rare. It's over. *Knight Ridder Tribune Business* News, 22 April, 1.

Waite, M. and Will, L. (2001). *Self-employed Contractors in Australia: Incidence and Characteristics.* Productivity Commission Staff Research Paper, AusInfo.

Walsh, J. and Deery, S. (1997). Understanding the peripheral workforce: an examination of employee diversity in the service sector. Working Paper No. 112, Department of Management and Industrial Relations, University of Melbourne.

Walton, J. (1999). *Strategic Human Resource Development.* FT Prentice-Hall.

WERS (2004). *Fifth Workplace Employment Relations Survey, 2004.* Department of Trade and Industry, London.

WF (2005) *In Less Mono? Flexible working, productivity and management.* Working Families.

World Employment Report (2005). International Labour Office. Geneva.

Wright, P., McMahan, G. and McWilliams, A. (1994). Human resources as a source of sustained competitive advantage. *International Journal of Human Resource Management*, **5**, 299–324.

Wright, P. M. and Gardner, T. M. (2002). Theoretical and empirical challenges in studying the HR practice–firm performance relationship. In: D. Holman, T. Wall, C. Clegg, P. Sparrow and A. Howard (eds), *The New Workplace: A Guide to the Human Impact of Modern Working Practices*, pp. 311–328. John Wiley & Sons.

Index